VE DAY 75

VE DAY 75

Printed in England by Pureprint Limited on 130gsm Lumi Silk. This paper has been independently certified according to the standards of the Forest Stewardship Council® (FSC)®.

A catalogue record of this publication is available from the British Library.

ISBN: 978-1-906670-85-6

"This is your victory. Victory of the cause of freedom. In all our long history we have never seen a greater day than this"

Winston Churchill, Victory in Europe Day 1945

PA

WINDSOR CASTLE

Sir Andrew Gregory, KBE, CB,
Controller,
SSAFA.

As Patron of SSAFA, the Armed Forces Charity, I am pleased to send my best wishes to the Beneficiaries, Volunteers, Employees and all those concerned with the Charity on the occasion of the Seventy-Fifth Anniversary of VE Day.

At this increasingly challenging time, I know that you have continued to provide support to members of the Armed Forces and Veterans, together with their families.

As you reflect on the Charity's One Hundred and Thirty-Five year history, my thoughts and prayers remain with you all for your continued safety and the future success of your important work.

ELIZABETH R.

8th May, 2020.

At the stroke of 11am on 8 May 1945, church bells rang out across Britain. In the worst days of the Second World War, when Hitler's armies were poised across the Channel, the bells would have rung only to warn the nation of invasion. Yet, 75 years ago, they resounded in joyful celebration of victory over Nazi aggression.

Our debt to those who were present at that moment — surely the greatest generation of Britons who ever lived — can be simply expressed. Without their valour and sacrifice, all that is good and right would have perished from the earth.

This was the generation who fought on alone in 1940, even after the rest of Europe had fallen into Hitler's orbit. If, at that moment, Britain had sought negotiation or compromise — or persevered but gone down to defeat — then the consequences hardly bear thinking about. Europe would not have been liberated, America would not have joined the struggle, there could have been no D-Day. Millions would have been abandoned to a wicked regime.

This catastrophe was avoided, but at a grievous price. Britain mobilised virtually the entire population for total war. Across the world, our armed services fought on land, sea and in the air. On the home front, women broke the Nazi codes, worked the factories, ran the hospitals and made the weapons. Pensioners served as air raid wardens. Children were evacuated from their homes. Everyone endured years of food rationing and shortages. Meanwhile, night after night, the enemy bombed London and other cities, killing over 40,000 civilians.

Today, we know that this supreme ordeal ended in victory. But at the time, nothing was inevitable. The pivotal episodes of the war — from Dunkirk and the Battle of Britain to the Normandy landings and the Battle of the Atlantic — could have ended tragically. Without the courage and ingenuity of remarkable people, they would have done. In Churchill's words: "The odds were great, our margins small; the stakes infinite."

Yet the greatest generation never flinched at the stakes. This anniversary is our opportunity to commemorate their sacrifice and celebrate their fortitude and achievement.

As we honour this anniversary, we should remind ourselves of the fragility of peace — and of our abiding duty to defend our way of life and our freedoms for generations to come.

Above all, this is a chance for those of us who were born in more recent decades to offer the greatest generation our heartfelt thanks. They came from every background and every walk of life. They faced the greatest ordeal in our history. And they won through to hear the bells of victory. To them we owe our peace and freedom.

The Prime Minister

Ministry of Defence

Seventy-five years after the end of the largest and bloodiest war in history, we remember with great pride and gratitude the inestimable courage and sacrifice of all those, both at home and overseas, who were called upon to defend and preserve freedom.

The cost in terms of life and suffering was enormous. The British Army experienced hundreds of thousands of casualties including the deaths of over 300,000 men and women. The fallen can be found in every corner of the world, from the military cemeteries of Europe to those of North Africa, and the Middle and Far East — from Normandy to Tripoli, Cairo, Singapore and Burma — and many of the names of those locations are evocatively etched into the battle honours of British Regiments.

The 75th anniversaries of VE Day and VJ Day are especially poignant, as they are likely to be the last major national commemorations in the lifetime of most of those who witnessed the ravages of that war. Those witnesses remind us of a time when the nation's freedom — and that of our friends and allies — faced mortal threat; and those veterans speak of what preserving that freedom cost in terms of the sacrifice by not just those serving in the Armed Forces, but also by civilians on the Home Front.

The victory in 1945 was a titanic shared endeavour and the freedom so hard won has subsequently been defended and fought for by generations of soldiers over the past 75 years. As the nation tackles the Coronavirus pandemic, those same qualities that ensured victory in 1945 are once more the currency of our Armed Forces. I am grateful to SSAFA for the hard work and dedication in supporting the person behind the uniform, and the invaluable contribution to the fabric of our Army, recognising the unique contribution our soldiers make every day in the defence of our country and in preparing to meet the challenges of tomorrow.

Mark Carleton-Smith

General Sir Mark Carleton-Smith KCB CBE ADC GEN
Chief of the General Staff

I am immensely proud to be President of SSAFA, a role I have held since 1982.

Established in 1885, SSAFA has been at the forefront of providing support to the Armed Forces community in every conflict this country has been involved in since that time.

As the Second World War progressed, keeping the country functioning was a huge responsibility. By 1944, SSAFA had a vast network of 50,000 volunteers providing support for our Armed Forces and their families. In a letter, General Montgomery, Commander of 21st Army Group, later to become the British Liberation Army (BLA) and British Army of the Rhine (BAOR), said of SSAFA:

"In the knowledge that his family at home are being well cared for by SSAFA, the soldier fighting overseas may wholeheartedly devote himself to his duty, without being worried by family troubles and consequently hampered in the efficient execution of his duty."

By the time VE Day, 8 May 1945, arrived we had been at war for many years. Much of the country, particularly London during the Blitz and strategic targets along the coast, had been raised to the ground by the Nazis. While we must not forget that the Allies were still at war in the Far East, the true horrors of which would be realised much later, VE Day was a day on which the country could, after such a long time, dare to breathe a sigh of relief and rejoice.

SSAFA was there during the last century and, having provided support to more than 85,000 people last year, we are very much here now.

Michael

HRH Prince Michael of Kent
President of SSAFA

Contents

Introduction

By Lieutenant General Sir Andrew Gregory KBE CB,
CEO of SSAFA, the Armed Forces charity

The lessons of the Second World War need to remain with us for generations. In terms of overall loss of life, it was the most terrible war the world had ever seen. The service and sacrifice of those in our Armed Forces, and of the communities that supported them, during nearly six years of conflict protected our freedoms and our way of life then, and are something we continue to benefit from today. For this reason, the nation's recognition and support of service personnel, veterans and their families remain as important as ever.

The Soldiers, Sailors, Airmen and Families Association — now SSAFA, the Armed Forces charity — was founded in February 1885, over 135 years ago. We have assisted those who served in the Boer War, the Great War, the Second World War and more recent conflicts. SSAFA was supporting those serving on VE Day and their families back at home, just as it does today.

Indeed, in 2020, the charity is as busy as ever. Last year, we assisted more than 85,000 members of the Armed Forces community in many different ways, helping them, as required, to regain their independence and their dignity. These persons ranged from our remaining Second World War veterans, through to those who served in recent campaigns in Iraq and Afghanistan.

At the beating heart of our work are over 5,000 volunteers, who act as "the frontline" of the military charity sector. Our volunteers visit those in need and help them receive the support they require, often bringing in assistance from Service Benevolent Funds and Regimental Associations,

without whom we could not be able to complete our work. And we are finding that our veterans face increasingly complicated issues that take more time and money to resolve; so your support for SSAFA has never been more important.

There is a duty to keep the events of the past alive now and in the future; hopefully this will ensure that a conflict on the scale of the Second World War never happens again. Hence, the nation should take a moment to reflect on the significance of the 75th anniversary of VE Day — it was a milestone that changed the course of history for the whole world.

The date has a personal connection for me, as both of my parents served throughout the war. My mother, a member of the Women's Royal Naval Service (WRNS), worked in the operations room of General Eisenhower's D-Day headquarters in Southwick House, before going across to France in September 1944. When Winston Churchill arrived in Paris just after VE Day, he saw her and two other WRNS with a White Ensign and gave them a thumbs up!

My father, a Royal Artillery Forward Observation Officer, landed on Sword Beach on 6 June 1944 and was badly wounded that evening, just south of Pegasus Bridge; on VE Day, he was still in hospital. Despite living with constant pain, he never complained through to his death in 2010 aged 93. He talked little about the war, as was the case for so many who had been involved in the fighting. I know that they would both be very proud of what I and others seek to provide through SSAFA.

Chapter one

THE BUILD-UP

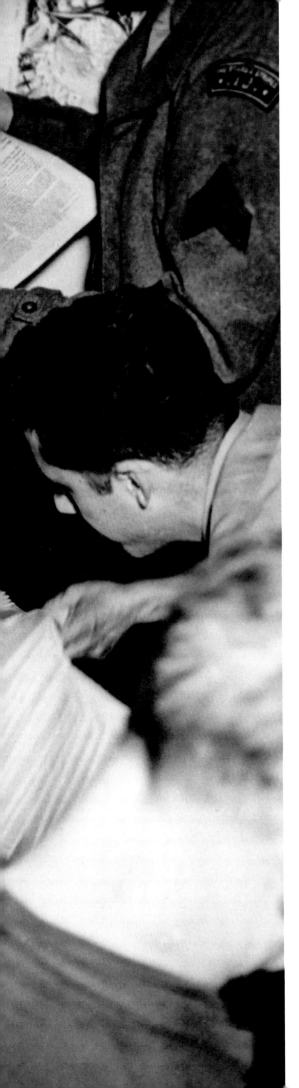

Peace at last

With the surrender of Nazi Germany came victory in Europe, and the promise of a much longed-for day of celebration

The news did not come as a huge surprise to the British public. But the announcement across the nation's airwaves that the war in Europe was effectively over, that the following day would be Victory in Europe Day, was met with a collective outpouring of joy and relief none the less. Crowds began to gather, bunting and banners were unfurled, and households the length of the land prepared to celebrate.

VE Day was the moment that the guns across Europe fell silent and the war with Nazi Germany came to an end. After nearly six years of conflict, which saw staggering losses on foreign front lines, as well as on the home front, hostilities officially ended at one minute past midnight on 8 May 1945. The conflict had cost the lives of millions and no other war had led to so much destruction on British home soil.

As news broke of the German surrender, the nation rejoiced. Prime Minister Winston Churchill, who had brought the nation back from the brink of defeat to ultimately topple Hitler, was able to finally make the speech he had longed for since taking power in 1940. The great orator's address to the nation — declaring the unconditional surrender of the Germans and victory in Europe — did not come until 3pm on the day itself, but the UK and its allies had been preparing for the victory for some time.

Unlike the seemingly sudden end of the First World War in 1918, there had been growing hope that the war with Nazi Germany was in its final stages since late 1944. History, and particularly the lessons of the First World War, had taught the British public that believing that it would all be over by Christmas could be wishful thinking. However, as 1945 dawned there was no denying the Allied forces had been gaining ground and the Axis powers in Europe — Germany and Italy — were in retreat.

Germany's military position appeared hopeless. The Eastern Front was a catastrophe, with Russia's Red Army driving the Nazis through Poland. In the west, Allied forces had taken Sicily, forcing the Italian government to sign an armistice in September 1943. As the Allies advanced north through Italy, the country's fascist leader and ally of Hitler, Benito Mussolini, was on the run. Then there was the heavy blow of the D-Day

Previous pages Military paper
The Stars and Stripes reports the
news of Germany's surrender on
the eve of VE Day, London

Left Field Marshal Montgomery
meets with high-ranking German
officers to negotiate the terms of
surrender in Germany

Opposite A North London local
celebrates the news that her
husband will soon be home
from the war in Germany

landings in Normandy, beginning on 6 June 1944,
which resulted in the subsequent liberation of
north-west Europe from Nazis occupation and
the march towards Berlin.

The Axis powers were on the back foot,
but Hitler had shown he was not likely to follow
in Mussolini's footsteps and flee. Instead, he
launched his V-weapons (V standing for *Vergeltung*,
or retaliation). A flying bomb and a long-range
rocket, the V-1 and V-2, were unleashed on Britain
days after the Normandy landings. By the end of
June, 100 "doodlebugs", as Londoners dubbed
them, had rained down on the capital, battering
buildings and morale alike.

As spring dawned in 1945, however, so
too did a new hope. A series of capitulations
suggested that the end was nigh for the Allies'
enemies. On the 28 April, the fleeing Mussolini
was captured by Italian partisans and shot; so
fell the first dictator of the Second World War.

Then came the news that all had longed for:
Adolf Hitler was dead. On 1 May 1945, this news
was broadcast to the nation by the BBC after
their monitoring team of translators intercepted
an official broadcast from Germany. The German

newsreader declared that the Führer had fallen
fighting Bolshevism in active combat rather
than admitting the truth, which was he had
taken cyanide before shooting himself in the
head in his underground bunker.

To admit the truth would have been to admit
defeat. Instead, the Nazi regime clung to the
illusion that it was still fighting. Grand Admiral
Karl Dönitz was named Hitler's successor and
declared that "Germany will fight on".

The announcement of Hitler's death came
after days of speculation about his declining
health, as well as his whereabouts, with some
reports saying he had fled Germany for safety.
In fact, he had been hiding in a bunker under
the Reich Chancellery in Berlin, surrounded by
Allied Forces. The Russian Red Army took the
suburbs of the capital on the 21 April. As the
Soviets advanced, Hitler married his long-term
partner Eva Braun in the bunker on 29 April.
The following day, the newlyweds took their
own lives and their bodies were then burned.

In the UK, the news of his death was met
with a mixture of celebration and hope. The *Daily
Express* ran with the headline "Germans put out

the news everyone hopes is true... 'Hitler is Dead'" The paper refused to run a picture of the deceased Nazi leader on the front page and in his obituary wrote: "The *Daily Express* rejoices to announce the report of Adolf Hitler's death".

As a figure, Hitler had cast an ominous shadow over the Allied nations, while for his own country, his fervour had driven the German war effort. The news of his death lifted the great spectre of his destructive force from the UK and simultaneously shattered the war spirit that his dictatorial presence had inspired in Germany.

Days later, on 2 May, German forces in Italy surrendered to the advancing British Army.

On the following day a high-ranking German delegation, including a senior admiral and a senior general, appeared at the headquarters of Field Marshal Sir Bernard Montgomery, located near Lubeck, Northern Germany.

After two days of negotiation under canvas and the flying Union Flag, the flashing bulbs of war photographers and a cameraman captured the historic moment. The unconditional surrender of German forces in North-West Germany, Holland and Denmark was signed over to "Monty" and the 21 Army Group on 4 May 1945.

Three days later, on 7 May 1945, at his French headquarters in Reims, the United States'

Supreme Allied Commander, General Eisenhower, accepted the unconditional surrender of all German forces. The document of surrender was signed on behalf of Germany by General Alfred Jodl. This was on orders of the Third Reich's newly installed Führer, Grand Admiral Karl Dönitz — despite his inauguration speech declaring Germany was still fighting, just six days earlier.

General Jodl's unconditional surrender on Monday 7 May at 2.41am formally ended war in Europe. However, fighting did not immediately cease: a German U-boat sank two merchant ships off the Scottish coast hours after General Jodl's surrender; some Germans continued to fight the

VE Day veteran

Joan Blair
Served in the Auxiliary Territorial Service
(ATS) in Hounslow, London; 96 years old

What are your memories of VE Day?
*When the news was blasted into our barracks
in Feltham that the war in Europe was over,
we made our way into central London by jumping
on the backs of lorries. There was plenty of traffic
going in and out.*

*We were at the front of Buckingham Palace,
with the masses of crowds behind us — everyone
wanted to be there. Somebody important had
got us to the front position, because we were
connected to headquarters in London. We saw
the royals come out on the balcony, and the
young princess who is now our Queen — everyone
screamed and clapped. We felt honoured to be
where we were. I wish I'd had a camera.*

*There was so much noise and singing. Then we
made our way to celebrate in Trafalgar Square.
Everybody got together and we partied at
night-time. We celebrated more than one night.*

**Do you remember making contact with
any of your family? Would you have tried
to call them?**
*My family? Well, you couldn't. It wasn't easy to
call in them days. It wasn't easy to get in touch.
Really, if you wanted to get in touch or send news
to anybody, it was by telegram. You couldn't just
phone, it was too expensive.*

How did you feel on the day?
*There was so much going on. We were just
rejoicing, knowing it was mostly over. You think
you'll always remember it, but there was so much
that happened it became a blur.*

Above Flags bearing the faces of
Allied leaders Winston Churchill
and Franklin D Roosevelt are dried
out in a factory in the East End of
London in preparation for VE Day

Left Crowds gather in Piccadilly Circus, London, on 7 May 1945

Right Spontaneous celebrations break out in anticipation of VE Day

Russians in an attempt to hold the Red Army's advance back; and British Forces were still on duty in the theatre of war. For those in the Far East — fighting the last leading Axis power, Japan — the war would not be over until August 1945, when the Japanese finally surrendered.

Hostilities in Europe could also not officially end, or the long-awaited Allied victory be announced to the world, on 7 May, as the three great Allied powers still had diplomatic matters to navigate.

As the Germans had surrendered to both the British in Northern Germany, and the Americans at Reims, the other main Allied player — the Soviets — needed to accept the surrender as well. As Soviet leader Josef Stalin did not have a senior military leader in Reims to sign on 7 May, a third surrender ceremony had to be arranged in Berlin on 8 May.

Churchill, however, was not going to bend to Stalin's will and allow him to hold up proceedings, or the much wished-for victory celebrations, any longer. Rumours of the surrender had spread across London on 7 May,

drawing large crowds to the gates of Buckingham Palace demanding to see the King. The Ministry of Information made a short announcement at 7.40pm that evening: "In accordance with arrangements between the three great powers, tomorrow, Tuesday, will be treated as Victory in Europe Day and will be regarded as a holiday."

The announcement was broadcast to the British people over the airways, with the BBC interrupting its scheduling programming with a news flash sharing the ministry's statement to the nation.

The British people, who had been on standby to celebrate, leapt into action. After six years of conflict, large death tolls that left few untouched by loss, bombed-out homes, rationing, austerity and war work, people were in need of a collective moment to rejoice. Within minutes of the announcement crowds had gathered in Parliament Square, Trafalgar Square and Piccadilly Circus. Great banners declaring victory were draped over monuments, out of windows and across streets. On the eve of Victory in Europe Day, a war-weary Britain was ready to party.

Chapter two

VE DAY ACROSS THE UK

The nation gives thanks

Whether cause for scenes of wild jubilation or quiet reflection, VE Day gave the people of Britain the chance to herald victory in Europe; a victory that had asked so much of so many

It was the biggest party in history, with half a million people pouring into London alone to celebrate VE Day. Similar scenes of mass gatherings were witnessed across the UK. Cities, towns, villages, and communities big and small came together to dance, sing and raise a glass to victory and survival — as well as to honour those whose sacrifice had brought peace.

There were moments of quiet reflection, commemorative thanksgiving and silent prayers for the souls of lost loved ones and those still on the frontlines or languishing in prisoner of war camps in Asia. Each person marked the day in their own way.

In the days leading up to the German surrender and as the government's confidence in victory grew, Winston Churchill responded to a question in the House of Commons regarding plans for peace celebrations with the remark that the British public could be relied upon to observe victory, when it came, in a suitable fashion without guidance from anybody. As it had been throughout the war, the Prime Minister's faith in the people of Britain was rewarded.

On VE Day, the nation was told by the Prime Minister to enjoy a "brief period of rejoicing" and that nothing should "prevent us from celebrating today and tomorrow as Victory in Europe Day". Churchill clearly felt that, after five and half years of suffering, the British people were entitled to mark victory as they wished.

Unlike other Allied nations, there were no planned or structured official events. It was not to be a celebration to be curtailed or carolled; police had been told to turn a blind eye to all but the most "flagrant excesses of ebullience". As a newsreel from VE Day stated: "For 48 hours, at least, rejoicing was off the ration."

London prepares to party
The scenes of celebration in London on VE Day would go down in history, with the sheer size and scale of the crowds across the city not witnessed before or since. Bonfires were lit that could be seen from miles outside of town, turning the sky red. Having seen the gathering throng, taxi drivers refused to operate, knowing that there was no way they would be able to

"Cars trying to press through the crowds emerged with dozens of men and women clinging to the bonnets, the sides and the back"

drive through central London. Streets, squares and whole sections of the city were blocked off by people dancing. It was a night that, in the words of a London reporter for *The Scotsman* newspaper, "will long remain as the prime instance of humanity's desire to rejoice in the mass".

As VE Day dawned, no one could have fully anticipated just how that desire to celebrate would ultimately manifest itself. There were crowds outside Buckingham Palace cheering for the King and people started to gather near Whitehall, Trafalgar Square and Piccadilly Circus, but the size of the crowds were only a fraction of what they would become. Even the small pockets of celebration on the eve of VE Day did not give much away.

On the Monday night, the city had been illuminated by red and green flares dropped from three Lancaster bombers prior to Churchill's 7pm address. Ships on the Thames hooted their sirens for two hours while small crafts raced up and down. A mile-long procession marched along the Strand during the night and then through Admiralty Arch and down the Mall to Buckingham Palace. The crowd was reported in *The Times* as being "cosmopolitan", with people of many nations represented. Cars could be heard sounding the letter V in Morse code on their horns when they came to a halt at traffic lights.

The Times reported that tens of thousands of people packed into Piccadilly Circus on the Monday and, despite the official warnings that the victory declaration would be postponed until Tuesday, they were determined to celebrate: "Cars trying to press through the crowds emerged with dozens of men and women clinging to the bonnets, the sides, and the back, and others standing on top trying to wave flags and hang on at the same time."

This was to be but a flavour of what was to come. A London reporter for *The Scotsman* quoted one observer who remembered the Armistice Day scenes of 1918 as saying: "This is altogether different. The crowds have not gone mad.

They are happy, but they are aware." The reporter with the benefit of hindsight followed the quote with the comment: "This observer might, later in the day at some points in London, have seen fit to revise his opinion…"

Jean Alys Campbell-Harris, the future Baroness Trumpington, was working as a codebreaker in Bletchley Park when peace was declared, at which point she quickly jumped on a train and headed to London. Jean spent most weekends in London during the war, and had become quite the city socialite; the band at the French restaurant The Bagatelle would even strike up a special tune whenever she entered. Speaking in the 2015 Channel 4 documentary *The Queen's Big Night Out*, Baroness Trumpington recalls the feeling in the city on VE Day: "There was a spirit of pure happiness, that we could live again, we were all going to live and we were going to live forever."

The capital comes to life

On VE Day, the city came alive once more. The grey veil of austerity, tribulation and mourning that had cloaked the capital for five and half years was cast off. Gone were the grey clothes, the stern faces and the black outs. Instead, the crowds looked like an over-saturated photograph, so vibrant were they in colour and spirit.

By midday a crowd of thousands had gathered on the steps of St Paul's Cathedral, one of the few London landmarks to escape the Luftwaffe's bombing attacks. They stood packed, listening to the music of a military band playing in the forecourt. Soon enough, listening turned to singing, as in one voice the crowd joined in with familiar songs from the First World War: "Pack Up Your Troubles", "Keep the Home Fires Burning" and "It's A Long Way To Tipperary" were sung heartily and with poignant emotion.

Many people gravitated to Trafalgar Square, the shrine to Britain's naval victory of the Napoleonic Wars. The first

Previous pages A packed Piccadilly Circus prepares to party

Right Revellers hitch a ride into town

service of thanksgiving got underway at 11am in St Martin-in-the-Fields, on the north side of the square, and the church was soon bursting beyond its capacity, with people spilling out of the doorway. Those wearing service uniforms were standing alongside people dressed in colourful outfits, not seen since the beginning of the war; others were draped in Union Flags and ribbons of the victory colours. The church held a service every hour until 9pm as the nation gave thanks to God for his great deliverance, and for being their "strength and shield" during the ordeal, as King George VI would later that evening phrase it.

Those attending the services at St Martin-in-the-Fields had to make their way through a crowd of tens of thousands in Trafalgar Square. Young people, crushed shoulder to shoulder, danced in and around the fountains through the night and into the next day. A news report of the scene published in the *Liverpool Daily Post* read: "They had scarcely room to move their feet but they managed it somehow."

As dancing was the order of the day, music was needed and military bands, local musicians and crowds of singers provided fine accompaniment at impromptu gatherings across the country. In Trafalgar Square a party of soldiers and sailors unearthed a barrel organ from somewhere and raced it to the front of the National Gallery, turning the square into an open-air dance hall.

As the music rang out and people danced, RAF bombers swooped and dipped over the centre of London,

Left Huge crowds gather in central London to join the VE Day celebrations

Above A happy horde brings Whitehall to a standstill

Left A couple share a VE Day
kiss in a London pub

Right Piccadilly Circus was at
the heart of the day's revelries

to the crowd's delight. It was the first time
since the start of the war that the sound of an
approaching plane had elicited cheers rather than
air-raid sirens. The triumphant RAF pilots flew
so low over the capital that, according to one
news report in the *Liverpool Daily Post*, they
"caused the revellers to catch their breath for fear
their wings should collide with Nelson's Column".

Joan Wyndham, the British writer and
memoirist, who as a teenager during the Second
World War had become part of London's bohemian
set, recalled the scene. "There was wild excitement
in Trafalgar Square, half of London seemed to
be floodlit — so much unexpected light was quite
unreal. There were people dancing like crazy,
jumping in the fountains and climbing lampposts,
and dull red glow in the sky from bonfires which
reminded us of the Blitz."

Piccadilly Circus also drew great crowds on
VE Day, particularly as it had become a mecca
for the city's out of towners. Visiting US Air Force
pilots had even been rechristening their fighter
planes with names like "Piccadilly Lily", and a
whole industry of clubs and bars had grown up
there to cater for the American GIs. On VE Day,
the crowd in Piccadilly Circus was dubbed a
"human maelstrom" with reports that it had

become unruly and wild, as some intrepid souls
produced death-defying acts to the delight of the
masses. English novelist Mollie Panter-Downes,
writing for *The New Yorker* magazine, described
one such incident: "A lad in the black beret of
the Tank Corps was the first to climb the little
pyramidal Angkor Wat of scaffolding and
sandbags which was erected early in the war to
protect the pedestal of the Eros statue," she wrote.
"The boy shinned up to the top and took a tiptop
Eros pose, aiming an imaginary bow, while the
crowd roared. He was followed by a paratrooper
in a maroon beret, who, after getting to the top,
reached down and hauled up a blonde young
woman in a very tight pair of green slacks.
When she got to the top, the Tank Corps soldier
promptly grabbed her in his arms, and encouraged
by ecstatic cheers from the whole Circus, seemed
about to enact the classic role of Eros right on
the top of the monument." The statue was soon
draped in a mass of bodies. "All jammed together
in an affectionate mass," reported Mollie, "calling
down wisecracks to the crowd."

Many among the throng, no doubt joyous at
having survived, showered others with amorous
affection. Memoirs of the day talk of the many
acts of passion that took place on 8 May 1945.

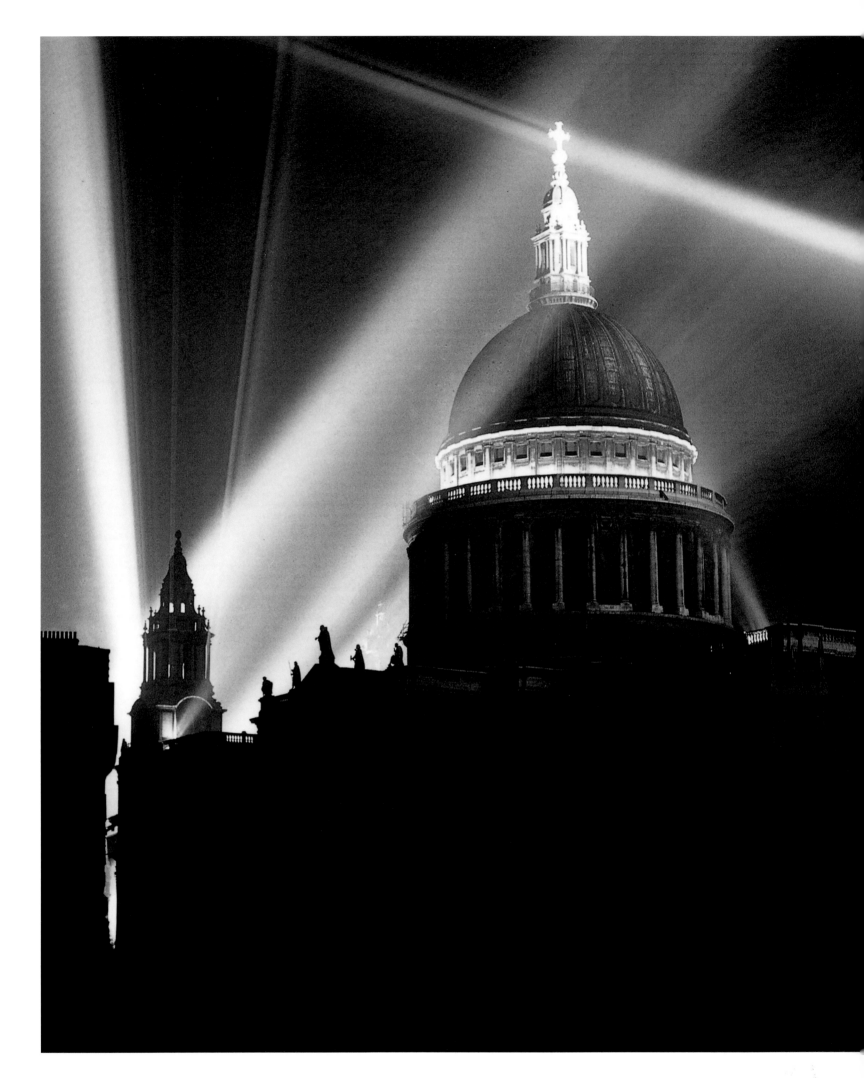

Baroness Trumpington recalls the licentious atmosphere of the night. "I had sort of picked up this naval commander, who did quite a lot of dancing around with me and quite a lot of kissing, but that was it," she said. "Bye-bye and never see again. But enjoy it while you may. I think that naval officer saved me from a lot of knicker trouble. He looked after me."

Surprisingly, the 48 hours of VE Day high-spirits passed with few injuries. According to a news report in the *Dundee Evening Telegraph*, the celebrations in London were remarkably free from accidents; the majority of incidents were due to fainting in the thickest parts of the crowd. The St John Ambulance Brigade had 2,000 members on duty in the West End and the City, and reported 241 cases. Interestingly, transport options were limited in the capital, with London Transport only running a Sunday service. Yet few showed any inclination to go home, and while the crowd around Buckingham Palace did peel off after the King's last appearance on the balcony around midnight, Piccadilly, Trafalgar and the other impromptu congregations seemed quite determined to party through the night and into the next day — which became known in the press at the time as "VE Day plus one". Those who did have to get home had to find more imaginative means of travel than public transport; such as hitchhiking or jumping on the back of passing wagons. Baroness Trumpington — who had to make her way back to Bletchley Park, near Milton Keynes — hitched a ride on a milk cart to get home the following morning.

One of the great enigmas of VE Day was where all the food and ribbon came from. Ribbon and material had been rationed for use in parachutes, uniforms and other war essentials. Yet, on VE Day, there was bunting hanging across streets, great victory banners, and crowds covered in red, white and blue ribbon. The half a million people who descended on the capital that night had to be fed and watered. Many had brought picnic boxes, and restaurants did a roaring trade offering "victory menus", but it remains a wonder how they managed to fill the orders at a time of rationing. "How the multitude was fed during the day is a mystery," observed a London-based reporter in The Scotsman. "Luncheon baskets were almost painfully obvious everywhere, but nonetheless every café and restaurant within miles of Charing Cross was besieged with hungry folk and long queues waited their turn outside." It was no surprise that, by early evening, many places had closed, announcing that they had "sold out".

Even the suburbs partied on VE Day. Many parts of the capital witnessed giant bonfires. The debris of bomb sites, wood piles, rubbish and sometimes effigies of Hitler were set alight. One of the biggest victory blazes took place on Hampstead Heath, where a dummy village of bungalows had been built in 1941, which was in flames by midnight at the end of VE Day. "The purpose of this construction was never explained," ran one article. "But according to rumour it was to be a decoy fire if ever London was blitzed again."

Blitz spirit

Many of London's communities gathered together to celebrate in their home streets, where they had lived and resisted the onslaught of the Luftwaffe. Those in the East End and Docklands, who had suffered the most during the Blitz and the doodlebug raids, showed the same capacity for celebration as they had for resilience. "To be a citizen of Poplar, Canning Town or Stepney is to be a member of a legion of honour," wrote *The Times* in its VE Day reports. "They sang and they laughed and they danced when the bombs were blasting their homes. They remained unafraid. They determined that on the day of triumph there would be flags and song and light and laughter. They showed their pride in their fortress by an amazing display of flags and bunting... An old man watching the dancers said: 'I've been bombed out of three houses, but I wouldn't live anywhere else than in Poplar. We showed 'em we couldn't be beaten.' And so they looked on their ruins with pride."

"The immeasurable relief felt by London citizens is not easily expressed," wrote *The Scotsman* on Wednesday, 9 May 1945. "High spirits and jubilation were but one and perhaps the least profound acknowledgement of the thankfulness which the people of London, with their grim memories, share at this great hour. To many Londoners walking these decked streets, the recollection must have occurred that four years ago, almost to the day, on 10 May 1941 the Germans made their last mighty bid to smash the defiant city. In the last great raid of piloted bombers, the House of Commons Chamber was destroyed, Westminster Abbey hit, as well as the Law Courts, the Mansion House and the Tower of London. Five of the ancient Halls of City Companies lay in ruins, and Londoners, who went to work the morning after, picked their way in practised manner round the craters, crumbled stone and piles of smoking rubble. Changed times indeed, and changed with a swiftness that, although unrecognisable four years ago, may well stand forth as not the least wonder of which the historians will write in future."

Since the declaration of war with Germany in August 1939 and the first bombing raid of the Luftwaffe's relentless attempt to force a surrender by bringing London to its knees, the city had known nothing but destruction, darkness and devastation. "It is no wonder people went a bit crazy," Pathe News announced after VE Day. "London has as much right as anywhere to celebrate and they certainly did."

At the end of the two-day-long party, Churchill was once again on the balcony of the Ministry of Health making another speech to the gathered crowd. This time his words were aimed directly at the residents of London. "My dear friends, I hope you have had two happy days," announced the Prime Minister. "You have been attacked by a monstrous enemy, but you never flinched or wavered. London, like a great rhinoceros, a great hippopotamus, saying 'Let them do their worst. London can take it'. London could take anything. Good old London! God bless you all. May you long remain as citizens of a great and splendid city. May you long remain as the heart of the British Empire."

The nation rejoices

VE Day revelries were by no means restricted to the capital, however. Birmingham celebrated "in a manner that was, in general, in keeping with the occasion," according to the Wednesday, 9 May 1945 edition of the *Birmingham Daily Post*. "The morning rain made the outlook dismal, and at first there was little to indicate that this was the day for which people had waited for more than five and half years, except the bunting, flags and other decorations with which the city was plentifully decorated."

People were reported as not knowing how to celebrate in the beginning, with the *Post* reporting that people were waiting for others to make the first move. Many turned to spiritual leadership, with people knocking on church doors in the morning. Eight services were held at the city's central place of worship, St Philip's Cathedral, on the day, attended by around 4,000 people, while other churches across the city and suburbs also held extra services.

Right Families take to the street in Northampton on 8 May 1945

Left Locals turn out to celebrate in (clockwise from top left): central Birmingham; Battersea, south London; Birmingham's Victory Parade; and Netherfield, Nottinghamshire

A great crowd gathered in front of the Council House on Victoria Square hoping to hear the Prime Minister's 3pm speech, but no arrangements had been made by the local authorities, as it "was not desired to attract people into the city centre", and the crowd were left disappointed. The Lord Mayor did his best by opening the window of his parlour and placing his radio set on the windowsill, "but the hubbub was too great and the power of the set too small." The crowd did let out a great cheer, however, when the Mayor and Lady Mayoress came out onto the beflagged balcony. By the time of the King's speech at 9pm, the square's relay system was in operation and the crowd listened in respectful silence.

"One could sense the atmosphere of anticipation," wrote the Post. Victoria Square, New Street, Stephenson Place, High Street and the Bull Ring seemed to attract people like a magnet and, long before lunchtime, carefree crowds began to throng the pavements and overflow into the carriageways. The *Post* tells of a "leather-lunged American" selling newspapers and extracting "whenever he could, kisses from buyers of the fair sex". Other characters depicted in the report included "two determinedly bright youths": one of the boys dressed in a woman's flowered skirt, a red, white and blue waistcoat and with a Union Jack chalked on his lounge jacket, another boy dressed in Scotch plaid and a tasselled beret. The tireless vendors of rosettes and red, white and blue posies were reported to be rather eclipsed by the one who did the thing in style from a pony and trap.

It was in Birmingham's back streets and in the city's suburbs that celebrations were most in evidence. Streamers, flags and bunting flew from almost every house in many streets, and the more technically minded had improvised electrically lit V signs. Effigies of Hitler hung from a few lampposts. Hundreds of bonfires were lit, wood and other waste having been gathered from bombed sites, and dancing took place.

By Wednesday 9 May, authorities in Birmingham had got their act together and made provision for the revellers. Brass band concerts were announced in the city parks and an illuminated tramcar and bus ran for the first time since the blackout. The following Sunday was given over to a victory parade, with contingents from all three armed services along with the Home Guard, the Civil Defence, the NFS, the Women's Land Army, the WVS and more all taking part.

On the south coast, Plymouth had been bombed 59 times during the Blitz, claiming the lives of 1,172 civilians and injuring more than 4,500 people, and VE Day prompted a commemorative spirit of gladness in the strategically important port town. "Plymouth paid a high price for her share in the glory of the victory," wrote H P Twyford, war reporter for *The Western Morning News*. It was no surprise, therefore, that the home of the Royal Navy dockyards, HMNB Devonport, would rejoice at the news of victory and the German surrender.

"Plymouth's reaction to victory was more in the sense of restrained emotion and heartfelt thanksgiving than in scenes of delirious joy and excitement," wrote Twyford. "There was colour and laughter, quiet gratitude and prayer, and there was heartbreak and tears rising from the rubble that was once the fair face of Plymouth. But there were not those hysterical outpourings which one saw when the ceasefire sounded in 1918."

Thousands did gather in the ruins of St Andrew Church in Plymouth Sutton, which in March 1941 had been bombed and badly damaged. Following the Luftwaffe's attack, a local headmistress nailed over the door a wooden sign with the Latin word "Resurgam", meaning "I shall rise again". A sign of the indomitable wartime spirit, the wooden sign was still in place as the VE Day congregation gathered in the ruins.

Plymouth Sound and Devonport Harbour had an almost regatta-like appearance, which came as a bit of a surprise to the thousands of dockyard

employees who had turned up for work unaware it was a general holiday. They found the gates to the yard shut for the first time and turned around either to return home or join in the celebrations.

It was not all quiet reflections of relief and remembrance in Plymouth, however. There was also dancing. At the city's south-facing public place, Plymouth Hoe, people were reported to have danced until midnight. Loudspeakers had been erected on both sides of the statue of Sir Francis Drake and recorded music was provided. It was estimated that at one time there were upwards of 1,000 dancers with perhaps 20 times that number looking on.

Northern soul

In Leeds, the crowds began to throng the streets on Monday 7 May, eagerly anticipating the announcement of Germany's surrender. News reports depict sellers doing a roaring trade with flags, with cries of "Get the winning colours here!" Kathleen Tozer was serving as a private in the ATS in 1945, and was on leave in Leeds when she heard news of VE Day on the radio. As a gunner, Private Kath had spent the war defending anti-aircraft bases on the home front. She had joined up in January 1941 at the age of 17, and had witnessed heavy losses and had even been

injured while testing mustard gas as part of her duties. "A lot of terrible things happened — like they do today," said Kath. "But you had to carry on and be strong. You can't just sit there and feel sorry for yourself." Years later, SSAFA, the Armed Forces charity, would fight for Kath to get a war pension, in light of the injury she sustained while on duty with the ATS.

On 8 May 1945, Kath was one of many celebrating in Leeds. "I went to the Town Hall, all the bands and drums were going," she said. "To think the war in Europe was over and we could all go back to civvy street. Thousands were on the street. It was packed all the way round. I never saw so many people."

She found herself in a city-centre pub, The Three Legs of Man on The Headrow. "It was so full it took an hour to get a pint," she recalls. "It was very exciting, everyone was screaming, shouting, laughing and making merry. It was wonderful. Shouting: 'The war's over!' 'No more killing!' 'It's over!' 'We can go back home!' At the same time as all the joy, I was nervous — I think most people were, wondering what was going to happen next. But we got over it. We had to push ourselves forward and look forward to another day."

For Kath there was the additional worry of a loved one still in conflict. "I met and married the

love of my life in a time that was harrowing," she says. Her husband, Bill, was in the Navy and had been posted to Hong Kong. "I wish my husband had been with me on VE Day. I had to wait until the war in Japan finished for him to come home."

Following two days of celebration in Manchester, *The Manchester Evening News* ran the headline: "The beer ran out, so did the cigarettes, but everyone was just grand". A sub-heading stated that "the only 'casualties' were eight flags".

In the Thursday 10 May 1945 edition, the newspaper described the VE Day festivities as "modest". It appears the city had anticipated more trouble than it got; less than a dozen people were brought into Manchester Royal Infirmary during the celebrations. The YMCA on Liverpool Road in Castlefield provided 8,010 servicemen with free meals.

Hundreds of people gathered in the city's Piccadilly Gardens to listen to the bands play, but a photograph that ran in the newspaper shows a relaxed scene of people sedately sitting on blankets or chairs with one woman seen to be reading a book or magazine.

Scotland celebrates

Across the border in Edinburgh, the celebrations were more effusive. "If the Scots celebrate with difficulty, they, or the younger portion of them, in Princes Street last night, made a praiseworthy effort to overcome this disability," wrote *The Scotsman* of the VE Day revelry in the Scottish capital.

The official recognition of the end of the war was a short meeting of the Town Council at which tribute was paid to those who played their part. This was followed by a service at the Mercat Cross in Parliament Square. However, the unofficial celebration was a far livelier affair.

Thousands of people paraded the city's streets. Additional police had to be called in to regulate the crowds that had gathered outside the American Red Cross Service Club, where chewing gum and chocolate were showered upon them from the club's windows. A US marine on the balcony of the club conducted the crowd in a mass sing-song, with both "The Yanks Are Coming" and "Land of Hope and Glory" being

among the song choices. As elsewhere, flags of all the Allied nations hung from public and private buildings while bunting fluttered in the air.

Princes Street is where the young gathered in Edinburgh that night, with the celebrations led by members of the Armed Forces. Those from the Navy seemed to be the most flamboyant in their jubilations. Newspapers report of three naval men putting on an undefined "public demonstration" on the Mound, while another group of sailors are reported to have circled an on-duty policemen, swinging and singing around him. The initially small circle of sailors become a calling beacon for all other naval men in the vicinity and soon the embarrassed policemen was at the centre of a singing mob. Nearby, a big party gathered near the Ross Fountain in West Princes Street Gardens, where hundreds joined in, including mothers with babes in arms, as a piper played eightsome reels.

Alcohol had run out in the early evening, but by that time the crowd were intoxicated on the spirit of mass rejoicing. On the other end of Princes Street, one newspaper reports how 30 sailors marched in solemn procession from the Leith Street direction. Each had a pint glass of beer and, at the word of their leader, they stopped in regimental fashion to take a drink.

As many of the pubs had already been drunk dry, a lorry loaded with beer barrels was surrounded by a party of sailors, who "liberated" its contents and proceeded to roll them down the street. The police — who had until that point maintained a tactful non-intervention policy — were forced to intervene, and ordered the barrels be returned to the lorry.

It was not only Scotland's capital that got into the spirit. The town of Wishaw in Lanarkshire, south east of Glasgow, had been preparing for victory for days and was transformed for VE Day. "As if by magic, the whole of Main Street was a blaze of colour," states a report in *The Motherwell Times* on 11 May. "The cinemas made a good show with neon light, clusters of lamps, flags and busts of the Big Three... On Tuesday VE Day opened with rain which lasted until late afternoon, when it cleared up and became a warm, close day. Soon the streets were crowded with groups in holiday mood, dressed to suit the occasion. One of the war's casualties was ribbon, but on VE Day there was no scarcity of it as young women were wearing it in their hair or made up in rosettes all in red, white and blue."

According to the paper, Wishaw's jolliest and most boisterous celebrations were at the East Cross, where a group of young men emerged from a pub singing Scots melodies and dancing to the music being played on the wireless.

Nearby Holytown went in for "bonfires whole-heartedly" on the evening of VE Day and as many as half-a-dozen blazed away. One huge bonfire on the side of a coal tip was an arresting spectacle for many miles around. However, not everyone in the town seemed to have heard the news of the two-day public holiday. One man in Motherwell turned out as usual to take his early-morning bus to work, despite noticing that his fellow commuters were absent. He arrived only to discover that his colleagues had been better informed than he was of the two-day break.

In some cases, it appears that whole towns failed to receive the official VE Day memo. A comment published in the *Montrose Standard* on 9 May said that the east-coast town did not share the wild abandon of Scotland's larger cities. "If anyone had said a year ago, or even a month ago, that VE Day would be celebrated in Montrose as quietly as it actually was, he would have been laughed to scorn. And yet, apart from the flags and bunting, there was very little outward sign of rejoicing. Crowds were to be seen in the High Street all afternoon, but they were silent crowds. The rain had a depressing effect and the knowledge that the dim-out was to continue and that floodlighting and bonfires were banned probably helped to remind everyone that the war was going on in the Far East. There was far more real excitement the previous day when the news was being hourly awaited."

There was also some initial confusion about how to embrace VE Day in Dumfries, in the south of Scotland. "How VE Day came to Dumfries will be a story retailed for many generations," ran the *Dumfries and Galloway Standard* on Wednesday 9 May. "The clockwork arrangements, which one had expected from the Home Office circular of the previous week, somehow went awry, and if the streets were not so full of people when the Provost made the official announcement at the Midsteeple at midday yesterday, certainly the hearts of the people were filled with an overwhelming thankfulness."

The delayed announcement of peace, due to diplomatic wrangling between Allied nations, created confusion about when people could celebrate. "VE Day had been eagerly anticipated, because it meant a release from those anxieties and strains which have been the portion

Right Members of the Canadian Women's Army Corps join the singalong on VE Day

"To think the war in Europe was over and we could all go back to civvy street. Thousands were on the street. I never saw so many people"

Left A jubilant group toast victory in the streets of Glasgow

Right A Scottish bus conductor gets in the VE Day spirit

of everyone for five long years," continued the paper. "The signs and portents were such that there was no doubt that it would be proclaimed this week. On Monday the radio, and particularly the Forces programming, kept repeating with increasing urgency that the announcement must be a matter of hours. Some people in their eagerness had it that it would be merely one hour. So there was an obvious tension in the town on Monday afternoon… Everyone had expected that the previous instructions would hold good, namely that people would carry on until after Mr Churchill had spoken. Thus did the confusion arise. Children went to school on Tuesday to be turned away. Shops were short of staff. Girls going to ministry factories decided not to set out… Others stood in queues seeking the liquid wherewithal to celebrate. Bakers were sold out in an hour or two."

Ultimately, though, once people realised that VE Day had finally come, the town embraced it wholeheartedly. "Dumfries folk are not traditionally demonstrative," ran the editorial, "but they are traditionally friendly, and their friendliness found its true expression on their great day of victory."

Another Scottish town may hold a clue to one of the mysteries of VE Day – how large

parties and gatherings of people were fed. In Kirkintilloch, just north-east of Glasgow, it seems that hoarding was the order of the day – resulting in a pre-VE Day bread famine in the town. "In Kirkintilloch on Saturday night it would have been easier to purchase a bottle of old-time Scotch whisky than to buy an ordinary loaf of bread," records the *Kirkintilloch Herald*. "Anticipating an early announcement of VE Day and anxious to lay in a good stock of food, housewives rushed to buy up loaves and other foodstuffs. We heard of homes with as many as a dozen loaves stored away and of others with not one extra VE Day slice stored in. In one of the unlucky households, the Sunday morning rasher of bacon and egg had to be partaken of with currant bread as a 'filler'."

Despite expectations of riotous celebrations in Dundee, most Dundonians maintained the civil order, with only seven men appearing before the police court for breaches of the peace relating to VE Day. The police were also congratulated for their "efficient and tactful policing". Archibald Bell, burgh prosecutor, paid tribute to the constabulary's "great tact", saying he had expected to have a very large court the day after VE Day but that had not, in fact, been the case.

VE Day veteran

Norman Lewis
Royal Engineers sapper; 100 years old

Opposite Sailors and soldiers join forces to in celebration

You were in action from the very start of the war, weren't you?
I joined the Territorials in May 1939, and got called up straight away when war was declared, getting sent to France. On 7 June 1940 I was captured by the Germans while blowing up a bridge 10 miles from Rouen. I was convinced I'd be shot dead. Others were. You really did see your life race past you.

We were forced to journey for hundreds of miles from France through Belgium, Holland, Germany and eventually to Poland, where we were put in a POW camp with 23,500 others. Heads shaved, all wearing the same uniform and clogs. You got a coffee in the morning, a bowl of turnip soup at dinner time and one slice of black bread at night, and that was that. An awful lot of prisoners committed suicide. Many others died of illness. We had to build bunks, beds and huts for each other — 60 men in each compartment, 20 to a platform. After a while I was taken out to work 12 hours a day on a sugar beet field, and after that I was one of 20 who worked on a farm. That saved my life, I think.

One day in 1945 we heard gunfire. It was the Russian Front. They got closer and eventually the German guards decided they would leave. They asked us to go with them and tell the Russians — if they caught up with them — that they were good to us. We all refused. At first they wanted to shoot us, but they changed their minds and they locked us in the prison and threw away the key. Some Poles came and broke the door down and hid us as the battle went on. When we came out of hiding the Russians were in charge.

How did you cope when you returned home to Stoke?
I got back on 1 April 1945. After five years on the floor I couldn't sleep in a bed for years, it was too soft. And I weighed just 8st 6lbs on my return — the Army gave me a medical and declared me as unfit for service, signing me off for six weeks.

How did you celebrate VE Day?
I remember seeing footage of Churchill standing up and telling us that the Germans had surrendered. I went into town and there were people in the streets dancing. It was wonderful. The shopkeepers put on a street party. I had a drink that night with my dad and my girlfriend, Dorothy. I was just so glad that Hitler was dead and there would be no more killing. We'd got rid of some nasty people.

For Ann Pont, who was serving with the Women's Auxiliary Air Force at RAF Crannoch Hill near Cullen in Banffshire, VE Day was one of mixed emotions. A farmer's daughter from York, Ann had enlisted in the WAAF aged 17 in 1944, and recalls going into the coastal village of Cullen with some of her RAF friends on the day. She had been working as a radar operator and was fortunate that she was not on duty that day. "We carried on exactly the same as normal," she says.

In Cullen, she remembers the celebrations being rather more subdued than in bigger towns. She was also concerned for her boyfriend, an RAF pilot called George Flanigan, who had been shot down in August 1943 and was being held in the Stalag IVB prisoner of war camp in Germany. Nevertheless, she recalls dancing in the pub with teenagers who were too young to be conscripted. "It was a Scottish dance," Ann recalls. "It was pretty merry and one of the few times that the RAF and WAAF mixed with the villagers. I remember there were no toilets and we had to pop out and find a dark corner when we needed to go!"

Wales warms to the occasion
VE Day was one of contrasting emotions in Wales. The headline in the *Western Mail and South Wales News* summed it up best as "Grave and Gay Moods". "One had the early impression that Cardiff was a little too subdued," wrote the reporters. Despite the fact the city was dressed in the colours of victory, apparently it was not until the thanksgiving service in the civic centre was complete that "people really let themselves go".

As many as 25,000 people were reported to have congregated at Cathays Park, near Cardiff Castle, where they listened to speeches from both Churchill and the King being relayed on loudspeakers. After an address from the Lord Mayor and some choir singing, the spirit of the day became much livelier, with hundreds marching through the city streets waving flags.

Just east of the castle, in Kingsway, American "Doughboys" (the nickname given to US infantrymen) and British "Jack Tars" (Merchant and Royal Navy seamen) held impromptu dances. One Jeep had every available inch of its roof and bonnet occupied by singing British and American servicemen. Some of the merrymaking in Cardiff turned into mischief as unknown individuals placed detonators — albeit non-explosive ones — along the tram lines, despite close police surveillance. Every time a tram moved along the line and set off one of the detonators there was an explosion and plumes of smoke filled the air. However, not all of Cardiff gave way to such joyous hedonism. For the Muslim community at the Docks, the day was spent in solemn thanksgiving. The majority of the men from that community were Merchant Navy and they had sustained heavy losses during the war.

Whether marked in joyous celebration or cause for deep reflection, the nation united in giving thanks on what was a day of monumental historical significance: 8 May 1945 — Victory in Europe Day.

CTJ 747

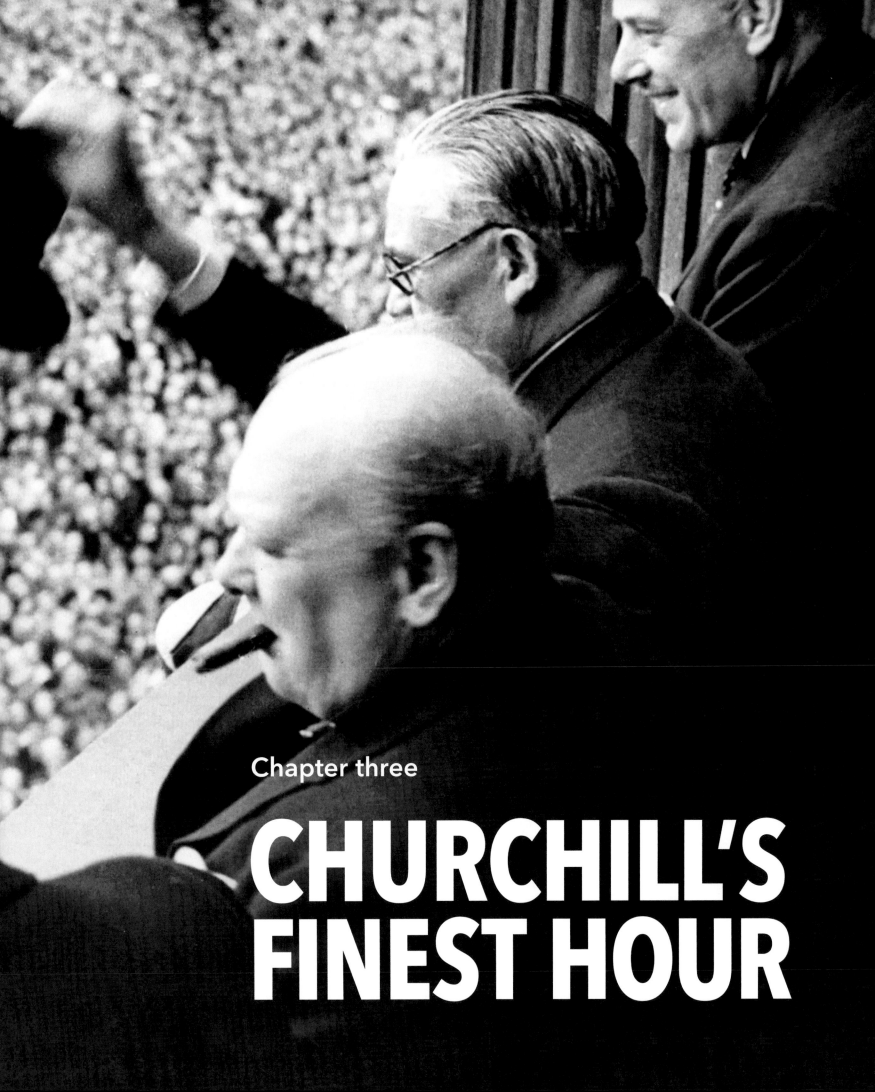

Chapter three

CHURCHILL'S FINEST HOUR

V for victory

A symbol of Britain's bulldog spirit throughout the war, Winston Churchill's declaration of victory in Europe sent the nation into scenes of joyous celebration

---

For Winston Churchill the Second World War would be his defining moment, one that elevated a maverick politician into Britain's greatest Prime Minister. Without the conflict with Germany, the First Lord of the Admiralty may never have been asked by the Conservative Party to be its leader.

By May 1940, the British government was in a state of disarray. The Prime Minister, Neville Chamberlain, who had signed the controversial Munich Agreement with Hitler in 1938, was now fighting a war with the Great Dictator that he had so desperately tried to avoid. The campaign to halt Hitler's advance through Europe was not going well. By May 1940, Britain had suffered a disastrous defeat in Norway. Then, on 10 May — as Germany simultaneously invaded France, Belgium, the Netherlands and Luxembourg — Chamberlain received a vote of no confidence in the Commons thereby forcing his resignation.

Churchill was the default successor after Lord Halifax, the Foreign Secretary, had taken himself out of the running. Churchill was the only member of the War Cabinet with the level of experience deemed necessary for the leadership. Crucially — unlike any other Conservative — he was supported by an extraordinary cross-party group of MPs, including most of the parliamentary Labour Party, who wanted a leader with a history of actively resisting fascism in Europe.

While he was successor by default, Churchill saw it as fulfilling his life-long ambition. As he would go on to write, "all my past life had been but a preparation for this hour and for this trial". Almost five years to the day of his appointment as Prime Minister, Winston Churchill was declaring the end of the war that had precipitated his leadership. The country, the Commons and the King had been rewarded for putting their faith in a man who had declared Britain would "never surrender". A man who, at first, had little more to fight with than the depleted military arsenal he had inherited, his rhetoric and his own stirring bellicosity. He had waged war against the might of the Nazis, a war he had often fought with words, and won.

As Tuesday 8 May 1945 dawned and VE Day began, the nation and the world were poised to hear what the great orator would say and how he would lead them in celebration. Before midday, MPs began to arrive at Parliament for the Prime Minister's anticipated address. According to the *Daily Telegraph*, many MPs had brought their wives and children and were congregating on the terrace overlooking the Thames.

The Prime Minister had lunch with the Royal Family at Buckingham Palace while fully booked hotels and restaurants across London offered special VE Day lunch menus such as the one at The Savoy Hotel, where Labour Minister Ernest Bevin gave a speech to mark the day. The Savoy's menu for the day included celebratory dishes such as "La Citronette Joyeuse Deliverances" (the lemon dressing of joyful deliverance) and "La Coup Glacee des Allies" (Allied ice cream) for five shillings.

Following his lunch at the palace, where he had been greeted by a great roar from the assembled crowd, the Prime Minister made his way back to the cabinet office at Number 10 to deliver his long-awaited address to the nation. The speech was broadcast across the airwaves into people's homes, and town squares, hotels and village halls across the country were packed to the rafters as people listened in. For those who had gathered in the capital, loudspeakers relayed the speech to the masses gathered outside Buckingham Palace, as well as to the throngs that lined the entire route from Trafalgar Square to Parliament Square.

As Big Ben struck three, the Prime Minister's words reverberated across the land:

"Yesterday morning at 2:41am at Headquarters, General Jodl, the representative of the German High Command, and Grand Admiral Doenitz, the designated head of the German State, signed the act of unconditional surrender of all German land, sea, and air forces in Europe to the Allied Expeditionary Force, and simultaneously to the Soviet High Command.

General Bedell Smith, Chief of Staff of the Allied Expeditionary Force, and General Francois Sevez signed the document on behalf of the Supreme Commander of the Allied Expeditionary Force, and General Susloparov signed on behalf of the Russian High Command.

Today this agreement will be ratified and confirmed at Berlin, where Air Chief Marshal Tedder, Deputy Supreme Commander of the Allied Expeditionary Force, and General de Lattre de Tassigny will sign on behalf of General Eisenhower. Marshal Zhukov will sign on behalf of the Soviet High Command. The German representatives will be Field Marshal Keitel, Chief of the High Command, and the Commanders-in-Chief of the German Army, Navy, and Air Forces.

Hostilities will end officially at one minute after midnight tonight, but in the interests of saving lives the 'cease fire' began yesterday to be sounded all along the front, and our dear Channel Islands are also to be freed today. The Germans are still in places resisting the Russian troops, but should they continue to do so after midnight they will, of course, deprive themselves of the protection of the laws of war, and will be attacked from all quarters by the Allied troops. It is not surprising that on such long fronts and in the existing disorder of the enemy the orders of the German High Command should not in every case be obeyed immediately. This does not, in our opinion, with the best military advice at our disposal, constitute any reason for withholding from the nation the facts communicated to us by General Eisenhower of the unconditional surrender already signed at Rheims, nor should it prevent us from celebrating today and tomorrow as Victory in Europe days.

Today, perhaps, we shall think mostly of ourselves. Tomorrow we shall pay a particular tribute to our Russian comrades, whose prowess in the field has been one of the grand contributions to the general victory.

The German war is therefore at an end. After years of intense preparation, Germany hurled herself on Poland at the beginning of September 1939; and, in pursuance of our guarantee to Poland and in agreement with the French Republic, Great Britain, the British Empire and Commonwealth of Nations, declared war upon this foul aggression. After gallant France had been struck down we, from this island and from our united Empire, maintained the struggle single-handed for a whole year until we were joined by the military might of Soviet Russia, and later by the overwhelming power and resources of the United States of America.

Finally, almost the whole world was combined against the evil-doers, who are now prostrate before us. Our gratitude to our splendid Allies goes forth from all our hearts in this island and throughout the British Empire.

We may allow ourselves a brief period of rejoicing; but let us not forget for a moment the toil and efforts that lie ahead. Japan, with all her treachery and greed, remains unsubdued. The injury she has inflicted on Great Britain, the United State, and other countries, and her detestable cruelties, call for justice and retribution. We must now devote all our strength and resources to the completion of our task, both at home and abroad. Advance, Britannia! Long live the cause of freedom! God save the King!"

A *Telegraph* columnist noted in the paper that the Prime Minister's speech began "with a plain recital of

facts" and "grew in emotion as it went on to its fine climax, 'Advance, Britannia'."

Following his speech to the nation, Churchill made his way to the House of Commons to address the Coalition government and the MPs that had served alongside him through the war. Due to the large crowds that lined Birdcage Walk, the short drive of just a quarter of a mile took the Prime Minister 30 minutes. As his car drove slowly along the route, Churchill stood on the front seat, displaying the victory sign he had become synonymous with, much to the delight of the gathered crowds.

The celebration of victory that was filling the streets of the London did not stop at the chamber doors of the Commons. As the Prime Minister entered to make his address almost the entire house was on its feet, cheering heartily and waving their order papers in celebration of the peace and the leader who had brought it.

As the then Labour MP for Leicester West Harold Nicolson wrote in his diary: "VE Day. Lunch at the Beefsteak. I then enter the House. The place is packed and I sit on the step below the cross bench. I see a stir at the door and Winston comes in — a little shy — a little flushed — but smiling boyishly. The House jumps to its feet, and there is one long roar of applause. He bows and smiles in acknowledgement." Churchill delivered the same speech to the Commons that he had made earlier across the airwaves, with a few additions at the end for his colleagues on the benches, as follows:

"That is the message which I have been instructed to deliver to the British Nation and Commonwealth. I have only two or three sentences to add. They will convey to the House my deep gratitude to this House of Commons, which has proved itself the strongest foundation for waging war that has ever been seen in the whole of our long history. We have all of us made

> **"Finally, almost the whole world was combined against the evil-doers, who are now prostrate before us. Our gratitude to our splendid Allies goes forth from all our hearts in this island and throughout the British Empire"**

our mistakes, but the strength of the Parliamentary institution has been shown to enable it at the same moment to preserve all the title-deeds of democracy while waging war in the most stern and protracted form.

I wish to give my hearty thanks to men of all parties, to everyone in every part of the House where they sit, for the way in which the liveliness of Parliamentary institutions has been maintained under the fire of the enemy, and for the way in which we have been able to persevere — and we could have persevered much longer if need had been — till all the objectives which we set before us for the procuring of the unlimited and unconditional surrender of the enemy had been achieved. I recollect well at the end of the last war, more than a quarter of a century ago, that the House, when it heard the long list of the surrender terms, the armistice terms, which had been imposed upon the Germans, did not feel inclined for debate or business, but desired to offer thanks to Almighty God, to the Great Power which seems to shape and design the fortunes of nations and the destiny of man; and I therefore beg, Sir, with your permission to move:

That this House do now attend at the Church of St Margaret, Westminster, to give humble and reverent thanks to Almighty God for our deliverance from the threat of German domination."

Commentators present at the time noted that the Prime Minister's voice faltered for the first time as he issued the motion to attend St Margaret's — part of the Westminster Abbey complex that was, at the time, the Anglican parish church of the House of Commons, and the place where Churchill had married Clementine Hozier in 1908. Other observers noted that some MPs were moved to tears during his speech. The reference to the liberation of the Channel Islands, which had been under German occupation since June 1940, elicited cheers from MPs.

Following the motion to give thanks, the Speaker of the House led a procession to St Margaret's Church. The Speaker was decked out in his state robes of Damascus silk and gold embroidery, which were normally reserved for coronations, jubilees and the state opening of Parliament. Headed by the Prime Minister and the deputy leader of the Labour Party, Arthur Greenwood, the procession made its way to the church, aided by mounted police who parted the cheering crowds to allow the MPs through.

Once inside the church, the service was led by the Speaker's Chaplain, Canon Don, whose sermon included the names of the 21 MPs who had lost their lives during the war. Churchill and his cabinet sat in the front row for the victory thanksgiving service. Following the service, the Prime Minister and the War Cabinet attempted to make their way to Buckingham Palace, but with celebrations now in full swing the roads were chaotic and the capital had become gridlocked by revellers. Churchill's car was mobbed.

In all the excitement of the day, Churchill realised he had forgotten his customary cigars. He asked his accompanying detective, Walter Thompson, to go back and get some saying: "I must put one on for them, they will be expecting it" — a nod to the importance of the well-established image he projected to the nation.

Eventually, the delegation made it to the palace, where they were received by the King in the Bow Room. Only a few months earlier, this elegant part of the palace had had all of its windows smashed by a flying bomb — a poignant reminder of how far Britain had come in the interim.

To the delight of the gathered crowds at the palace gates, Churchill joined the Royal Family on the balcony of Buckingham Palace for the royals' third and by no means last appearance of the day. The crowds cheered at the sight of their elected leader standing alongside the nation's leading family.

Other crowds elsewhere in the city continued to wait eagerly for their promised glimpse of the Prime Minister. Over in Whitehall, where official reports estimated that a crowd of 50,000 had gathered, there were chants of "We want Winston/

W-I-N-S-T-O-N", "We want Winnie" and "Five, six, seven, eight/Mr Churchill's always late!" Their chants did not go unanswered and, as promised, although almost an hour after he was expected, Churchill arrived in Whitehall.

According to a contemporary report in *The Times*, Churchill stood at the balcony of the Ministry of Health, flanked by the Coalition cabinet that had assisted him throughout the war, and addressed the nation:

"God bless you all. This is your victory. Victory of the cause of freedom. In all our long history we have never seen a greater day than this. Everyone, man or woman, has done their bit. Everyone has tried. None has slipped. Neither the long years, nor the dangers, nor the fierce attacks of the enemy, have in any way weakened the unbending resolve of the British nation. God bless you all!"

A pause after the opening lines of his speech allowed the crowd to punctuate the air with the roar of: "No, it is yours!" after Churchill told the nation it was their victory. The roar from the crowd paying homage to Churchill's personal part in their victory was indicative of the wider national sentiment. *The Scotsman* ran the headline "Mr Churchill's Hour" on page three of its Wednesday 9 May 1945 edition above photos of the Prime Minister and the celebrations in London, including one of him being mobbed in his car by the crowds.

Even through the most difficult and devastating periods of the war – Dunkirk, the Battle of Britain and the Blitz – when the country was brought to its knees and on the brink of defeat, Churchill's approval rating in the opinion polls never fell below 78 per cent.

"He won us the war," Joan Cuff nee Pearce from Bristol would often say whenever the conversation turned to Churchill, echoing the sentiments of many of her generation. Joan was nearly 16 when war broke out. Her father, a former Royal Marine who had fought in the First World War, had had the honour of chauffeuring the Prime Minister when he visited Bristol during the war.

For Ann Pont, a member of the Women's Auxiliary Air Force (WAAF) who was working as a radar operator at RAF Crannoch Hill in Scotland when VE Day was declared, the sound

"We may allow ourselves a brief period of rejoicing; but let us not forget for a moment the toil and efforts that lie ahead"

Previous pages A throng of well-wishers gathers around the Prime Minster as he walks across Parliament Square

Opposite Crowds look on as Churchill addresses them from the Ministry of Health

of Churchill on the airwaves was powerful. The memory of his VE Day broadcast stays with her to this day.

"I can't remember hearing the King's speech, but I do remember Mr Churchill's," says Ann. "I thought he was magnificent as Prime Minister during the war. He could deliver a speech and make people feel things were getting done. I was very young and didn't know a lot about politics in those days but I can't imagine anyone else doing the job at that time. He gave everyone a purpose in life."

The pride and reverence that Churchill inspired was noted by *The Times* in its following observation of his appearance at the Ministry of Health on VE Day:

"One of the most moving and remarkable scenes in the national rejoicing took place just before six o'clock when Prime Minister Churchill spoke from a balcony in Whitehall to a great crowd, whose self-disciplined orderliness and gaiety were so typical of the proud, unconquerable spirit of London through the dark and perilous days now left behind."

This appearance by Churchill was not the last address he made that day. As the evening turned into night, the city had never been so alive. After almost six years of darkness due to national blackouts, the capital was illuminated again. Floodlights, torches, beacons, fires and household lights shone bright; breaking through the bleakness of war and lighting up the city. St Paul's Cathedral was lit by the search lights of two young Auxiliary Territorial Service girls while Big Ben basked in the glow of 36 1,000-watt bulbs, according to the Telegraph. Other landmarks, including Buckingham Palace, Trafalgar Square and the Houses of Parliament, were also lit up for all the capital to see.

Churchill once again stepped out to celebrate with the crowds at Whitehall, this time clad in his famous boiler suit and iconic black top hat. Great roars from the crowd welcomed the Prime Minister as he made his way back out onto the balcony of the Ministry of Health. Carrying off this trademark sartorial ensemble required an audacity only the Prime Minister possessed, according to one radio broadcaster at the time: "Nobody can say that the black hat goes with the boiler suit, but you heard what a cheer it raised from the crowd."

The Guards' band, which had been playing to the Whitehall crowds, struck up a chorus of "For he's a jolly good fellow" and once again the Prime Minister found himself serenaded by the crowd. As he waved his hat above his head, cheers erupted once again. When the band started to play "Land of Hope and Glory" Churchill, now jubilant with victory, began merrily conducting the singing — a contrast to his persona of the past six years of bulldog statesmen. Following his impromptu musical performance, the great orator turned again to words. The Times reports that he addressed the crowds thus:

"My dear friends, this is your hour. This is not victory of a party or of any class. It's a victory of the great British nation as a whole. We were the first, in this ancient island, to draw the sword against tyranny. After a while we were left all alone against the most tremendous military power that has been seen. We were all alone for a whole year.

There we stood, alone. Did anyone want to give in? [The crowd shouted "No."] Were we down-hearted? ["No!"] The lights went out and the bombs came down. But every man, woman and child in the country had no thought of quitting the

Right Churchill, flanked by his cabinet, receives the cheers of the crowd from the balcony of the Ministry of Health

struggle. London can take it. So we came back after long months from the jaws of death, out of the mouth of hell, while all the world wondered. When shall the reputation and faith of this generation of English men and women fail? I say that in the long years to come, not only will the people of this island but of the world, wherever the bird of freedom chirps in human hearts, look back to what we've done and they will say "do not despair, do not yield to violence and tyranny, march straightforward and die if need be — unconquered." Now we have emerged from one deadly struggle — a terrible foe has been cast on the ground and awaits our judgment and our mercy.

But there is another foe who occupies large portions of the British Empire — a foe stained with cruelty and greed — the Japanese. I rejoice we can all take a night off today and another day tomorrow. Tomorrow our great Russian allies will also be celebrating victory and after that we must begin the task of rebuilding our hearth and homes, doing our utmost to make this country a land in which all have a chance, in which all have a duty, and we must turn ourselves to fulfil our duty to our own countrymen, and to our gallant allies of the United States who were so foully and treacherously attacked by Japan. We will go hand and hand with them. Even if it is a hard struggle, we will not be the ones who will fail."

VE Day veteran

Bert Turner
Served in the RAF; 96 years old

Can you tell us a little bit about your wartime experience?
I volunteered for the Air Force in 1942 and trained as a flight engineer at RAF St Athan in South Wales. I did about four bombing runs but mainly we were supplying the SOE [Special Operations Executive], towing gliders, dropping paratroopers. Action started when you got in the aeroplane in England and it didn't stop until you landed again. When you got to a target, you saw the flak and you thought "how can you get through that?" But some way or another you did.

When we went to Arnhem [the Battle of Arnhem, Netherlands, September 1944], we took the gliders — a Horsa glider on the Sunday and the Monday, and they weren't bad trips — a bit of flak. We went on the Tuesday and it was very rough. We were very badly damaged. We went again on the Thursday and by 3pm we had been across to Arnhem and had been shot down; the skipper and rear gunner were dead.

How did your family react?
I'd got married on 14 September 1944 to a WAAF on the same station, and she was told seven days later that she was a widow. I said goodbye to her on 21 September at about half past ten and the next thing she knew, we had been shot down and she was told nobody had seen us bail out. So, they thought we had gone down with the aircraft.

I got back on the Sunday morning and I was in a state. I had a hole in me ankle, no hat, no collar and tie, my jacket and trousers were torn and I hadn't had a decent wash since Thursday. The first thing she said to me was "you stink", which wasn't very polite!

Do you remember where you were when you were told that the war in Europe was over?
I was at RAF Keevil in Wiltshire serving behind the bar in the Sergeants' Mess. We were all confined to camp — we had just had a party in the mess. We knew it was coming, it was on the cards. We were just waiting for it to finish. Somehow there was disappointment — the majority of us were expecting to go to the Far East.

Chapter four

THE KING'S SPEECH

A kingdom united

Just as the Royal Family bolstered the country's spirit of fortitude in wartime, so in victory they became the focus for scenes of national jubilation

The Royal Family, headed up by King George VI, was held in high regard and was of great significance to the nation and the wider Commonwealth during the Second World War.

Following his elder brother's abdication, Prince Albert, known as "Bertie" by those closest to him, found himself on the throne. A shy man, he had sought a quieter life and never anticipated that he would one day become king. However, the ultimate royal duty was thrust upon him at a time of great unrest for both the British monarchy and Europe as a whole. As King George VI was crowned in 1937, Adolf Hitler was holding meetings about "acquiring living space for Germans" — a moment that marked the radicalisation of his expansionist plans for the Third Reich. Two years later, the newly crowned king and his nation would be forced into a world war against Germany, the second in living memory.

At the outset of his reign, there was a feeling among some in the country that George VI was not fit for the throne. These doubts were, at times, shared by the King himself. Since childhood he had struggled with a stammer, a life-long battle depicted in the 2010 film *The King's Speech*. As a prince, his few attempts at public speaking had been torturous affairs. While he had shown his commitment to his people and displayed a deep, paternal sense of royal duty, there were concerns he could not shoulder the burden of leading a kingdom.

Yet, as with Churchill, the Second World War was to be the making of him. Over the course of the conflict, George VI demonstrated a quiet strength of character, becoming a symbol of courage and resilience for the nation.

The King and Queen gained approval for remaining at Buckingham Palace during the war, even after it was bombed during the Blitz. On one occasion it was hit when the royal couple were at home preparing for bed, prompting the Queen to write to her mother-in-law, Queen Mary: "It all happened so quickly that we had only time to look foolishly at each other when the scream hurtled past us and exploded with a tremendous crash in the quadrangle."

Buckingham Palace was hit twice during the Blitz, and then again by the V-weapons — the flying bombs known as "doodlebugs" — in the final weeks of the war. This gave the King and Queen a commonality with the bombed-out communities they regularly visited. "I am glad we have been bombed," said the Queen, after the Palace received a direct hit from the Luftwaffe in September 1940. "It makes me feel that I can look the East End in the face."

The fact that the royal couple also chose to keep their beloved daughters Princess Elizabeth (the future Queen Elizabeth II) and Princess Margaret in England, rather than sending them to North America as many of the aristocracy did, further endeared the royals to the nation. "The children will not leave unless I do," the Queen explained in a letter to her mother-in-law, Queen Mary. "I shall not leave unless their father does, and the King will not leave the country in any circumstances whatever." The Royal Family determined to stand shoulder to shoulder with their people and endure the ordeals of the war.

The King visited his troops on several battle fronts during the Second World War. He had military experience of his own, having served in the Royal Navy from 1913 to 1917, and had been briefly deployed during the First World War. He was even mentioned in dispatches for his role in the Battle of Jutland. Ill-health shortened his naval career, however, and when the Royal Air Force was established in 1918 he transferred, becoming the first member of the Royal Family to be certified as a pilot and rising to the rank of Squadron Leader.

Once crowned king, he represented all three of the Armed Forces, holding the ranks of Admiral of the Fleet for the Royal Navy, Field Marshal in the British Army and Marshal of the Royal Air Force. Throughout the war he and the Queen would inspect the troops, with the King always appearing in uniform. On VE Day itself, the King chose to wear the uniform of the Royal Navy — the first of the forces he had served.

The Royal Family had a long association with the Armed Forces charity the Soldiers, Sailors, Airmen Families Association

Opposite The VE Day crowd looks on as the Royal Family make their way onto the Palace balcony

Right King George VI calls on the British people to "stand calm, firm and united" following the declaration of war on Germany in September 1939

(SSAFA). The King and Queen were both patrons of the charity, while the King's mother, Queen Mary, was its President. All three visited SSAFA branches, clothing stores and events to witness the work the charity did to support serving personnel and their families during the war. The Royal Family took a keen interest in the organisation's efforts; in 1945, following the release of a report by Lord Munster into the conditions for British military personnel in India and Southeast Asia, Queen Mary sent a telegram asking what SSAFA was doing to alleviate the suffering. The charity's chairman was able to respond that, in line with the report's request for an increase in the number of SSAFA volunteer staff, the SSAFA branches or offices in those commands had been expanded and more volunteers were undergoing training to be deployed.

The Royal Family boosted the nation's morale, even when it was at its lowest ebb. Knowing the positive impact they had, the King and Queen made frequent visits to factories that were supporting the vital war effort, visits that the Ministry of Supply found invariably boosted weekly production figures, according to the Imperial War Museum. The King and Queen also ventured out to meet the victims of the Luftwaffe's raids.

As a newsreel report on the VE Day celebrations remarked, the Royal Family were "the great family of Britain". The nation turned to them as one might to a parent in times of need for guidance, support and an example of how to keep going. It was only natural that, on the day that victory was declared, the people would want to celebrate with the family who had become the epitome of British endurance and resilience.

As 8 May 1945 dawned, Buckingham Palace was, like much of the nation, going on as normal. An investiture ceremony had already been planned for the morning, and even the official declaration of a long-awaited victory over Nazi Germany was not going to halt official proceedings. The King held the first peace-time investiture at Buckingham Palace with more than 270 men and women decorated. The arrival of the delegation of newly invested OBEs, MBEs and Knights at the Palace caused cheers to erupt from the crowds that had already started to gather outside. However, the jubilant throng's chants to see the King remained as yet answered.

Reports describe the Palace crowds as a sea of red, white and blue. Every other woman seemed to sport a ribbon or rosette — something of a mystery given the apparent scarcity of ribbon during wartime. Yet on VE Day, the streets were draped in red, white and blue fabric, banners and bunting. "Seen from above they by no means corroborated the gloomy report that London had become a place of tired-looking people wearing tired-looking clothes," *The Times* noted.

The tulips that lined the Mall added yet more colour to the occasion. On that sunny May day, people sat among them picnicking and waiting for a sight of the King and the official speeches from the newly erected loudspeakers in the Palace forecourt. The presence of these speakers, as well as the full size Royal Standard — normally reserved for special occasions and last flown on the day of the King's Coronation in 1937 — flying above the King's residence were the only outward signs from Buckingham Palace that there was anything different about that morning.

And yet, the crowd that was gathering would become the biggest seen outside Buckingham Palace since the Silver Jubilee, according to *The Times*, even outnumbering that seen at the King's Coronation.

The sight of Prime Minister Winston Churchill arriving at Buckingham Palace for

Opposite The King and Queen survey bomb damage to Buckingham Palace, September 1940

Right The royal couple visit London's East End during the Blitz

lunch with the Royal Family excited the crowd once more, with everyone cheering his name and whipping up renewed calls to see the King. But the King kept the crowds waiting until after Churchill's address to the nation at 3pm, which officially declared that war with Germany was over.

The Royal Family listened to the Prime Minister's speech from their private apartments and, following Churchill's address, the King appeared on the balcony of Buckingham Palace to the delight of all assembled. At first, stood alone on the gold and scarlet-draped balcony, the King waved to the crowds, who had been chanting his name throughout the day. He was then joined by the Queen, who wore powder blue, Princess Elizabeth dressed in her khaki Auxiliary Territorial Service (ATS) uniform and Princess Margaret who, like her mother, wore blue. "This was the central scene of it all," wrote *The Scotsman*'s London reporters of the sight of the Royal Family on the balcony.

A Guards band led the crowd in the National Anthem. George VI was reported to be smiling widely as the crowd before him flung hats into the air and sang in united voice, "They are jolly good fellows" to the Royal Family.

Throughout the remainder of the day and late into the night, the Royal Family would return to the balcony again and again to wave to the crowds and take part in the collective celebration of the day. As one news broadcaster commented at the time: "Never was there a deeper and more heartfelt expression of joy than this … We had won through … Britain and the great family of Britain throughout the world rejoiced as never before."

In total, the King appeared on the balcony eight times that day. Once the Royal Family were even accompanied by Churchill, who returned to the Palace with his War Cabinet to meet with George VI ahead of the King's own address to the nation.

King George VI had battled with a stammer his whole life, a stammer he thought might alienate him from his people but which, in fact, only endeared him to them. They witnessed his steely resolve to overcome the debilitation and were inspired by it, as he addressed the nation at 9pm on VE Day. Across the radio airwaves and transmitted via the many loudspeakers erected in the capital and elsewhere around the world, he made the following public address:

"Today we give thanks to Almighty God for a great deliverance. Speaking from our empire's oldest capital city, war-battered but never for one moment daunted or dismayed, speaking from London I ask you to join with me in that act of thanksgiving. Germany, the enemy who drove all Europe into war has been finally overcome.

In the Far East we have yet to deal with the Japanese, a determined and cruel foe, and to this we shall turn with the outmost resolve and with all our resources. But at this hour, when the dreadful shadow of war has passed far from our hearts and homes in these islands, we may at last make one pause for thanksgiving and then turn our thoughts to the tasks all over the world, which peace in Europe brings with it.

Let us remember those who will not come back. Their constancy and courage in battle, their sacrifice and endurance in the face of a merciless enemy. Let us remember the men in all the services, and the women in all the services, who have laid down their lives. We have come to the end of our tribulations and they are not with us at the moment of our rejoicing.

Then, let us salute in proud gratitude the great host of the living who have brought us to victory. I cannot praise them to the measure of each one's service. For in the total war, the efforts of all, rise to the same noble height and all are devoted

"As your King I thank, with a full heart, those who bore arms so valiantly on land and sea or in the air and all civilians who shouldering their many burdens have carried them unflinchingly without complaint"

to the common purpose. Armed or unarmed, men and women you have fought, striven and endured to your utmost. No one knows that better than I do, and as your King I thank, with a full heart, those who bore arms so valiantly on land and sea or in the air and all civilians who shouldering their many burdens have carried them unflinchingly without complaint.

With those memories in our mind, let us think what it was that has upheld us through nearly six years of suffering and peril. The knowledge that everything was at stake. Our freedom, our independence, our very existence as a people, but the knowledge also that in defending ourselves we were defending the liberties of the whole world, that our cause was not the cause of this nation only, not of this empire and commonwealth only, but in every land where freedom is cherished and law and liberty go hand in hand. In the darkest hours we knew that these enslaved and isolated peoples of Europe looked to us. Their hopes were our hopes.

Their confidence confirmed our faith. We knew that if we failed the last remaining barrier against a worldwide tyranny would have fallen in ruin. But we did not fail. We kept faith with ourselves and with one and another. We kept faith and unity with our great allies. That faith, that unity carried us to victory, through dangers which at times seemed overwhelming.

So, let us resolve to bring to the tasks which lie ahead the same high confidence in our mission. Much hard work awaits us, both in the restoration of our own country after the ravages of war and in helping to restore peace and sanity to a shattered world.

This comes upon us at a time when we all have given of our best. For five long years and more, hearts and brain, nerve and muscle have been directed upon the overthrow of Nazi tyranny. Now we turn, fortified by success, to deal with our last remaining foe.

The Queen and I know the ordeals which you have endured throughout the Commonwealth and Empire. We are proud to have shared some of these ordeals with you. And we know also that together we should all face the future with stern resolve and prove that our reserves, our will power and vitality are inexhaustible. There is great comfort in the thought that the years of darkness and danger in which the children of our country have grown up are over. And please God, forever. We shall have failed and the blood of our dearests will have flowed in vain if the victory which they died to win does not lead to a lasting peace, founded on justice and goodwill.

To that then let us turn our thoughts on this day of just triumph and proud sorrow, and then take up our work again. Resolve, as a people, to do nothing unworthy of those who died for us and to make the world such a world as they would have desired for their children, and for ours. This is the task to which now honour bids us.

In the hour of danger we humbly committed our cause into the hand of God, and he has been our strength and shield. Let us thank him for his mercies and in this hour of victory commit ourselves, and our new task, to the guidance of the same strong hand."

Following the King's broadcast and in response to it the Buckingham Palace crowd erupting yet again into chants of "We want the King". The King and Queen reappeared on the balcony, the King still in his naval uniform while the Queen was now reported to be wearing a white ermine wrap over her evening gown and a diamond tiara, according to *The Times*. For five minutes there was a tumult of cheering.

Watching from among the crowd were two daughters who beamed with pride and bubbled with the excitement of the night — the 19-year-old Princess Elizabeth (to become Queen Elizabeth II) and her 14-year-old sister, Princess Margaret. The two had spent little time in London during the war, having lived in Windsor Castle for the majority of the conflict. Despite having taken part in war work, with Princess Elizabeth joining the ATS at the beginning of 1945 at her own insistence, the princesses had spent most of the past five and half years cloistered away. They were eager to experience the excitement of VE Day and, in a move that still surprises many to this day, the King granted his daughters permission to head out into the streets of the capital to see for themselves how the nation was celebrating.

Previous pages An expectant crowd gathers before the gates of Buckingham Palace

Left The King is joined by the Prime Minister and members of the cabinet in the grounds of Buckingham Palace

VE Day veteran

Leslie Edward Kershaw
Served in the RAF as a glider pilot; 97 years old

What had your war been like up until May 1945?
I signed up in my first year at university, joining the RAF's Cadet Core and training in Canada until September 1944. In March 1945 I had been part of a glider regiment during the Rhine Crossing. They were desperate to have an airborne regiment to get the troops over the Rhine, so they got RAF pilots and gave them khaki uniform and boots — after landing, you were expected to get out of your glider and fight like an ordinary soldier.

That Rhine crossing was a huge success and established our air supremacy in the final weeks of the war. I did get shot at by the German snipers, but made it back unscathed.

What are your memories of VE Day?
I was at RAF Netheravon, on Salisbury Plain. There were four pilots flying two gliders — two to each glider. We were concentrating on what they call "snatch pickup" — flying a plane over the top of a glider that has a rope strung out in front of it and a hook on the end. If you were in the glider, it whipped you from 0 to 60mph in no time. You might be flying over the glaciers or in a place where you couldn't land a plane, but you could land a glider, and rig it up so you could pick up an injured soldier, or someone who needs to return home.

However, not long after the end of the war, the development of the helicopter rendered the glider obsolete. When we heard about the German surrender, we got an old glider and all sorts of things, piled them onto the parade ground and set fire to them.

You actually set fire to your glider?
Well they were only bits of plywood, with a small amount of metal in the undercarriage. Who was going to want them? So we had a bonfire until midnight. It was incredible.

We knew that there was still work to do, in rescuing prisoners of war in Europe, and not to mention the war in Asia. But it was just great fun for everyone around the bonfire. I don't think anyone had any moans or groans to express.

"Resolve to do nothing unworthy of those who died for us and to make the world such a world as they would have desired for their children, and for ours"

The princesses were escorted by 16 trusted members of the Royal Household, including their cousin Margaret Rhodes, lady in waiting Jean Woodroffe, members of the Grenadier Guards and the King's newly appointed Equerry Group Captain Peter Townsend (whose successes as leader of the RAF's pathfinder team locating German bombing targets during the war had made him a war hero and something of a heartthrob). Yet even with this entourage, stepping out into a crowd of thousands to wander through a celebratory London was an unprecedented risk.

In a rare radio interview for the BBC's *The Way We Were* in 1985, Queen Elizabeth II recalled how, as she was about to step out into the midst of the crowd and pretend to be an ordinary member of the celebrating public, she become nervous. "I remember we were terrified of being recognised," said the Queen. She went on to describe how she pulled her ATS uniform cap down low over her eyes in a bid to cover her face, but a Grenadier Guard officer among the group accompanying her informed the Princess, who was now a Junior Commander in the ATS, that he would not be seen in the company of another officer improperly dressed, so the princess had to wear her hat according to regulation.

Around 9pm, as their father was making his broadcast, Princess Elizabeth, Princess Margaret and their accompanying party slipped out of the Palace and joined the crowd beyond the gates, chanting for the King and Queen. After cheering and waving like all those assembled, the royal party moved away from Buckingham Palace and danced the entire length of The Mall, mixed in among the celebrating public. On foot, the royal party would cover five miles that night, visiting the liveliest VE Day celebration hotspots of the evening.

"I remember lines of unknown people linking arms and walking down Whitehall, all of us swept along on a tide of happiness and relief," the Queen recounted for the BBC. By 10.30pm they made it to Trafalgar Square, which was jammed with people and a scene of absolute "whoopy", as Margaret Rhodes described it in an interview for the Channel 4 documentary *The Queen's Big Night Out*, which first aired in 2015.

From Trafalgar Square the partying princesses and their entourage were swept along to Piccadilly Circus, which was reportedly one of the most riotous and rowdy spots in London on VE Day. "It was a very one-off sort of occasion," Margaret Rhodes told Channel 4. "It was a wonderful escape for the girls."

Imbued with the VE Day spirit of freedom and liberation, the royal party decided to conga through The Ritz. Unlike the youthful hedonism on show at Piccadilly Circus, the hotel was a place of polite standards, and the temporary wartime home of many European aristocrats, world leaders and politicians. As older residents drank tea and ate sandwiches in a formal atmosphere, the royal party danced merrily and exuberantly through the reception and the dining areas. Few of the older residents of The Ritz would have realised that one of these high-spirited young people was actually the future Queen of England. "I think we rather electrified the stuffy individuals inside," said Rhodes.

From The Ritz, the dancing royal party made its way back towards Buckingham Palace, weaving its way through Green Park. Before returning to the confines of the Palace, the Princesses joined the crowd cheering for the King and Queen once again. Thanks to a message sent by the princesses, as search lights lit the night sky and the Palace was illuminated by flood lights, their parents appeared on the balcony for the final time that evening.

It was a thrilling and electrifying night for the two young princesses and their entourage. They had partied with their public and shared in the nation's celebration of victory. Forty years on, when interviewed by the BBC, Her Majesty still fondly remembered the day that she danced through the streets of London along with a gleeful public. "I think it was one of the most memorable nights of my life," she said.

Opposite, top
Princess Elizabeth ventures out into the VE Day celebrations

Opposite, bottom
As darkness descends, flood lights illuminate the Palace and the still bustling throng

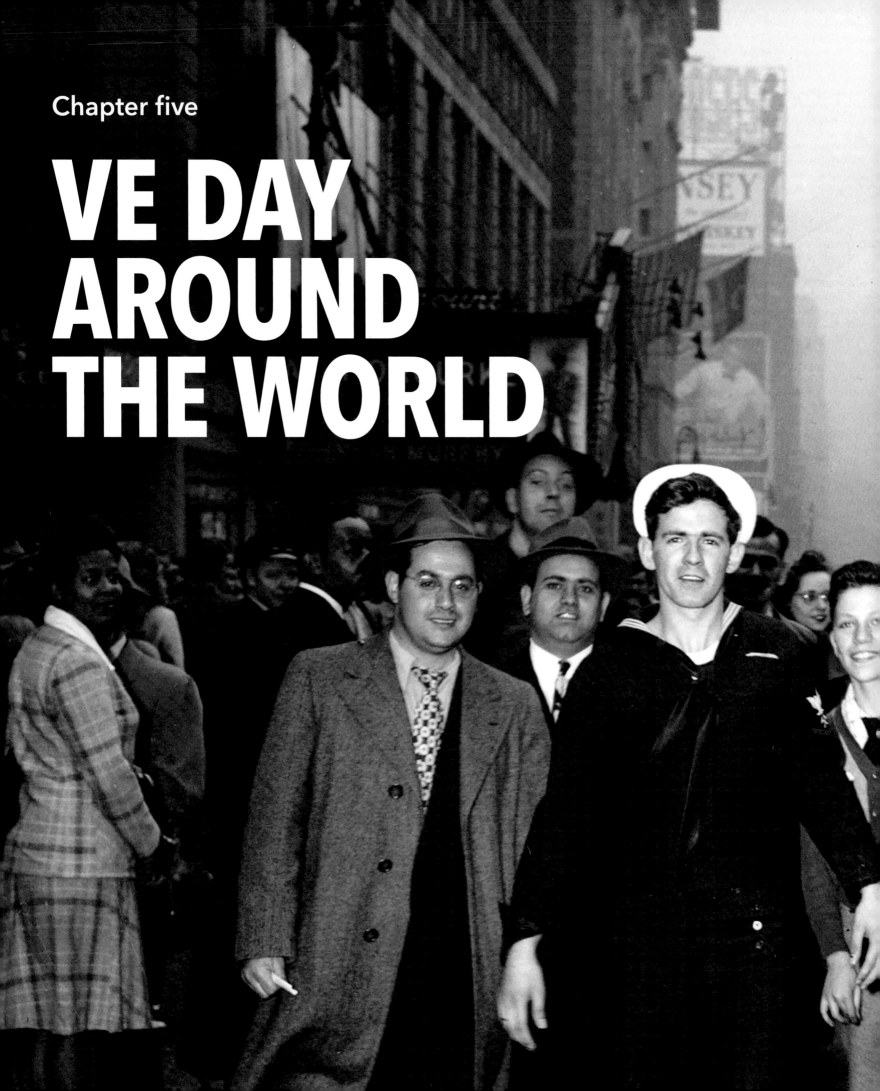

Chapter five

VE DAY
AROUND
THE WORLD

Celebration
and solemnity

For many around the world, VE Day was cause for revelry and rejoicing, but for others it was a day of remembrance and grim realities

The declaration of peace in Europe was received in different ways in the different countries and regions of the world. Although the Germans had instigated the Second World War and their defeat was welcomed by all opposed to their tyranny, for many the conflict did not end with the surrender of the Third Reich. The war was still raging in the Far East and, as Churchill noted in his speech from the balcony of the Ministry of Health, there was still another enemy to vanquish.

As one report from Burma — now known as Myanmar — in the *Liverpool Daily Post* illustrates, VE Day did not mean victory for all, such as those in the Far East. It reads: "A small group of mud-splashed green-uniformed British soldiers gathered round a signals truck in a flooded Burmese paddy field listened in silence to the news that the War in Europe was ended. 'V-Day at last,' one said. 'No, Chum, VE-Day; we have got to wait for VFE Day,' another replied."

Yet for those nations that had been occupied by Nazi Germany, that had suffered the onslaught of the bombing raids or had faced the constant threat of destruction, it was a moment to rejoice.

Scandinavia
While Sweden had maintained a policy of neutrality throughout the Second World War, its geographical proximity to occupied countries, such as Norway, and the horrors that were taking place on the other side of its borders meant its people were only too aware of the misery of war. Sweden had also provided a haven for those fleeing German occupation, including 50,000 Norwegians, while nearly all of Denmark's 8,000 Jewish citizens fled there to escape being deported to concentration camps.

With so many refugees in their country fleeing German tyranny, it was not possible for Swedes to be unaware of the brutality of the Nazi regime. Despite its policy of neutrality, the country secretly trained Norwegian resistance fighters.

It also helped connect Hjemmefronten — the Norwegian resistance movement — to London, ensuring that supplies, reinforcements and military intelligence flowed between the occupied Nordic countries and the Allied powers.

During the war, Sweden had been forced into providing support to Nazi Germany, selling it iron ore and allowing it the use of Swedish railways. However, towards the end of war, the Swedes started providing operational support to the Allies, even allowing them to use Swedish airbases — something that threatened to provoke a violent response from Germany. It is little wonder, then, that on VE Day, Swedish Prime Minister Per Albin Hansson was reported as saying: "It feels as if a long nightmare has lost its grip on us and we can breathe again."

While Sweden could breathe again, the fall of the Third Reich elicited more lively celebrations in both Norway and Denmark. Having been occupied since April 1940, both countries had suffered under the yoke of Nazi rule. Even for Denmark, which did not have to endure military occupation until 1943, the capitulation of Germany in May 1945 and the announcement of the Allied victory was long overdue. The Norwegian Telegram Bureau reported that in Oslo on VE Day throngs of people filled the streets, laughing and singing, and the "excitement reached boiling point" late in the evening. Freed patriots, who had been languishing in German prisoner-of-war camps, were carried shoulder-high among the crowds in the Norwegian capital.

In Denmark, people were reported to have stormed news-stands, fighting to get copies of papers announcing the German surrender. Giddy on freedom, some Danes went a little too wild for their Allied friends in the city. "Terrified Britons and Americans sought to escape as people kissed them and hoisted them on their shoulders," read a report from Copenhagen that ran in the *Liverpool Daily Post* on Wednesday 9 May.

France

When the announcement of the German surrender came on 7 May, Paris exploded into celebration — similar to the mood in August 1944, when the French capital was liberated after four years of occupation. As on liberation day, crowds filled he streets rejoicing and cheering the Allies. Even more significantly for the city dubbed *La Ville-Lumière* ("the City of Light"), Paris shone bright once again. After years of observing night-time blackouts, the city's buildings and monuments were bathed in floodlight.

The Eiffel Tower, the city's most iconic structure, had remained a symbol of resistance throughout the war, even when it was being used as a German broadcast station. As the Germans entered the city in 1940, citizens sabotaged the tower's lift cables, meaning that the Germans had to climb the 300-metre tall structure, and it was never open to the public during the occupation. The cables were not fixed until 1946. In addition, German attempts to hang a giant swastika from the top of the tower were thwarted; within hours of the Nazis soldiers climbing up the tower to raise the flag, it was ripped away by the wind.

In 1944, as the Allies approached Paris, Hitler ordered his military governor of the city, Dietrich von Choltitz, to demolish the tower along with all of Paris's other surviving religious, cultural and historic icons; the Führer's demands were ignored. The Eiffel Tower and the rest of the city remained intact and, on the day of liberation, 24 August 1944 — less than nine months before VE Day — six firefighters climbed the tower to raise the French Tricolour. This time, the flag wasn't removed by the wind.

"Crowds paraded the boulevards last night singing 'It's A Long Way To Tipperary' and 'The Marsellaise,'" on VE Day, according to Paris-based journalists reporting in the *Liverpool Daily Post*. Spontaneous celebrations filled the beflagged streets with parades and cheering crowds. For Nicola Treharne, who had been working with the Resistance in occupied France since she was 16, VE Day was thrilling, filled with "great rejoicing". Born in England to a French mother and fluent in French, Nicola had become quite practised in parachuting in and out of occupied France, and was later awarded both the Croix de Guerre with Palm and the Medaille de la Reconnaissance Francaise for her wartime work.

After the war, Nicola volunteered with the Armed Forces charity SSAFA, and was eventually awarded an MBE in recognition of her 30 years of service as a SSAFA caseworker. Celebrating the 50th anniversary of VE Day in 1995, Nicola told the *SSAFA News* magazine that she had spent the day hurtling down the Champs Elysees in a convoy of trucks, with horns blaring in true Gallic fashion.

Belgium

For Belgium, one of the first countries invaded by German forces, in May 1940, and the scene of the last major German offensive campaign on the Western Front, the Battle of the Bulge (16 December 1944 to 16 January 1945), the news of victory in Europe could not have been sweeter. While Brussels, the country's capital, had been liberated by Allied Forces on 3 September 1944, before the Battle of Bulge began, the presence of German forces in other parts of the country up until February 1945 meant that true relief could only come with the announcement of peace.

Opposite Evening
VE Day celebrations
in Sydney, Australia

Above, left
Crowds gather in the
Place de la Bourse
in Brussels

Above, right
Children look on at the
scene of celebrations in
Wellington, New Zealand

In Brussels, it was announced that all public buildings and private houses were to be dressed with flags for eight days. Children were given three days off school. On their return to lessons, the first order of the day was to gather around the national flag to hear about the meaning of victory.

For Mary Blood (nee Pettit), who was in Brussels with the WAAF, the sight of the city on the eve of VE Day was one she will never forget. Recording her memories for the BBC's *WW2 People's War* project, Mary recalls the scene after the 7pm news flash came announcing the following day as Victory in Europe Day, with the whole city lit up by searchlights, rockets, fireworks and flares, and the streets bedecked with British, Belgian and American flags. People stood and danced on the roof of trams and car horns were honked. Mary recalls being invited to the house of a Belgian family for a "thanksgiving" dinner, before riding on an American Jeep and partying until two o'clock in the morning in various Brussels nightclubs. "VE Day had been a very long, but a very happy day," she said, "one never to be forgotten."

Australia and New Zealand
A reporter based in Sydney, Australia observed in the *Liverpool Daily Post* that "People were in bed when the news came last night, but those still in the city nightclubs and theatres took up the revelry, cheering and yelling." However, while those already out on the tiles may have embraced the victorious spirit, it seems that the general tone in the country was one of solemn remembrance and battle hardening. For Australia, the Second World War was far from over — Japan, its Pacific Ocean neighbour, had posed more of a threat than Nazi Germany throughout the war, and continued to do so.

"Since when has it been customary to celebrate victory halfway through a contest?" wrote *The Sydney Morning Herald*.

Despite this, the newspaper also reported on the scenes of mass jubilation in Sydney. Tickertape, in the form of discarded and ripped up documents from the Taxation Department, filled the air and by dusk the streets were 12 inches deep in paper. The *Herald* also told how a crowd formed a dance ring around a Scottish member of the Royal Navy and a WRNS girl to allow the couple to perform a Highland fling.

On 9 May, some 100,000 people attended a service at the Shrine of Remembrance in Melbourne. On the same day, in the capital city of Canberra, the editorial writer of *The Canberra Times* described the floodlights over the Australian War Memorial as being "in bright relief against the darkness which is now passing from Europe, and soon from the entire world".

New Zealanders were more prepared for a celebration, but one that was to be an organised commemoration rather than a spontaneous outpouring of wild jubilation. Acting Prime Minister Walter Nash refused to allow celebrations to take place until Winston Churchill had officially announced peace from London. Due to the time difference between the two nations, the confirmation of peace did not come to New Zealand until one o'clock in the morning on 9 May 1945. As a consequence, although there was some spontaneous dancing in the streets, cities in New Zealand did not erupt as their counterparts had in Europe.

Preparations for the victory celebrations had actually been underway for some weeks in the country, with planned events including speeches, thanksgiving services and the singing of the national anthems of New Zealand, Britain, the US and the Soviet Union. A People's Victory March in Christchurch drew 25,000 people. Crowds gathered in front of the parliament building in Wellington, with the mass of people extending from Parliament Grounds to the government building, many brandishing the Union Flag.

"Russians danced and sung where once the feet of soldiers had marched to war"

In Dunedin, a Highland Pipe Band led a victory parade through the city. "It has often been said that Dunedin is the dour Scotch city, but there's been nothing of dourness about it on this occasion as the people have let themselves go properly," remarked a broadcaster on Radio New Zealand. "It started on Tuesday, and the enthusiasm is still running high."

The Soviet Union
As one of the three main Allied forces, the Soviet Union — which entered the war in 1941 — played a pivotal role in the victory over Nazi Germany. The Red Army also bore the greatest death toll; one estimate puts it that for every American soldier who died fighting the Germans, 80 Soviet soldiers suffered the same fate. The Soviet Union was decimated by the Nazi war machine, bearing the brunt of Hitler's genocidal plan to depopulate the east of its native citizens for "*Lebensraum*" — living space for an expanding Third Reich.

In his memoir, General Eisenhower recalls his visit to the USSR in the weeks after VE Day: "When we flew into Russia, in 1945, I did not see a house standing between the western borders of the country and the area around Moscow. Through this overrun region, Marshal Zhukov told me, so many numbers of women, children and old men had been killed that the Russian Government would never be able to estimate the total."

So devastated were the nations of the Soviet Union that its citizens were too war-weary, too shell-shocked and too broken to reach the jubilant heights of its fellow Allies' celebrations. They were also still living under their own dictatorship. Few could have forgotten Josef Stalin's Great Terror of 1933-38, during which 3 million people were accused of opposing communism and sent to gulags, and around 750,000 were summarily killed. Nor would they forget Stalin's infamous Order No. 227 of July 1942, also known as "Not a step back", which stipulated that each front must create "penal battalions" — comprising soldiers who had faced court-martial — who would be forced to serve at the front line. These were accompanied by "blocking detachments" at the rear of the front, which were ordered to shoot anyone who retreated.

A Reuters special correspondent in Moscow, Duncan Hooper, reported that it was "All Quiet in Moscow" on VE Day, unlike in other Allied nations. "Monday began quietly in Moscow with the newspapers giving no hint that any special announcement was expected. Overnight, as Tuesday dawned, the shops were crowded with people laying in small extras for victory parties."

Instead of 8 May, the date celebrated by the rest of Europe, Stalin declared that the Soviets would mark victory on the following day. Nor would they use the term VE Day — instead the Red Army's victory in "the Great Patriotic War" would be called simply Victory Day. Unlike Churchill, Stalin did not appear in public in a jubilant mood. When his underling, Nikita Khrushchev, telephoned him to congratulate him on his victory, Stalin reportedly responded: "Why are you bothering me? I am working." It was not until June that the USSR held any official victory parade. On that day, lines of soldiers paraded past Stalin throwing defeated German banners, flags, standards and insignias at their dictator's feet.

Nevertheless, the battered and depleted Soviet population did turn out on Victory Day. Crowds gathered in Red Square — a poignant commemorative moment given that it was from Red Square that the Red Army had marched straight to the front when it looked as if Moscow may fall to the Germans in 1941. Four years later, Russians danced and sung where once the feet of soldiers had marched to war.

The Far East
For many of those British forces who had been to the Pacific theatre of the Second World War, VE Day passed without much in the way of recognition at the time, although years later some still recall how they spent the day. For Ian Ronald,

Above A woman holds the Soviet and Union Jack flags outside her window on VE Day

Opposite, top and bottom Fireworks light up the night sky above the Kremlin in Moscow on 9 May 1945

EGYPTIAN MAIL

No. 9663.   CAIRO. — TUESDAY, MAY 8, 1945. — ALEXANDRIA.   10 MILLIEMES.

It was officially announced last night that today would be V-E Day, and that the whole day would be regarded as a holiday. This is in accordance with arrangements with the three Great Powers. Mr. Churchill will broadcast at 13.00 hours G.M.T. (16.00 hours Cairo summer time), and the King will broadcast to the peoples of the British Empire and the Commonwealth at 19.00 hours G.M.T. (22.00 hours Cairo time). Parliament will meet at the usual time. — Reuter.

GERMANY SURRENDERS

WORLD WILL CELEBRATE 'V.E. DAY' TODAY

Churchill To Speak From No. 10 This Afternoon

THE instrument of Germany's unconditional surrender to the Allies was signed yesterday by Colonel General Jodl for Germany and three Allied Generals, including a Russian and French delegate. Today is V-E Day, it was officially announced last night.

AFTER THE SIGNATURE, GENERAL EISENHOWER RECEIVED GENERAL BEDELL SMITH AND THE GERMAN NAVAL COMMANDER-IN-CHIEF, ADMIRAL VON FRIEDBERG. THE GERMAN EMISSARIES WERE REPEATEDLY ASKED: «DO YOU UNDERSTAND THE SIGNIFICANCE AND SERIOUSNESS OF THE TERMS?» AND THE GERMAN OFFICERS REPLIED «YES».

Although the war in Europe is over, there will be no official announcement of this until this afternoon. As Parliament will be sitting today, the Prime Minister may make the announcement first in the House of Commons.

The delay in announcing V-E Day is occasioned by the agreement which has been reached between Mr. Churchill, President Truman and Marshal Stalin that the announcement, when it comes, shall be made simultaneously in London, Washington and Moscow.

It is believed that another reason delaying the announcement of V-E Day is that the Allies wish to make sure Admiral Doenitz can enforce his surrender on all German battlegroups before telling the world the war is over.

Colonel General Gustav Jodl, the new German Army Chief of Staff, signed the unconditional surrender of all German Forces at 2.41 hours yesterday morning at a little town about which is little about Eisenhower's headquarters.

First news of Germany's total surrender was a broadcast by the German Hamburg radio early yesterday afternoon in which it was reported that Admiral Doenitz had ordered the unconditional surrender of all German fighting troops.

Message to the Germans

Soon after the German radio broadcast a special message to the German nation. It said:

"This is the German nation. We're now broadcasting an address by the Reich Minister, Count Schwerin von Krosick, to the German People. German men and women — The High Command of the Armed Forces has to-day, on order of Grand Admiral Doenitz, declared the unconditional surrender of all fighting German troops.

This news came soon after the Danish radio had announced that the German forces in Norway had capitulated.

Yesterday the German-controlled Flensburg radio reported that Grand Admiral Doenitz had ordered all U-boats to cease activity. The cease fire order to U-boat commanders was given in an Order of the Day on Sunday the radio said.

Shortly after 1 p.m. yesterday President Truman went into conference in Washington with Mr. Grew, acting Secretary of State, and Mr. William Clayton, Assistant Secretary of State.

Crowds in Downing Street

Urgent last minute talks between Germany's surrender kept the radios humming between London, Moscow and Washington.

The cabinet met yesterday morning and ever since there have been comings and goings of the Ministers in Whitehall. A large crowd formed at the end of Downing Street waiting for the news to break last night.

There were wild scenes of joy within a few minutes of the report that Germany had surrendered unconditionally. Ticker tapes and bits of torn telephone books started fluttering down from sky-scrapers in the city's traditional manner of celebration.

Patton Makes A Final Dash—To Prague

A dash for Prague is being made by General Patton's famous Fourth Armoured division which carried out the spectacular race across France, said a late message last night.

It is speeding on in two columns, and although no details are being given at the moment, Prague Radio reported that American tanks were 15 miles south of the Czech capital.

This followed the earlier broadcast by the German-controlled Prague radio that the German commander in Czechoslovakia does not recognise Doenitz's surrender. The broadcast added that the Germans in Bohemia will continue to fight until they receive free passage out of the country.

Considerable Forces

A curfew for civilians from 10 p.m. to 5 a.m. has been imposed. Civilians found in possession of fire-arms will be summarily shot. Any excesses against the German civil population will be answered by reprisals against Czechs in German hands.

This came after the statement by Prague Radio that owing to the strength of resisting Czech groups, the German authorities had decided to put considerable forces into action to restore calm and order in the capital.

Unrest arising out of political developments has interrupted negotiations between the German authorities and the Czech protectorate Government the announcer said.

Another broadcast said: The rebellion in Prague renders it impossible to spare the city the destruction of war, although it had been declared a hospital city by the German state and military leaders.

"The leaders of the rebellion, acting against the interests of the majority, bear the sole guilt. — Reuter.

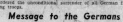
COLONEL GENERAL JODL
He replied, "Yes"

CHURCHILL'S MICROPHONE WAS READY

MR. CHURCHILL prepared last night his historic statement to announce the end of the European war and was ready to go to the microphone at a moment's notice.

A special squad of B.B.C. engineers and technicians were ordered to stand by to ensure the most perfect reception.

The B.B.C. arranged to put out the news in about 30 languages by a corps of announcers who included many patriots driven from their European countries by Hitler.

B.B.C. Stood By

These are the men who have been playing a vital part in Allied propaganda work to occupied Europe during the Hitler regime.

Mr. Churchill had received direct 'phone reports on the situation from Europe and made frequent 'phone calls to President Truman and Mr. Eden.

According to the "Daily Herald", Mr. Churchill admitted to friends that he had "never imagined an end so swift and complete." — A.N.A.

The Portuguese Government yesterday closed all German diplomatic and official property on the ground that the national German government no longer...

BEGINNING OF THE END

THIS was the beginning of the end . . . . In Field Marshal Montgomery's tent at Luneburg Heath at 6.25 p.m. on Friday last General Admiral von Friedeburg, Supreme Commander of the German Navy, signed the surrender instrument by which nearly a million Huns lay down their arms. This official war office photograph shows Montgomery looking sternly on while the German chief signs his name to the document.

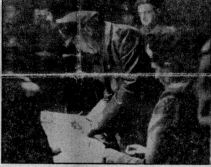

THE BIGGEST SURRENDER IN ALL HISTORY

By Jon Kimche, Reuter's Correspondent

THE six years war in Europe has ended with the greatest surrender in history. It is estimated that about 10,000,000 Germans will now become prisoners of war. The Western Allies will hold more of them than they have troops in the field. They may remain prisoners for years.

Under the rules of war prisoners are held until the signing of peace which is not anticipated for some considerable time. Some of them, however, will be released early for work on the land to tackle the economic difficulties of Central Europe and the Russians have again said that German prisoners should be used to make good some of the damage they have done.

Despite Admiral Doenitz's unconditional surrender, it is probable that at the last minute that Grand Admiral Ernst von Schorner will order his cliché in Czechoslovakia to retire and surrender to General Patton's Third Army.

Meantime Allied military circles are taking every care to ensure that last-minute German plans to drive a wedge between the Soviet Union and the Western Allies do not succeed.

Every German action in the east has been designed to stimulate mistrust in the Soviet. — Reuter.

MONTY MEETS ROKOSSOWSKY

Field Marshal Montgomery lunched yesterday with Marshal Konstantin Rokossowsky at Wismar.

This was their first meeting and very cordial greetings were exchanged. Toasts were drunk to the Allied armies, the Prime Minister, Mr. Churchill, Marshal Stalin, and President Truman. — Reuter.

Commission Will Now Take Over

The next stage in dealing with defeated Germany is for the Allied Control Commission to take over.

A detailed programme for the administration of Germany has already been drawn up and the Commission's duty will be to see that Allied policies are carried out.

The plans arranged may have to be readjusted because of the chaos now reigning in the Reich.

It is understood that there will be no attempt yet to bring into existence a German Government. The Germans will have to obey the orders of the Commission, under which will work various sub-commissions covering all the phases of public and economic life.

One of the main tasks will be the elimination of all Nazis.

BRITISH 2nd. ARMY'S FINE RECORD

TWENTY-SEVEN British and American divisions which fought under the command of the British Second Army have destroyed seventy-nine German divisions—at the rate of one per day over one period.

They have liberated 11,000 square miles of Europe and conquered 70,000 square miles of Germany, including 110 German towns.

These figures are included in what may be termed the official statistical story of the British Second Army, from D-Day to its own Victory Day—May 5 — a total of 335 days.

In those eleven months of battle, General Sir Miles Dempsey's men have opened and maintained 11,000 miles of road, constructed 76 airfields and built 677 bridges which, placed end-to end, would stretch sixteen and a half miles.

How necessary were these bridges was shown by the fact that the Germans wrecked 2,876 in their park.

Allied sappers sowed 95,000 mines and lifted 350,000 German mines. One hundred and six towns, with populations of over ten thousand, acclaimed the British Second Army as liberators. — (Reuter)

New York radio yesterday announced that U.S. Ninth Army troops have withdrawn from the territory east of the Elbe in accordance with the demarcation agreement with the Soviet Union.

GERMANY IS TOLD 'ENEMY WAS TOO STRONG'

'WE NOW HAVE TO FACE OUR FATE SQUARELY'

COUNT von Krosigk, the German Foreign Minister, announcing Germany's surrender, said: As the leading Minister of the Reich Government, which the Admiral of the Fleet has appointed for dealing with war tasks, I turn at this tragic moment of our history to the German nation.

After an heroic fight of almost six years of incomparable hardness, Germany has succumbed to the overwhelming power of her enemies.

To continue the war would only mean senseless bloodshed and futile disintegration. The Government, which has a feeling of responsibility for the future of the nation, was compelled to act on the collapse of all physical and material forces and to demand of the enemy the cessation of hostilities.

It was the noblest task of the Admiral of the Fleet and of his Government, after the terrible sacrifices which the war demanded, to save in the last phase of the war, the lives of the maximum number of fellow countrymen. That the war was not ended immediately simultaneously in the west and in the east is to be explained by this reason alone.

In this gravest hour of the German nation and its Reich we bow in deep reverence before the dead of this war. Their sacrifices place the highest obligations on us. Our sympathy goes out above all to the wounded and bereaved and to all on whom this struggle has inflicted blows. No one can be in doubt about the severity of the term to be imposed on the German people by our enemies. We must now face our fate squarely and unquestioningly. Nobody can be in any doubt that the future will be difficult for each one of us and will exact sacrifices from us in every sphere of life.

This Burden

We must bear this burden and stand loyally by the obligations we have undertaken. But we must not despair and fall into mute resignation. From the collapse of the past, of all relations between material lines in the years of war have found their biggest expression in the spirit of comradeship at the front and readiness to help one another in all the distress which has afflicted the homeland.

In our nation, justice shall be the supreme law and the guiding principle. We must also recognise law as the basis of all relations between nations. We must recognise it and respect it from inner conviction. Respect for treaties will be as sacred as the claim of our nation to belong to the European family of nations, as a member of which we want to mobilise all human, moral and material forces in order to heal the dreadful wounds which the war has caused.

Then we may hope that the atmosphere of hatred which today surrounds Germany all over the world will give place to a spirit of reconciliation without which the world cannot recover. — (Reuter).

Spain To Freeze Assets

German assets in Spain will be frozen shortly, reliable sources reported yesterday.

It is understood that the German Embassy and Consulates are being closed down. Reuter.

Danish Traitors Arrested

TRAITORS are being quickly rounded up. Fritz Clausen, leader of the Danish Nazi Party, Moeller, leader of the German military party, Knudsen, director of the Danish State Railways, and Col. Martinsen, leader of the Schleswig Corps, are all under arrest.

A Bill has already been prepared and will shortly become law introducing the death penalty for murder and sabotage by Nazis and for denouncing Danish citizens to the German authorities. It will apply retrospectively.

Capital punishment, even for murder, did not exist in Denmark before the war, and the new Bill may be taken as an indication of the Danish fury against traitors and Germans.

Heavy shooting took place on Sunday afternoon in Copenhagen. One unit of the Danish Gendarmerie arriving from Sweden was attacked by Hipomen (German auxiliary police). Several were killed, among others four women belonging to the Women's auxiliary corps. — Reuter.

COUNT VON KROSIGK
"To continue would only mean senseless bloodshed"

AN EPITAPH
Third Reich Is Dead

Alan Moorehead, British war correspondent, who has followed the Allied armies from invasion to victory, cabled this epitaph on Germany:

HITLER wanted Germany to go down with him in utter ruin — a colossal sacrifice to a colossal vanity. He has done it.

Around us in Germany are things too monstrous to grasp. Starvation. Fifty great cities in ruins. Ten, 20, perhaps 30 million people roaming helplessly through the countryside without homes, with relatives lost and with all normal hope gone.

Greater Germany is extinct. The third Reich is merely a dead carcase and there is no need for any of our generation to think we can again be hurt by it in our lifetime.

Something else might arise — but will not be Germany. — A.N.A.

PARIS IS READY...

Paris is ready to celebrate V-E day. Extra rations of wine and meat will be granted to Parisians for a whole week's victory week.

Frenchmen will celebrate in a sober mood of thankfulness. The black-out will be lifted entirely, searchlights will play on outstanding buildings, and Paris will assume something of its pre-war appearance. — Reuter.

Above The Egyptian Mail reports the news of victory in Europe

stationed in Burma, 8 May 1945 was a relaxing one. "I was sitting under a tree drinking rum," he told *SSAFA News* magazine in 1995. Ian, who in later years volunteered as a Divisional Secretary for the Hampshire branch of SSAFA, had started his military career in the Royal Navy but, at the outbreak of the war, aged just 19, he found himself in the British Army. He had been in "the deep end of Dunkirk" and ultimately wound up in Burma as peace in Europe was declared.

Ian was still only 23 years old by then, and the rum he was drinking with fellow British soldiers had quite literally fallen out of the sky. It had been dropped by an American aircraft, instead of urgent supplies such as boots, and was not going to go to waste. They knew nothing about the German surrender and were just enjoying a rare moment of peace, having not seen any Japanese soldiers for a few days. It was a different story to VJ — Victory over Japan — Day on 15 August, when Ian was in Singapore and watched the official ceremony take place.

For Arthur Lane, who had served in the Manchester Regiment, VE Day did not pass in quite such a peaceful fashion. He was being held as a prisoner of war by the Japanese and would go on to dedicate his life to the memory of his fellow prisoners. During his captivity he played "The Last Post" more than 3,000 times for those who fell in front of him while they were forced to construct the notorious Thailand–Burma Railway — among the 13,000 Allied prisoners and up to 100,000 civilian forced labourers who died in its construction.

Speaking to *SSAFA News* magazine in 1995, Arthur recalled how — on what turned out to be VE Day — he and a group of 100 other prisoners were on their way to Chiang Mai in Thailand's Golden Triangle to repair bomb damage on the railway that they had built with primitive tools and their own sweat, blood and tears. In later years, he would write books about his experiences, donating the proceeds of his writing to SSAFA.

Egypt

Egypt adopted a position of neutrality during the Second World War but this did not protect it — or the wider North African region — from the ravages of conflict. Partly, this was due to the key strategic role of the Suez Canal — a link between Asia, North Africa, Europe and the assorted colonies of Britain and France. But it was also due to the region's proximity to Italy and southern Europe.

Almost as soon as the war began there were skirmishes in North Africa between British and Italian forces. In February 1941, Hitler deployed his army to North Africa in a bid to gain the strategic territory and within weeks the British had been pushed back into Egypt from Libya. However, in October 1942, General Bernard Montgomery, one of the war's best-known British military figures, inspired the dispirited Allied force to victory at the Battle of El-Alamein. In less than three weeks, and despite suffering significantly more losses than the German and Italian forces, "Monty" had forced the enemy into full retreat and 30,000 soldiers surrendered. Churchill saw the victory as a turning point in the Allied campaign, stating "this is not the end, it is not even the beginning of the end. But it is, perhaps, the end of the beginning".

Less than three years later, on VE Day, British Armed Forces personnel attended a thanksgiving service at the aptly named El -Alamein Club in Cairo to commemorate the end of the war in Europe. A report from Cairo-based foreign correspondents published in the *Liverpool Daily Post* described the VE Day celebrations in Egypt: "In Cairo the soldier's dream is coming true. For 48 hours there will be no reveille and no fixed mealtimes. Entertainment has been arranged on a large scale, including a running buffet, victory games, and all-night concert parties. The most popular event is expected to be High Command Stakes for donkeys jockeyed by brigadiers or officers of still higher rank."

British forces had remained in North Africa and the Middle East throughout the conflict. "Cairo was the crossroads of the world — a kaleidoscope that was always changing," recalled Virginia Stuart in a 2019 article in *New York Times Magazine*. Virginia worked for the Office of Strategic Services [OSS] — a clandestine espionage organisation set up to gather intelligence against the Axis powers — and was based in Cairo from 1944.

Cairo was also the location of the first overseas bureau of SSAFA, the Armed Forces charity, which opened in September 1941. The bureau was manned by volunteers, many of them women. In February 1943, a special message was received from General Harold Alexander, Commander in Chief of Middle East Forces, in which he praised SSAFA and the importance of its work saying it "was contributing directly and in no small measure to the victory".

While the war had moved out of North Africa in the final year of the conflict, pursuing the retreating Axis forces into Italy and Greece, Egypt remained a hub for military intelligence and activity well after the German surrender. The RAF's 205 Group would regularly fly into Cairo as they transported the personnel of the South African Army and Air Force, and other Allied military personnel, and former prisoners of war would use Cairo as a hub when being transported around the Commonwealth.

The United States

President Harry Truman announced that, unlike in most of Europe, including its ally Great Britain, VE Day would not be a public holiday in the US. In fact, he announced that Sunday 13 May — Mothering Sunday — would be the official Victory in Europe day, setting a thanksgiving rather than rejoicing tone. For the United States — which had not suffered the bombing raids of the Blitz, been invaded and occupied by enemy forces, or suffered the civilian death toll of its European allies — there was not the same level of collective relief that news of Germany's surrender evoked in others. Instead, America's focus remained on the enemy that had brought it out of isolationism and into the war: Japan.

"It obviously will be no time for unrestrained rejoicing," announced Thomas E Dewey, the Governor of the State of New York, according to the *Kirkintilloch Herald* on 9 May 1945. "Many brave Americans will die, many hundreds of thousands will be wounded before we have completed the subjugation of the Japanese. Thus victory over Germany will in truth be the occasion for prayers."

Since Pearl Harbor, which saw the death of 2,403 Americans in a single day, the US war machine had been the biggest international player in the Far East. War propaganda called up the memory of the Japanese attack on 7 December 1941, with posters bearing slogans such as "Avenge December 7" as an American sailor raised a clenched fist. As President Franklin D Roosevelt famously stated to US Congress the day after the attack, it was "a date which will live in infamy". While American GIs who found themselves in Britain on VE Day embraced the celebrations, often to be found at the centre of the action, for those deployed in the Far East or in the United States, the day was more a moment to give thanks.

Right, clockwise from top left
A woman throws tickertape onto the street below in New York on VE Day; an aerial view of Wall Street; New Yorkers in the city's financial district crowd the steps of the Sub Treasury Building

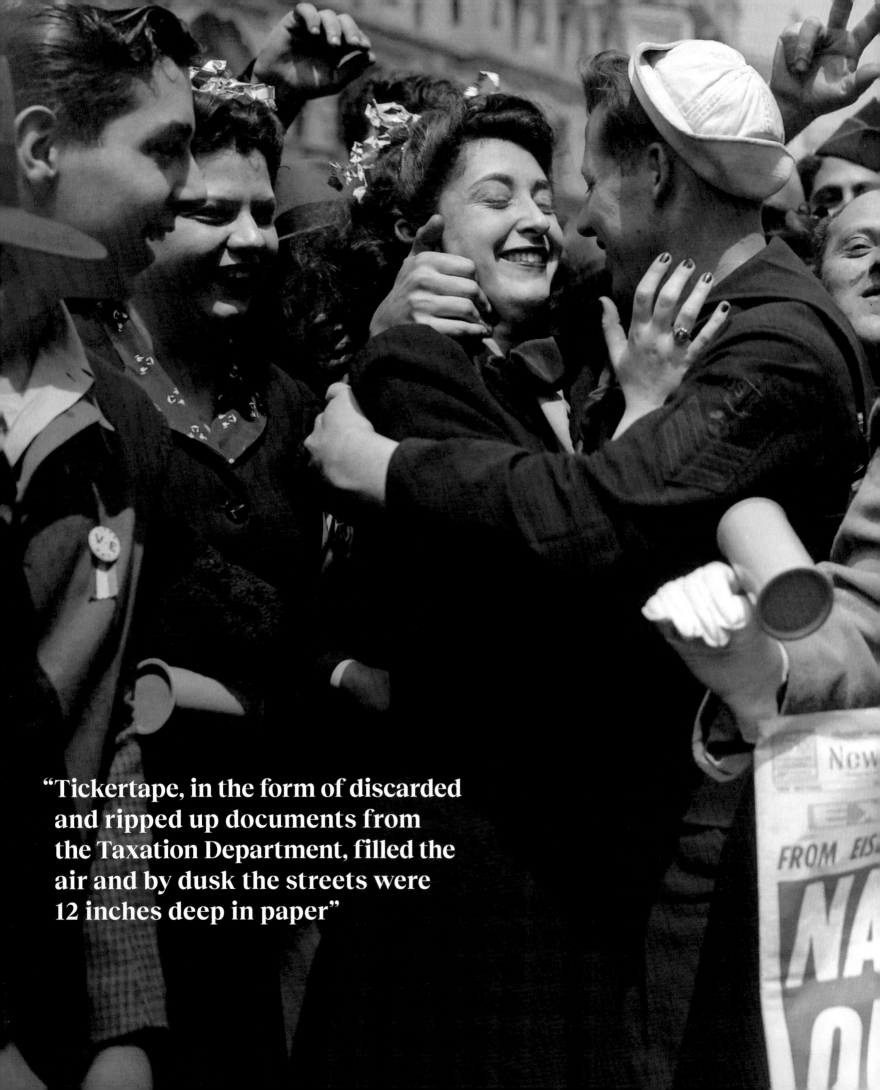

"Tickertape, in the form of discarded and ripped up documents from the Taxation Department, filled the air and by dusk the streets were 12 inches deep in paper"

As 8 May dawned in the United States, flags across the country were still flying at half-mast to mark the passing of the much-loved President Roosevelt, who had died in office on 12 April 1945. His successor, Harry Truman, made it clear that VE Day was not a time for partying, nor to forget there was still a job to be done. In his address to the American people that day, Truman set a commemorative, sober tone and reminded his nation not to forget the battle they still faced and those who had already lost their lives.

"Our rejoicing is sobered and subdued by a supreme consciousness of the terrible price we have paid to rid the world of Hitler and his evil band," he said. "Let us not forget, my fellow Americans, the sorrow and the heartache which today abide in the homes of so many of our neighbours — neighbours whose most priceless possession has been rendered as a sacrifice to redeem our liberty… If I could give you a single watchword for the coming months, that word is work, work, and more work. We must work to finish the war. Our victory is only half over."

Heeding that message, *The New York Times* reported that in Washington DC "Thousands of War and Navy employees, some uniformed but mainly civilians, greeted the V-E news as soberly as their chiefs gave it to them. There was thankfulness, but no cheering. Perhaps it was in recognition that this nation had only passed the halfway mark in its global war." However, huge crowds did gather in New York's Times Square after news of the surrender, and managed to stop the traffic. Other celebrations also took place in cities across the nation, including New Orleans, which reportedly took on the appearance of a Mardi Gras parade.

Canada

One million men and women — nearly a 10th of Canada's population — served in the Canadian Armed Forces during the Second World War, and more than 45,000 Canadians gave their lives in the conflict. When VE Day came, along with declaring a public holiday for 8 May, the government also announced the end of military conscription — despite the fact that Allied forces were still actively engaged in conflict with Japan in the Far East.

According to a news report from *The Globe and Mail*, celebrations in Toronto began on the 7 May as the city "let loose a tidal wave of enthusiasm that drowned out the government's expressed desire to have VE-Day observed the day following the announcement of the unconditional surrender of Germany." Thousands danced in the

"Europe has been brought to misery and famine by Germany, the German nation must not expect to fair better than the nations they have overrun"

Opposite US and Soviet troops link up near Griebo in Germany

streets as tickertape rained down from windows of buildings and from three Mosquito aircraft that circled overhead. A piper and drummer led a group of revellers through the lobby of the King Edward Hotel where "girls received hearty kisses from total strangers, men and women clasped hands, throats became rather choky."

While there were exuberant celebrations from the young, for those who had experienced the conflict first-hand, the mood was less jovial. *The Globe and Mail* noted that: "The men in uniform were less demonstrative, less exuberant, especially those who wore ribbon and whose eyes told of things that the bobby sox brigade would not have to see." The newspaper reported that the business that had its most successful day on VE Day was The Bell Telephone Company, as people called loved ones to share the news of peace but also to remember those who they had lost. While the streets filled with "marching, singing people" in the churches and privacy of homes, there were people who prayed and wept and the day became one of remembrance and commemoration.

As Toronto marked VE Day with a mixture of celebration and reflection, elsewhere in Canada the day proved to be one of tension. There were even riots in Halifax and Dartmouth in Nova Scotia, where a total of 564 businesses suffered damage and 207 shops were looted. The population of Halifax had nearly doubled during the war as service personnel poured into the port city, creating overcrowding and resentment between the locals and the military personnel. On VE Day, when poor preparations by both the military and local authorities resulted in restaurants, bars and cinemas being closed for the celebrations, there was little for those in the port town to do. "It was a real problem to get a meal," said one local commentator. A brewery was broken into, almost every bar, restaurant and liquor store was looted, and large-scale vandalism ensued.

According to *The Globe and Mail*, only one store remained unbroken in the city's miles of downtown thoroughfares — Jack Sutherland's barber shop. Its survival was down to the building's owner, Emma Mackay, who stood in front of the store for 15 hours defending it from the rioters and "diplomatically talking at least a dozen people out of breaking her window". The store had stood for 56 years and Mrs Mackay was not going to let a mob of drunken revellers change that.

Germany

For the Allied Forces in Germany, the day of surrender was one of mixed emotions. As the Germans surrendered to Montgomery's 21st Army Group in Luneburg, Allied military personnel briefly celebrated before listening to the updates from their commanding officers. The 8th Hussars (part of 7th Armoured Division), also known as the "Desert Rats", celebrated VE Day in northern Germany with a church parade followed by rum punch, drunk beside bonfires on which swastikas were ceremonially burned.

The BBC reported that a Scottish battalion let off some flares when the news of victory reached them. Later on, rum was issued and one platoon held a sing-song. However, some German forces who refused to believe the surrender continued to fight, meaning that — even in victory — the Allied Forces in Germany could not let their guard down.

A *BBC History* article tells the story of Stuart Hills, a British officer with an armoured regiment, who found himself in Germany at the time of surrender. On hearing the news he immediately felt exhilaration and "liberated" some champagne. Then, like many others who just hours before were still seeing the horrors of war, Stuart thought of the friends he had lost and his desire for celebration waned.

Further back from the front lines, there were more jubilant celebrations, which on occasion descended into wildness, with

men going AWOL and reports of some alcohol-fuelled fatalities. But, on the whole, the British military maintained their discipline. There were no stories of British pillage or of violent British retributions against the Germans. However, the reality of conditions in Germany — a near-starving civilian population, the flattened ruins of towns and cities, and the horrors of the death camps —had a sobering effect on British troops.

British forces had liberated the notorious concentration camp at Bergen-Belsen on 15 April 1945. The scenes they saw there would haunt them and the world forever. Thousands of bodies laid unburied and some 60,000 starving and fatally ill people were packed together in the most inhumane and appalling conditions. While the camp was liberated that day, it did not empty. Many of the inmates were too ill to move; the British Army and relief workers stayed in the camp for months treating those who remained. Nearly 100 British medical students arrived after VE Day to assist with the relief effort.

RAF Sergeant JC Thompson was attached to the Second Army, which formed part of the 21st Army Group under Monty. For the BBC's *People's War* project he recalled the feelings he had when he arrived in Luneberg, having first travelled through the concentration camp at Belsen and then witnessed a grenade attack on some Tyne Tees Guards. Sergeant Thompson recounted still feeling sick and angry about Belsen and the attack when they got news of the German surrender on 7 May. "Our mood changed as we celebrated with a tot or two and fired off some Verey lights on the strip," he reported. "That evening, the General's Adjutant comes over to us and thanks us for our efforts and the commanding officer has a talk with us on the strip about how important our work had been." However, for the men of the 21st Army Group, dubbed "the British Liberation Army", or BLA, there was the sense that the war was not over, with servicemen grimly jesting that BLA stood for "Burma Looms Ahead".

VE Day veteran

Leslie Norman Collins
1st Assault Brigade; 95 years old

What were your memories of the war?
I grew up on the Old Kent Road. My war started in 1938 when I was 14, as a message boy for the Auxiliary Fire Service. Everyone was gearing up for war. I then joined a cable manufacturing company whose headquarters in High Holborn got bombed during the Blitz.

In June 1943 I got called up. I trained in Canterbury and then Aldershot as a driver and wireless operator. I then moved on to train in Suffolk with the Assault Engineers — Royal Engineers who were assault troops. We were training for the Normandy landings, equipped with special tanks and guns to attack the Germans' West Wall.

On 6 June 1944 we landed on Gold Beach, in a field outside Bayeux. We were bombed and shelled but we managed to take Bayeux on the first day, and eventually on to Caen. Then there was the failed Battle of Arnhem in September 1944, where we had to retreat — I ended up spending most of the winter in a tobacco factory in Nijmegen.

What are your memories of VE Day?
After the Rhine crossings in March 1945, we could tell victory was close. The week before VE Day I remember we captured a drum of cherry brandy somewhere outside of Bremen. So when news of the German surrender came, we decided to broach this barrel! Naturally, we all got drunk, but the news was a massive relief.

But your war didn't end there?
We got moved Hamburg. The devastation was terrible. You could travel five or six miles and you wouldn't find a building that was standing. Then it was back to Canterbury and we started training to go to Japan, because they needed assault troops like us. But then, of course, they dropped the atom bomb, so we didn't have to go. So they sent us to Germany where we became the army of occupation. We were stationed at a barracks at Hamelin.

When did you leave the Army?
Not until 1952. At the end of the war, my brother returned from a mission to Yugoslavia, and found out he'd contracted tuberculosis. Our dad had dies from it, so I immediately got an X-ray. They found a lesion on my lung. I had to have a medical procedure called a pneumoperitoneum every single week for five and a half years, and spent some time in a sanatorium. So, for all the celebrations on VE Day, it wasn't quite over for many of us.

Right Red Army soldiers march to meet the Allies' military delegation for the signing of the German Instrument of Surrender in Berlin

Travelling with the 21st Army Group was a group of civilian volunteers from SSAFA. In 1944, Montgomery had requested that SSAFA provide a bureau to accompany them – the first of its kind to be recruited. It came into official existence on 13 April 1944. By the end of June of that year it was dealing with 200 new cases a week, rising to 950 by end of July. The SSAFA caseworkers travelled with the troops as they advanced through France and then Germany. Camping out in the bombed-out buildings of the fallen German cities, they supported the service personnel in the field and also helped families back home remain in touch with their serving loved ones via the SSAFA branch network.

Like the soldiers of the 21st Army Group, the SSAFA volunteers saw for themselves the state of ruin and deprivation Germany found itself in. Wynford Vaughan-Thomas reported from Luneburg for the BBC on VE Day. In his despatch he describes the scene of "docile" crowd of Germans massing around the main square. Before the old town hall, in the hot May sun, the crowd waited to hear the announcement, which was scheduled for 4pm.

"We have got no flag or bunting out. Instead a single white sheet hangs from a window of the town hall," reported Vaughan-Thomas. He describes an endless line of German soldiers that "no one even bothers to notice anymore", as they troop by on their way to the nearest prison camp. German citizens are said not even to raise their heads to look as their soldiers go by. "The war for them is over," Vaughan-Thomas reported. "All these people want to do now is hear the official announcement."

For the Germans it was a time of great anxiety and dread, with many citizens particularly fearing the wrath of the Red Army. The announcement that rang out to the crowd at Luneburg and others around the country stated it was for the German civil administration and the German people to restore order to civil life and rebuild the country. The public were told that they would be "treated with justice". The agent of the commanding forces told the crowd: "Europe has been brought to misery and famine by Germany, the German nation must not expect to fair better than the nations they have overrun. On your efforts and cooperation with military government depends the standard of living and the amount of nourishment you will get."

Dr Hans Graf von Lehndorff, a German surgeon, recalled hearing the news of the Germany defeat in Königsberg – now the Russian city of Kaliningrad but which was part of the German empire until 1945. "On 8 May we hear that the war is over," he wrote. "The loudspeakers ring out a bit more piercingly than usual. In the halls a few sceptical German soldiers are talking about the liberation from National Socialism and the blessings of Bolshevism. Outside the commandant's door – where can it have come from, in this wilderness? – an opulent flower arrangement is being constructed. Otherwise we aren't really aware of the final victory."

While the German surrender was met with a more tempered reaction from Allied troops in Germany than in other parts of Europe, there was also a lot to be grateful for. On Tuesday 8 May, VE Day, RAF Lancasters landed in Germany to fly the first wave of freed British prisoners of war home. On that first day of peace, 4,500 soldiers were repatriated.

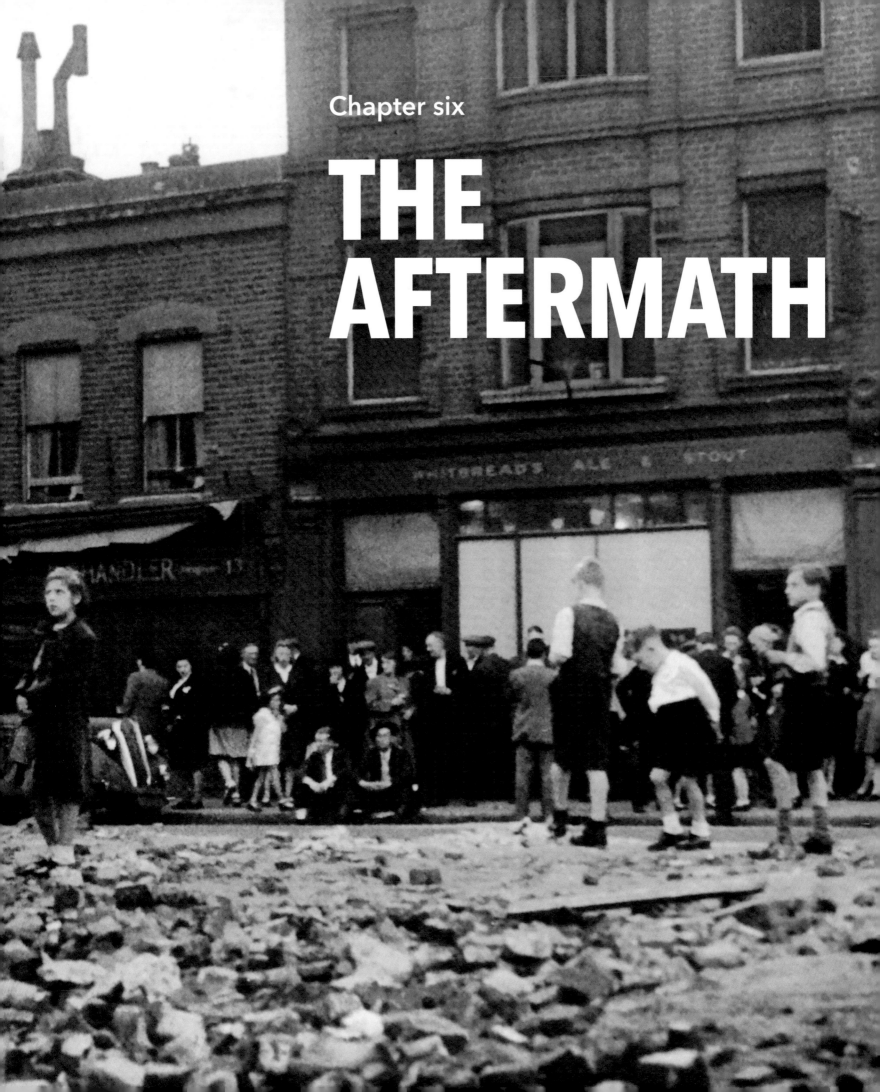

Chapter six

THE
AFTERMATH

Winds of change

The weeks and months that followed VE Day witnessed a momentous British General Election and, eventually, an end to the war in the Far East

As VE Day came to a close, an age of austerity dawned in Britain. The nation was now at peace with Germany but there was still a war to fight in the Far East, and a welfare war to fight at home.

The Second World War had cost the nation greatly. Britain suffered 264,433 military and 60,595 civilian deaths during the conflict. Many others were physically and mentally scarred by the war and unable to resume normal life. Thousands of houses had been destroyed by bombing raids while many factories and shops had suffered. People were sleeping in army camps or in emergency homes.

In addition, 177 merchant ships and two-thirds of the Royal Navy's fleet had been sunk, so importing food supplies was a problem. Ironically, rationing became tighter after the war. Many Europeans were surviving on less than 1,000 calories per day — around a third of the recommended amount — and rationing was set to continue for another 10 years.

The war had largely bankrupted Britain. The national debt had risen from £760 million to £3,500 million, and the country had spent close to £7 billion, or a quarter of its national wealth. Even as war spending was coming to a close, more government spending was desperately needed to repair and rebuild a devastated nation. In addition, the public demand for social and welfare support had never been greater.

The shared suffering and sacrifice of the war years strengthened the belief that governments had an obligation to provide basic care to the masses. The need to treat large numbers of civilian casualties from bombing raids gave people access to healthcare they had never experienced before. War had also provided evidence for the benefits of state intervention in welfare. Indeed, rationing during the Second World War had actually improved the diet and health of the poor in Britain.

The changing attitude to welfare was further demonstrated by the release of high-profile recommendations, including the 1942 report to Parliament by the Liberal politician William Beveridge, entitled *Social Insurance And Allied Services*. With its mantra to "Abolish Want" the Beveridge Report (as it became known) set out plans for the future of post-war Britain. It identified the main issues facing British society as want, disease, ignorance, squalor and idleness. The radical report laid the foundations of what would become known as the Welfare State and was embraced by many sections of the British public that desired reform and change.

"The Conservative party slogan 'Help him finish the job' next to a picture of Churchill did not chime with voters who wanted to move on from the war"

This desire for social reform is thought to be one of the many factors that led to the shock landslide victory for the Labour Party in the July 1945 elections. Winston Churchill was a successful wartime leader and a hero. Yet, for all the cheering and public adoration directed towards "the man who won us the war", the winds of political change were strong in Britain. Churchill's personal popularity was not enough to win the Conservative Party new supporters. His speech on 4 June about a socialist government requiring "some form of Gestapo" to achieve its plans was seen as hugely disrespectful to his loyal Labour colleagues in the wartime coalition, including the Labour leader Clement Attlee, who had served as Churchill's deputy prime minister.

The Conservative party had also run a flawed campaign: its slogan "Help him finish the job" next to a picture of Churchill did not chime with voters who wanted to move on from the war. The Labour party responded by using a similar slogan next to a picture of three returning British servicemen — "Help them finish THEIR job! Give THEM homes and work!" — which appealed to the national mood for a brighter future and a sense of change.

The very war that had been Churchill's defining moment would also be the cause of his political defeat. It had brought a change in public expectations, with people becoming more accepting and expectant of state intervention and support. The Labour Party's plans for a welfare state reflected these new needs, as did election slogans such as "Let us face the future together" and "A non-stop drive to provide a good home for every family". The promises of a welfare state, based on the Beveridge Report, and immediate nationalisation of the Bank of England, coal, power, transport, and iron and steel industries attracted voters to Labour.

While the official election date was 5 July, voting did not close until 19 July to enable soldiers stationed abroad to vote.

Previous pages
Labour Party leader
Clement Attlee enjoys
a cup of tea with
constituents in the
build-up to the 1945
General Election

Left Campaign
posters for the 1945
General Election

Right Attlee joins US President Harry Truman and Russia's leader Josef Stalin at the Potsdam Conference in Germany, August 1945

The results of the election were announced a few days into the Potsdam Conference near Berlin, a meeting of the key Allied figures of Churchill, Stalin and Truman to establish the principles of the Allied occupation of Germany. Potsdam would be Churchill's last international outing as wartime Prime Minster, and he was reported as being in decline. The 71-year-old was depressed and anxious about the impending results of the General Election. "I don't want to do anything," he told his doctor. "I have no energy. I wonder if it will come back." He is reported to have refused to look at briefing notes prepared by Foreign Office experts for the conference, and indulged in lengthy and irrelevant discourses during the discussions. Labour's landslide victory meant that, halfway through the conference, Churchill and his Foreign Secretary, Anthony Eden, were replaced by Attlee and his Foreign Secretary, Ernest Bevin.

In the decades that followed the Second World War, there was a long period of "post-war consensus" in British politics. All parties agreed on the country's main priorities and generally worked together to achieve post-war recovery. Attlee's Labour government immediately set out on a course of radical welfare reforms. He announced the introduction of the Welfare State as outlined in the Beveridge Report, including the establishment of a National Health Service in 1948.

On the global stage, of course, there was an even more immediate challenge to be met in the wake of VE Day — the ongoing conflict in the Far East.

On 6 August 1945, the first atomic bomb, known as "Little Boy", was dropped on the southern Japanese city of Hiroshima by a US B29 Superfortress bomber, the *Enola Gay*. The blast devastated an area of five square miles, destroying more than 60 per cent of the city's buildings and killing around 140,000 people. Three days later a second atomic bomb, "Fat Man", was dropped on another city in southern Japan, the military port of Nagasaki, killing a further 74,000 people.

These devastating attacks, which helped bring about the surrender of Japan and the end of the Second World War, came after several years of intense military research into the potential of atomic explosions. European physicists who had fled Nazi Germany, including Albert Einstein, had warned American officials that Germany was developing its own atomic weapons, while the British military had been running a programme code-named "Tube Alloys". It led to the founding in 1939 of the Manhattan Project, the United States' secret programme to develop the atomic bomb. The project was so secret that even Harry Truman, who had been Roosevelt's Vice-President since January 1945, only found out about the work when he took up the presidency following Roosevelt's death in April 1945.

Even at the Potsdam Conference in July 1945, less than a month before the first atomic bomb was used, the US withheld the true nature of its arsenal from its allies. A week into the conference, Truman told Stalin, rather ambiguously, that the US possessed "a new weapon of special

"The US Secretary of War advised Truman that the nuclear bomb could act as a deterrent against expanding Soviet influence in Eastern Europe"

destructive force", but omitted to reveal that this weapon was a nuclear one. Stalin apparently responded saying he hoped they would make "good use of it against the Japanese".

The Manhattan Project had initially been triggered by fears of Germany's own nuclear developments. While it would ultimately be used against the Japanese, there is evidence that the real motivation was the growing concern over Soviet dominance. The US Secretary of War Henry Stimson advised Truman that, after VE Day, the nuclear bomb could act as a deterrent against expanding Soviet influence in Eastern Europe. Truman reportedly agreed, adding: "I'll certainly have a hammer on those Russians."

From the Potsdam Conference, Britain, the United States and China issued the Potsdam Declaration to Japan (the Soviet Union did not sign this declaration as it had not actually declared war against Japan at this stage). The declaration threatened the Japanese with "prompt and utter destruction" if they did not immediately surrender unconditionally. However, the Japanese military leaders did not heed the warning.

Japan had been at war with Britain and the US since December 1941, when it had launched attacks on British, Dutch and American territories in the Asia and the Pacific. Japan occupied vast swathes of southeast Asia, and under its occupation prisoners of war and enslaved local civilians suffered very harsh treatments. The conflict had played out in battles across China, Burma and New Guinea, on land, in the air and at sea. Allied troops drawn from across the British Empire not only had to contend with the brutality of the Japanese military but also the tropical conditions and diseases that this particular theatre of war presented. According to the Imperial War Museum, in 1943, for every soldier evacuated due to battle wounds, 120 soldiers were evacuated due to sickness.

The war in the Far East presented Britain with some of its greatest military disasters. In February 1942, Allied forces had surrendered Singapore, a British colony of strategic importance to the Japanese. Churchill would later call it "the worst disaster in British history". After the surrender, thousands of Allied servicemen became prisoners of war and were forced to build the notorious Burma–Thailand railway, dubbed "Death Railway" as more than 100,000 civilian labourers and prisoners of war died during its construction.

Even with the onslaught of American bombing campaigns targeting Japanese cities from the summer of 1944, the Japanese Imperial Army showed no sign of surrender. Military leaders favoured continuing the war, while the country's civilians wanted peace. Emperor Hirohito had little power with military officials when it came to national policy.

While the atomic bombs were kept a secret, the US military did attempt to warn the citizens of the targeted cities that they would be dropping destructive bombs, though they never mentioned that these would be nuclear in nature. Prior to the bombings, a leaflet drop was made over several Japanese cities. Known as "LeMay leaflets" they warned citizens to evacuate, though the historical record is unclear about whether the citizens of Hiroshima and Nagasaki actually even received these drops, and some reports claim the Nagasaki leaflet drop happened after the nuclear bomb had hit.

These leaflets stated that: "in accordance with America's humanitarian policies, the American Air Force, which does not wish to injure innocent people, now gives you warning to evacuate the cities named and save your lives… We cannot promise that only these cities will be among those attacked but some or all of them will be, so heed this warning and evacuate these cities immediately."

Even after the bombs had hit and the atomic plume had lifted, revealing the nuclear devastation, the Japanese government still considered fighting on. However, Emperor Hirohito appears to have insisted on the surrender and on 15 August 1945 made his first ever broadcast to the Japanese people. In his speech he announced the end of war by imploring his subjects "to endure the unendurable and bear the unbearable".

Opposite A jubilant
US crowd celebrate
VJ Day in Chicago on
15 August 1945

VE Day veteran

Daniel Harrison
Army Corporal; 97 years old

What kind of war did you have before VE Day?
I was doing an engineering apprenticeship before getting drafted into the Army in February 1943. Ours was one of the companies who took part in the D-Day landings in June 1944. I was sat in a fishing boat with my company on the English Channel for hours before landing at Gold Beach. I eventually got a Légion D'Honneur medal.

Then I spent the next year, on and off, around Europe — assisting with supply and transport in the months leading up to VE Day. After the war I witnessed a completely flattened Dresden. I got lost and some German drivers gave me a lift back to base, which was nice of them. I remember them speaking very good English. I spent a lot of time in Germany helping with the post-war rebuilding. It took me a long time to get demobbed.

Where were you when VE Day was announced?
I would have been stationed just outside Hamburg with 103 Company. It was while we were at this barn. We were going out into a forest to do some repairs to a road along with some nearby Canadian troops with whom we got on well. Our officers or sergeants were some distance away — 10 minutes' walk away — so it was easy enough, no pressure. We got back, cleaned up and had a meal, and we were told about the German surrender shortly afterwards. We were removed from where we were billeted, out of the barns and down into some building that the officers had taken over. We could tell that something was up because we could hear the Canadian Army troops celebrating.

What was the mood like?
Oh, it was gorgeous. There were tears and everybody was happy. A bit surprising, considering how long it took before we had a chance of going home. But we all celebrated.

Chapter seven

THE BEST OF BRITISH

Together in spirit

VE Day has always been an opportunity for the nation to come together to pay tribute to the fortitude, sacrifice and unity of "the greatest generation", and this year's 75th anniversary is no exception

This year marks 75 years since VE Day. It's a landmark anniversary that is being honoured across the country, as befits a day of such huge historical significance. And while many of the planned celebrations have had to be rethought or rescheduled due to the Covid-19 pandemic, the nation's desire to pay tribute to those who gave so much to claim victory in Europe remains as strong as ever. If anything, it has been only fortified by the spirit of unity and resilience that the current crisis has spawned.

One of the anniversary's key celebrations — the VE Day 75 concert at the Royal Albert Hall — is a case in point. While the commemorative evening has been moved to a later date, the occasion will be no less stirring or symbolic, and its setting no less significant.

The Royal Albert Hall has been the scene of many national celebrations since the iconic venue was opened in 1871 by the Prince of Wales — later King Edward VII — in honour of his father Prince Albert. During the First and Second World Wars, the Royal Albert Hall hosted a series of fundraising concerts for those serving in the Armed Forces and their families. Prime Minister Winston Churchill stood on its hallowed stage on 23 November 1944 to rally the audience with one of his morale-boosting speeches as part of the "To You, America. A Thanksgiving Day Celebration" held to honour the nation's great ally, the United States.

On VE Day 1945, as the ticker tape and confetti settled, plans were already underway for the Festival of Empire at the Royal Albert Hall on 24 May. The first Empire Day since the

announcement of peace with Germany became an unofficial indoor victory parade, with representatives from across the Empire who had joined with Britain in the fight. King George VI, Queen Mary and the two princesses — Elizabeth and Margaret — all attended. Above the great pipe organ of the Royal Albert Hall were suspended intertwined ribbons of red, white and blue in the shape of a V sign. On either side of the organ were draped the emblems of the Union Jack.

The parade included not only representatives of Allied Armed Forces — including the Merchant Navy and Royal Marines — but also Chelsea Pensioners, "Children of the Empire" (cadets from across the world) and unsung heroes such as two lighthouse keepers and members of the Women's Land Army. There were also men and women who had fought the fires in the Blitz, and nurses from Britain and the Commonwealth who had tended the wounded in Italy and on the beaches of Normandy. Wrens, Auxiliary Territorial Service (ATS) and the Home Guard also joined the parade.

The Festival of Empire's victory parade would not be the only commemorative event the Royal Albert Hall would host for the Second World War. The venue would also become the host of the annual Burma Reunion events, held for the men of the 14th Army, who had fought in the four-year-long Burma campaign against the Japanese during the Second World War. The first reunion of the "Forgotten Army", as they were dubbed, was held on 2 June 1947 and included performances by Vera Lynn and an

"Columns of marchers passed under Marble Arch and trooped their way to the Mall. In all, 20,000 marchers took part"

11-year-old Julie Andrews. The Burma Reunion concerts commemorated the fallen and paid tribute to all those who had fought in the longest and bloodiest campaign of the war.

The Royal Albert Hall has since become the natural home for commemoration. The Festival of Remembrance is held there every November to mark Armistice Day. Landmark anniversaries of other historic wartime moments have also been marked at the venue, including the 70th anniversary of D-Day in 2014, when the BBC joined forces with SSAFA, the Armed Forces charity, and other charities to host a special edition of Radio 2's "Friday Night is Music Night".

The first anniversary

In 1946, a year after VE Day and with the war in the Far East officially over, the government turned to celebrating the first anniversary of victory. However, the plans for a victory parade and a re-enactment of the carnival feeling of the events of 8 and 9 May 1945 were not universally welcomed. The House of Commons debated whether or not they were what the country needed and a motion was put down for the government to reconsider its plans.

The Conservative MP for Sutton Coldfield, Sir John Mellor, speaking in a parliamentary debate in April 1946, stated: "On VE Day we celebrated, and rightly celebrated, the brilliant victory of our forces in Europe and on VJ Day we celebrated, and rightly celebrated, the equally remarkable achievements of our forces in the Far East. To try to celebrate anything a second time always results in an anti-climax… So far as feeling in the country is concerned, I do not appreciate any desire for such celebrations; on the contrary, there appears to be prevalent an acute disappointment at the slow progress made at home towards reconstruction and equally severe disappointment at the slow progress towards the solution of the many difficult problems which confront our government overseas."

Despite such reservations, the government's plans to mark the anniversary of victory went ahead. "V Day" was set for 8 June 1946. Kensington Gardens was designated a camp area for visiting troops from oversees for the Victory Parade, as it had been used on former occasions such as the Coronation, the 1919 Victory Parade and the Silver Jubilee. A royal procession made its way from Buckingham Palace down the Mall, and the Prime Minister Clement Attlee arrived at the Mall together with wartime leader Winston Churchill in an open-top horse-drawn carriage.

Footage of the Victory Parade survives in a Movietone newsreel. "Just over a year ago the people celebrated their deliverance, today they honour the men who made it possible," announces the broadcaster. "And what better place to do them honour than from their own streets in their own capital. London. The centre of the Empire. London. Battered but triumphant."

A column of the mechanised machines that helped secure victory set off from Regent's Park and made its way to the Mall to salute the King. It was not just tanks and military vehicles among the procession but also vehicles and machinery of the Land Army, the National Fire Service and transport services — including London's iconic double-decker buses — and other non-combat organisations. Even Movietone recording cars, which had recorded war footage, joined the parade.

Leading the marching column of service personnel were the Americans. Forces from the Empire were also present but the biggest moment was the sight of the British Armed Forces and then the men and women of the Home Front. Columns of marchers passed under Marble Arch and trooped their way to the Mall. In all, 20,000 marchers took part, which, at the time, was the largest military procession seen in the capital.

Rain set in later that evening, which meant that a planned synchronised searchlight and air display of nine Lancaster bombers had to be abandoned. However, one brave pilot, Flight-Lieutenant Dennis James Lundy, a 24-year-old from east London, did take to the skies that night accompanied by the BBC's Richard Dimbleby who broadcast from the air a description of the West End crowds on Victory Day night. It was not the first time that day that Lundy had taken to the air. Earlier, in far better weather conditions, he had flown the radio commentator Raymond Glendenning, two press photographers and a Reuters reporter over the crowd, going as low as 500ft above the parade to give the press pack a bird's-eye view of the historic scene.

"London looked marvellous from the air," Lundy later told his local newspaper, the *Walthamstow Guardian*. "We must have had the best view of the parade. We saw the King and Queen leave Buckingham Palace, and we could pick out the people on the saluting base." Lundy notes that he later flew Glendenning to an air station in Lincolnshire. "All the way northwards we saw bonfires blazing," he said, which suggests that the nation was very much in a celebratory mood.

Right Troops of the Royal Engineers parade in central London to mark Victory Day, June 1946

Left The Queen, the Queen Mother and Princess Margaret appear on the balcony of Buckingham Palace as part of the VE Day 50 celebrations, May 1995

The 50th anniversary

Fast forward 49 years and a quarter of a million people gathered on the Mall to watch the Queen Mother and her daughters take to the balcony of Buckingham Palace on Sunday 7 May 1995, just as they had done half a century earlier. According to BBC court reporter Jennie Bond, the sight of the Queen Mother, aged nearly 95, and her daughters Queen Elizabeth II and Princess Margaret "encapsulated the mood of the three days of celebration… the Queen Mother a poignant link between past and present".

VE Day 50 was very much seen as a tribute to the Queen Mother, the woman who in the words of Jennie Bond "had commanded the admiration of a country at war by refusing to leave London even when the Palace was bombed." The BBC footage of the day showed the Queen Mother visibly moved by the sight of the crowds and the musical performance that took place from a stage at the gates of the Palace. She is seen singing along to "The White Cliffs of Dover" and shedding a few tears.

"It gives me very great pleasure to inaugurate the 50th anniversary of VE Day," said the Queen Mother at the beginning of the weekend, addressing the crowds before a remembrance parade. "This day will bring back many memories to many people, and I do hope that all those who go to the many ceremonies arranged will remember with pride and gratitude those men and women armed and unarmed whose courage really helped to bring us to victory. God bless them all."

On VE Day 50, London was once again the scene of the greatest street party in the world. Veterans were seen dancing on the Mall, while the Red Arrows performed a flypast, their famous red, white and blue trails streaming behind them. St Paul's Cathedral, a symbol of defiance during the war, hosted a thanksgiving service for visiting dignitaries and heads of state. Among the order of the service was a reading by Field Marshall Lord Bramall, Vice-President of SSAFA.

There was a large gathering in Hyde Park throughout the day, where the crowds were treated to tea dances, a Workers' Playtime concert and a display from the Red Devils, the British Army's parachute display team. In the evening, the royal park hosted a ticket-only 1940s-style concert as the grand finale to the celebrations. Dame Vera Lynn, the Tiller Girls, Cliff Richard and Elaine Paige all performed with the proceedings compered by the actor Robert Hardy. The concert ended with Dame Vera leading all the performers and the crowd in a rendition of "We'll Meet Again".

At 8:38pm on VE Day 50, a two-minute silence was held, before the Queen lit the first of a chain of beacons across the country. As a lone piper played, Her Majesty was handed a flaming torch with which she set off the first beacon in Hyde Park. At this point, across the country — from London to the Scottish Highlands — 2,000 beacons were lit.

Pageantmaster Bruno Peek LVO OBE OPR, who had organised the national beacon lighting, was alongside the Queen as she lit the first one. He recalls: "It was an enormous honour to be asked by the Ministry of Defence to organise the lighting of beacons for this special anniversary, involving local communities throughout the nation. The end of the war in Europe was celebrated by millions of war-weary people on the 8 May 1945, so to pay tribute to them and those that fought for our freedom must never be forgotten. The concept of the lighting of the beacons was warmly embraced by the country. It had its challenges but these were overcome."

The events on VE Day 50 were the brainchild of Major Michael Parker CVO MBE. After serving in the Queen's Own Hussars, Major Parker went on to organise the Royal Tournament at Earls Court Exhibition Centre for 27 years, as well as three Edinburgh Tattoos, and the Queen's Silver and Golden Jubilees. The VE Day 50 celebrations — which included daytime fireworks at Buckingham Palace, church services in both St Paul's and Westminster Abbey, the lighting of the beacons across the country, the concert in Hyde Park and a laser projection from Hyde Park to the BT Tower, which set off a firework display — were described as "extremely ambitious" and the result of Major Parker's "reckless imagination".

One of the most memorable moments of the celebrations came when a choir of children performed for assembled world leaders as part of the remembrance event. The youngsters were all dressed in white, bearing sashes that depicted the various nations that had fought in the war. In a moment that was described as "sending a tremor of nervousness through crowned head and commentator alike", the Queen and Prince Phillip led the dignitaries into the throng of children. Each head of state and country representative sought out the child that bore their nation's sash to present them with roses. They then joined the procession to a giant globe made up of 2,000 flowers, where they were met by children from their own country. It was an unprecedented moment: never before had so many heads of state mingled with ordinary schoolchildren in such an informal way.

Opposite and left Veterans and well-wishers alike join the 50th anniversary party in Hyde Park, London

I do hope that all those who go to
the many ceremonies arranged will
remember with pride and gratitude
those men and women armed and
unarmed whose courage really helped
to bring us to victory"

Previous pages V for victory
searchlights pierce the
night sky in front of Big
Ben, London, May 2015

Opposite, top and bottom
Flag-waving crowds
gather in front of
Buckingham Palace
to celebrate VE Day 50

Among those at Hyde Park was Doreen Burley, Chairman of SSAFA Lancashire. Doreen was one of the charity's representatives on the day, while others were in the royal box for the events in Hyde Park. SSAFA also took as much pride in its local acts of celebration and commemoration, with the charity's branches assisting and participating in a variety of ways. SSAFA Oxfordshire raised £1,400 at a VE Day concert. Clwyd branch helped to arrange a "wartime lunch", while a 1940s-themed concert at Brierley Hill Civic Hall in the West Midlands — including a big band, a ladies choir and variety acts, attended by war veterans and serving personnel — was sold out and raised £1,300 for SSAFA Dudley.

In Painswick, Gloucestershire two veterans donned their original Second World War uniforms to rattle SSAFA collection tins. Major John Sutton was wounded and captured at Arnhem, but later escaped. On VE Day 1945, he flew out to Denmark to disarm German servicemen. His wife Reigh served with the First Aid Nursing Yeomanry in Ceylon throughout the war. She recalled for *SSAFA News* that in 1945, VE Day was "just another working day for me".

One especially moving episode of the celebrations — both emotionally *and* physically — was the BBC'S *Challenge Anneka* television programme, presented by Anneka Rice. SSAFA and the Royal British Legion had been requesting that a war memorial at the top of a steep hill in West Lothian be moved. The cost of relocating the monument — estimated at around £94,000 — was too great to be met by the charities or the local town council. Thankfully for the Second World War veterans who wanted to visit the monument but could not make the climb, the show took up the challenge. Anneka and her team toiled, day and night, for four days around the VE Day weekend. Old mine workings meant they had to drill out the new site and concrete the platform. Every stone was numbered and cleaned. A new site for the monument was landscaped with trees and plants, and a path was laid. The task was completed just minutes before the scheduled VE Day parade to the monument got underway. "Anneka was just amazing," said SSAFA's West Lothian Branch Publicity Officer, Vanda Collins. "Nothing was too much trouble for her. She set up another 17 projects in the town and never stopped all weekend."

VE Day 50 also served as the poignant start for a 413-mile tandem Victory Push wheelchair race from Edinburgh to London. The race, undertaken by wheelchair athletes Paul Guest and Ian Lea, took 11 days to complete and saw the pair stopping at all mainline InterCity railway stations to obtain signatures on the SSAFA Tribute and Promise scroll. The scroll was then presented by Paul and Ian to the charity's President Prince Michael of Kent at the SSAFA AGM. As the athletes rolled into the AGM, the 400 delegates greeted them with a standing ovation.

Even though it had been 50 years since the Second World War, SSAFA'S help for the wartime generation was never more in demand. "In 1945 they thought the worst was over," wrote *SSAFA News.* "Sadly that is not so. Savings have dwindled, loved ones have passed on, health and vigour are waning, homes are falling into disrepair." In 1995, there were nearly 1.75 million surviving Second World War veterans. At the time, the Ministry of Defence was predicting that by 2020, the 75th anniversary of VE Day, that number would be 52,000, all of whom would be more than 93 years old. The knowledge that this cohort would need support for the future saw SSAFA join with 129 other organisations to launch the Tribute and Promise campaign.

This aimed to highlight the needs of the surviving ex-service and wartime civilian generation, and ensure that they had someone to turn to for help and companionship. The campaign was officially launched at the Cabinet War Rooms by SSAFA's patron Dame Vera Lynn. "I was also there," said Dame Vera. "I saw and understand what ordinary people went through. I am delighted and honoured to sign this letter."

SSAFA's then Controller, Major General Charles Grey, was appointed as Director of Tribute and Promise. "The needs of the surviving wartime generation are many and varied," he said at the launch. "As official government figures show, up to 700,000 pensioners are not claiming income support to which they are entitled. There may be as many again who need practical help or are suffering from the most corrosive threat to health and old age — simply acute loneliness." In August that year a special Tribute and Promise Parade took place in London in front of the Queen along the Mall to mark the joint 50th anniversaries of VE Day and VJ Day,

Left The Red Arrows put on a patriotic display in the skies of central London, May 2015

Right Anfield Stadium in Liverpool plays host to a tribute to Merseyside's war generation, May 2015

and cement a national pledge to be there for the wartime generation for as long as they needed support.

Before the parade, a service led by the Archbishop of Canterbury in the presence of Her Majesty saw the following promise declared: "We, the voluntary organisations of Tribute and Promise, pledge ourselves anew to work in support of the wartime generation. We promise to do everything possible to help where there is need and to ensure that they may enjoy the years that lie ahead in comfort, dignity and contentment. This we promise as a lasting token of our appreciation and gratitude."

Among the floats, marchers and cavalcade of historical military and wartime vehicles was a wartime bridal-party-themed float, a reminder of SSAFA's life-long help to service families. Another float, from the London Homeless Division, told of SSAFA's wartime clothing distribution service. Above the parade flew vintage aircraft from the Battle of Britain Memorial Flight.

The Tribute and Promise celebration of VE Day and VJ Day was not only marked in London. Local communities held luncheons, with members of the wartime generation as guests of honour. Liverpool FC's Anfield Stadium was the scene of a tribute to the people of Merseyside who had played a part

in the war. A crowd of 10,000 attended the event, which was organised jointly by SSAFA Merseyside and the West Lancashire Royal British Legion. Massed bands played, aircraft flew past and the Promise was made. A 60-minute film of the event was sold with proceeds from the sales going to SSAFA.

The 70th anniversary
On 8 May 2015, three days of commemorations and celebrations began with a Service of Remembrance at the Cenotaph at 3pm — the date and time that, 70 years earlier, Winston Churchill famously broadcast the immortal words that it was the nation's "victory day". The service was followed by the national lighting of beacons.

As it had been on the 50th anniversary, the beacon lighting was started by the Queen, this time from the Long Walk in the grounds of Windsor Castle. Pageantmaster Bruno Peek, who had been choreographing national beacon lighting for three decades, was at Her Majesty's side once again. The Queen's beacon set off a chain reaction that saw a total of 235 beacons lit across the nation and in British territories overseas. Precisely two minutes after the Queen lit her beacon in Windsor at 9.30pm the other beacons were ignited, symbolising the light emerging after the darkness of the Second World War in Europe. The beacons stretched

"It is our duty to keep the events of the past alive in collective memory, including future generations — this is how we ensure that such a conflict never happens again"

from Unst in the Shetland Islands to St Michael's Mount off the south-west coast of Cornwall, and all the way out to South Georgia and the Falkland Islands.

By the evening, London was awash with victory lights. St Paul's Cathedral, the Houses of Parliament and Trafalgar Square were lit up with V-shaped beams of light, with the latter display, which recreated that of 1945, taking place on each evening of the three days of celebration.

While there were recreations of poignant moments from 1945, the celebrations also embraced new developments. At 11am on Saturday 9 May, a "V for Victory" Thunderclap went live on Twitter and Facebook, with more than one and a half million people sharing an archive audio clip from May 1945 of cathedral bells ringing and drums beating out the Morse code for "V" across social media platforms.

A "Party to Remember" concert was held at Horse Guards Parade, and was attended by thousands. Alongside members of the Royal Family and the Prime Minister the audience included nearly 1,000 veterans and their families. Also in attendance were representatives of Allied and Commonwealth nations who had fought alongside Britain in the conflict.

On the final day of the anniversary weekend — Sunday 10 May — the Queen led the nation in marking the 70th anniversary of VE Day with a Service of Thanksgiving at Westminster Abbey. Among those who attended was Lieutenant Chris Chew, Commanding Officer of *HMS Trumpeter*, from Skipton in Yorkshire. His grandfather,

the late Sergeant Arthur Attwood, served during some of the pivotal moments of the Second World War. His grandmother, Hazel Attwood, was a Land Girl during the war.

"It's important to remember what our ancestors did during the Second World War," said Lieutenant Chew in an interview on the Department for Digital, Culture, Media & Sport website. "My grandfather served in the Army and he inspired me to join the military. I'm incredibly proud of his actions during the war to make sure I could have everything I have today. We should never forget the hardship he and thousands of others went through to preserve the nation and I feel honoured to join the VE Day celebrations in his memory."

The 75th anniversary

In 2019, to honour the sacrifices of the wartime generation and to celebrate peace, the government announced that Friday 8 May 2020 would be a bank holiday. Only once before had the early May bank holiday been moved — on the occasion of the 50th anniversary of VE Day in 1995.

"VE Day marked an historic moment in not only our nation's, but the world's history and it is important that we commemorate this great occasion on its 75th anniversary, honouring those who did their duty — whether on the battlefields of Europe or through their efforts and sacrifices here at home," commented the Business Secretary at the time, Greg Clark. "Moving next year's early May bank holiday to VE Day itself is a right and fitting tribute. It will

Above The Queen attends a Service of Thanksgiving at Westminster Abbey to mark the 70th anniversary of VE Day

Opposite, top and bottom Veterans of the Second World War take part in an anniversary parade in central London, May 2015

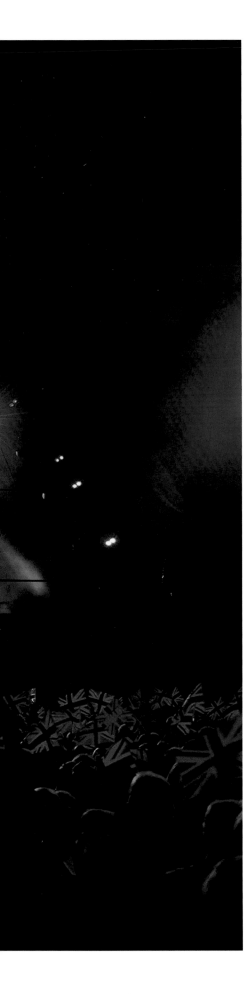

Left An appreciative
audience looks on during
the VE Day "Party to
Remember" concert at
Horse Guards Parade,
London, May 2015

ensure as many people as possible have the opportunity to remember and honour our heroes of the Second World War and reflect on the sacrifices of a generation."

While Covid-19 has called for a rethink of how VE Day 75 should be marked, the spirit of celebration endures. For instance, the Nation's Toast, which along with a host of other anniversary events has been organised by pageantmaster Bruno Peek, was originally intended to take place in pubs and at community events, tea dances and street parties up and down the country on 8 May at 3pm. An opportunity to raise a glass, or a tea cup, to the men, women and children of the Second World War, the toast is now being held in homes across the UK in an alternative but no less poignant moment of national unity and commemoration.

"I wanted to do something extra special for the 75th anniversary of the end of the war in Europe as I believe it will be the last time that veterans of the Second World War will be involved in such historic moments," says Bruno. "I wanted to ensure that a number of activities planned for VE Day could still take place if the country was in a crisis of one kind or another, as we all live in troubled times. These events will bring our country together at various moments in time — a very much needed experience of togetherness. Those who fought and died for our freedom deserve the

best we can all provide and I believe that VE Day 75 will fulfil this aim."

SSAFA was honoured and grateful to be invited by Bruno to be the chosen charity partner for his VE Day 75 series of events. As the UK's oldest tri-service military charity, which supported both service personnel and their families throughout the Second World War and continues to support that wartime generation to this very day, SSAFA was keen to take an active part in the nation's VE Day celebrations.

"It is our duty to keep the events of the past alive in collective memory, including future generations — this is how we ensure that such a conflict never happens again," says SSAFA Chief Executive Sir Andrew Gregory. "It is our hope that the nation takes a moment to reflect on the significance of this date, as a milestone that changed the course of history for the whole world."

It's a sentiment shared by Prime Minister Boris Johnson. "The 75th anniversary of VE Day marks a historic moment for our great country to come together and reflect on the heroes of the Second World War. No one will ever forget what they sacrificed in defending our freedom and securing peace across Europe, and we will continue to honour those who contributed at home and abroad.

"By commemorating these moments, we can remember and remind ourselves of the fragility of peace, and the need for us all to collectively uphold this."

Scent and service

Hand finished to perfection in Britain, Elegantes perfumes convey timeless elegance, underpinned by one family's proud military heritage

www.elegantes.co.uk

Across a 16th-century granite archway in Prague is inscribed a motto that translates as: "Elegant people of our time are honourable people who pass on their values to others". This maxim has lent itself to Elegantes London, a British perfumer founded by Dagmar Smit, who hails from the Czech capital, and her British husband Thomas. Their fine perfumes — showcased in Harrods and Fortnum & Mason as well as boutiques in Los Angeles, Bucharest and Milan — are housed in stunning handcrafted crystal flacons and are unlike anything else on the market.

"We are not a corporation," says Thomas Smit. "We have heart and passion about what we do." For his values he looks back to his days in the infantry. "In the military there is no place to hide failure. The Army emphasises hard work, discipline, integrity and determination. These are also essential qualities for success in business."

Before launching Elegantes London, the couple developed and managed a number of successful luxury hotels, including the Augustine in Prague, which they built from an old monastery. One of their ambitions is to develop a premium hotel in the UK, which they hope can be staffed and managed entirely by former military personnel — after all, soldiers of any discipline are trained to serve. Thomas comes from a family of soldiers, dating back to 1694 with the famous Waldeck Regiment. He and his wife have supported military charities as part of a strong sense of social commitment.

"When sniper training, one has to collect used cartridges to return to the quartermaster so they can be recharged," says Thomas, "and when combat training in the jungle, one learns to appreciate Mother Earth's kaleidoscope of colours and plethora of aromas. Elegantes London is 99.8 per cent plastic free and we have made a commitment to be 100 per cent plastic free by the end of 2020. All of our oils are natural and we will use zero artificial preservatives. We want to educate the consumer about the quality and integrity of the products they use and the effect they have on them and the planet."

The Elegantes London collection was created by French master "nose" Julien Rasquinet, who spent four years finding the most exotic and rare ingredients while working to unusual instructions. "We wrote a brief that encompassed the qualities found in people we admire and value," says Thomas, "and asked them to be portrayed in the character of our perfumes. It was a completely new approach."

The elegant flacons, which come in clear and black crystal, have an air of vintage glamour. One of the more masculine lines — Chesterfield Club — has proved popular with American veterans, who appreciate its strong, smoky tones. Elegantes London will soon launch a body care range as it continues to expand.

Thomas likens his experience managing the hotel to organising a small army, with operations commencing each morning at 6am. Similarly, creating a perfume house from scratch has required dedication, diligence and strong leadership from the couple. "In the army you have all the different disciplines that come together as a team," he says. "To be effective, you have to understand what the others do; and a successful business has vision, integration, communication and execution — like a military exercise. We have inner strength, discipline and a determination to create something better and help others achieve more. We are setting very clear milestones and want to become a hallmark for British success and excellence."

Thinking hats

Christys' has been making high-quality
British headwear for nearly 250 years

www.christys-hats.com

As the north of England was building the foundations for an industrial revolution in the mid-18th century, a man named Miller Christy was making Stockport an unlikely fashion capital. After completing an apprenticeship in what was referred to as the "Art and Mystery of Felt Making", Miller travelled south from Edinburgh, and in March 1773, Christys' Hat Makers was born.

Almost 250 years on and Christys' is firmly established as an emblematic marker of British tradition and craft, a brand that has been proudly worn by Prince Albert, Sir Winston Churchill and young, scooter-driving fashionistas of the 1960s alike. Christys' has now relocated to Witney, Oxfordshire, but its dedication to the craft remains. Each Christys' item is passed through a small factory team of 10 or so people before reaching the head of its wearer.

"This is not fast fashion," says Laura Thomas, Finance Director at Christys' London. "We still do everything in the traditional ways. A lot of our machines are at least 100 years old."

From berets and bowlers to trilbies that echo the elegance of vintage film noir, Christys' has a hat for every occasion possible. In recent years, as the official headwear suppliers for the Royal Ascot, Wimbledon and the English FA, Christys' has become as much a part of British summertime as strawberries and cream. International clients include Juventus FC, Paris St-Germain FC and the Kentucky Derby.

The Christys' name has been further bolstered by the success of British television shows *Sherlock* and *Peaky Blinders*, with the hat maker having been enlisted to design the now iconic caps that are so synonymous with the two programmes. "The cap has become a lot more fashionable and commercial as a result," says Thomas. Indeed, it has earned its place in modern pop culture thanks to a new generation of fans eager to pay homage to their on-screen idols.

"In the past, hats were very much a symbol of class," says Thomas. "Ladies wouldn't take them off when they were inside while gentleman always would. Men would walk around in top hats, but now you wouldn't wear one unless you're at a wedding. That has completely changed. People wear hats not because it's a necessity or it's polite, but because they like them and it's fashionable. It's become a part of people's outfit again."

Hops for the future

At Harvey's Brewery, the oldest beer producer in Sussex, independence and self-determination come with the territory

www.harveys.org.uk

"We wunt be druv" may mean nothing to outsiders; but as the unofficial motto of the county of Sussex, this dialect phrase — which translates as "we won't be driven" — is an unabashed declaration of freedom. And Miles Jenner, Head Brewer and Joint Managing Director of Harvey's Brewery, believes the local statement is also an avowal of the company's principles.

"I think it does run through Harvey's," he says, sitting in the brewery's grade II listed home in the Sussex county town of Lewes. "We think it personifies the independence — the dogged independence — that we've had for generations in the brewery."

He has a point. Established by John Harvey in 1790, the brewery — the oldest in Sussex — is still a family-run business. Direct descendants of John Harvey are still involved in the company to this day. And despite many breweries being taken over by larger, corporate companies, Harvey's is determined to preserve its independent spirit.

Sussex's radical temperament extends to the Harvey's beers too — of which its most famous, Sussex Best, has twice been named Best Bitter at CAMRA's Great British Beer Festival. "I think a lot of the character of our beers is determined by our water supply and our yeast," says Jenner. "Our yeast strain is unique to us and the water we use for brewing comes through an aquifer below the brewery. So it is fresh spring water, filtered through the South Downs. Any brewer can brew the same recipes, but brewing with your own yeast and water gives it a different quality." And, as part of what Jenner calls "the fabric of local sustainability", the hops used by Harvey's are sourced within a tight radius of the brewery.

While the beer industry is often hostage to any number of negative stories — mostly arising from pub closures — Jenner believes Harvey's nimble operation and self-determination will result in its beers being enjoyed and cherished by new generations of beer drinkers to come.

"As long as we remain alert to the marketplace and embrace trends that keep us relevant," says Jenner, "there is a future for Harvey's as independent brewers. We have a heritage to preserve and that is important."

In other words, Harvey's Brewery: it wunt be druv.

Nuclear vision

The Nuclear Advanced Manufacturing Research
Centre makes UK manufacturers fit to win work
across the nuclear sector

www.namrc.co.uk

Andrew Storer knows the British nuclear sector inside out. Having begun his career as an apprentice with a firm that manufactured reactor components for Sizewell B, Storer moved to Rolls-Royce to service the Royal Navy's Trident submarine fleet. Now he drives innovation across the industry as Chief Executive of the Nuclear Advanced Manufacturing Research Centre — commonly abbreviated as Nuclear AMRC — the national research and development hub responsible for enhancing the UK's nuclear manufacturing capability.

"Our mission is simple," says Storer. "It's to deploy our R&D talents to enable UK companies to win work in the nuclear and adjacent sectors; whether it be in defence, civil nuclear, decommissioning or advanced fusion reactors."

The trouble is that much of Britain's nuclear industry comprises companies that are only partially committed to the sector because they struggle to win as much work as they would like, either because of price or lack of capability. To that end, Nuclear AMRC has invested heavily in research centres up and down the UK that specialise in niche areas of nuclear manufacturing, from modular construction and large-scale

machining to digital instrumentation. "It's there that we convert ideas into reality," says Storer, "and then we give it to industry to go and apply it."

The results have been spectacular. Nuclear AMRC's Civil Nuclear Sharing in Growth programme, concluded in 2017, saw the organisation assist 10 companies looking to enter the nuclear market. "By the end, orders worth nearly £700 million had been won by these firms," says Storer. "In government speak, that's just short of 7,000 jobs created or sustained."

That effort is now being replicated on a much larger scale in its new Fit for Nuclear (F4N) campaign, which has seen the Nuclear AMRC work with 1,200 SMEs to prepare them for entry into Britain's civil nuclear sector. Ultimately, Storer wants to use his organisation's expertise to enable the UK's nuclear industry to compete effectively with its rivals abroad.

"If we can ensure that the right jobs stay in Britain, then we can look at expanding other areas of expertise that we currently can't deliver," he says. At the moment, the British nuclear industry is at the cutting edge of small reactor design, pushing the envelope when it comes to research into fusion and modular technology.

Larger reactors capable of producing electricity in the gigawatt range, however, have not been built by UK manufacturers since Sizewell B in the 1980s. Lacking the domestic resources and expertise to build them, the British government has since reached out to Chinese and French firms to construct its newest generation of nuclear power stations.

This, Storer says, is an intolerable situation for the UK's nuclear industry, and one that Nuclear AMRC is seeking to rectify. "What we need to do is constantly hold a mirror up to government and to developers, and ensure that Britain will be able to accomplish this feat," says Storer. "At the Nuclear AMRC, we sit in the space of trying to create an intervention to allow that to happen."

The 75th anniversary of Britain's victory in the Second World War is an inspiring reminder of the true potential that resides in the country's civil nuclear sector. It was, after all, a conflict that saw the fundamentals of atomic power generation being explored in British laboratories. "Think about the innovation and the pace that people worked at then," says Storer. "The same effort and pace of work, in my opinion, should apply today."

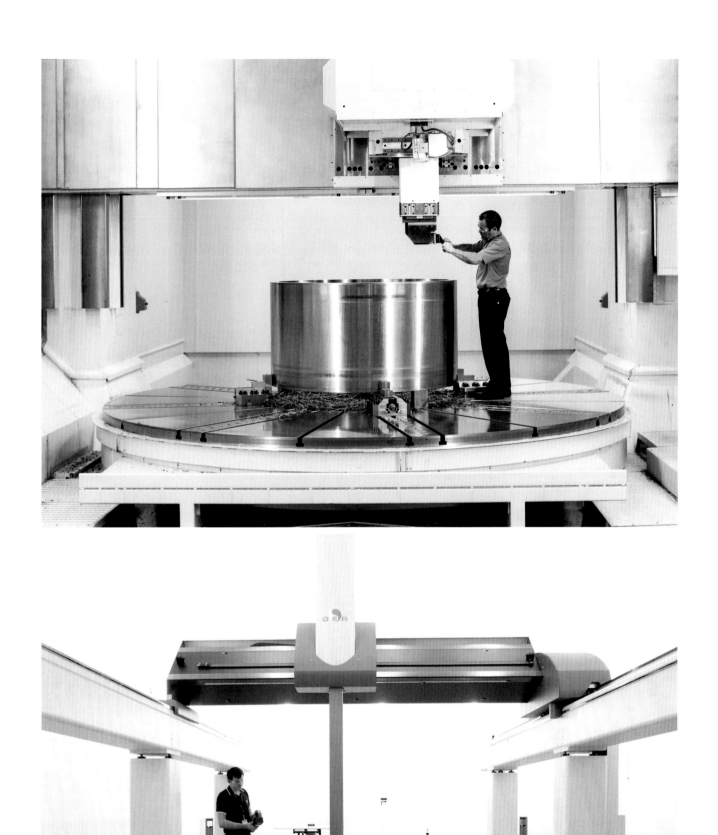

Cyber house rules

Templar Executives supplies human beings with the weapons needed to fend off future cyber attacks

www.templarexecs.com

"Technology develops all the time but humans don't change and you need to factor that in to produce the best cyber security," says Andrew Fitzmaurice, CEO and founder of Templar Executives. For 14 years the company has helped clients to develop resilient cybersecurity systems in an increasingly complex threat landscape, in which the human element is of utmost importance. Once armed with Templar Executives' advice on best practice, those clients stand to gain a significant competitive advantage.

Fitzmaurice specialised in air command and control in the military. "My final role in the services was in a military think tank where we were predicting the next 20 years," says Fitzmaurice. "From there I went to GCHQ and then up to the Cabinet Office, always driven by the question of what was going to come next."

This experience in predicting progress informs everything Templar Executives does. "We bring something very special to the market in that we're assessing what lies 18 months ahead and we design strategies to take that into account," explains Fitzmaurice.

The company name is a very considered choice, deliberately reminiscent of the Knights Templar, the 12th century Catholic military order which played a major role in the Crusades. Fitzmaurice has a long family history involved with the Templars and reaching back to Richard the Lionheart. It's no coincidence that the Templars were considered to be the elite fighting force of their day — highly trained and motivated, with the finest equipment to hand. Their mission was also to support and provide the right resources, all of which chime with the ethos behind Templar Executives.

Today the company develops cyber security and information assurance strategies across all critical sectors including financial services, healthcare, telecommunications and utilities. It won Best Cyber Security Company 2016

European CEO awards, entirely decided by client votes; and *CEO Insight* magazine named it Best Cyber Security Firm UK in 2018.

Fitzmaurice also sets great store by the pro bono work he does throughout the Commonwealth, further echoes of the traditional chivalrous behaviour expected from the Knights Templar of old. Since Cyber Champions launched in 2011 Templar Executives has been actively supporting this not-for-profit organisation in delivering best practices and online safety awareness interactive workshops to schoolchildren and parents through a network of young professional volunteers. "Supporting not-for-profit organisations is very important to us and thus far we've trained 40,000 children and 20,000 adults in cyber safety," says Fitzmaurice "One of our smartest moves is to send someone to a school they've recently left, so young people have an instant connection."

Normally the company specialises in board-level engagement, setting up minimum standards to be followed throughout the organisations it assists. "Cyber security should be built into every company now," says Fitzmaurice, "and at board level people tend to understand the value of it and how to look after it. That understanding then gets fed down to non-executive staff. These days everyone's aware of breaches in security, such as the malware that infected the NHS in 2017, leading to 19,000 cancelled appointments. That really brought it home to the man or woman in the street and showed what a massive disruptive impact a cyber breach can have."

Templar Executives now runs its own Cyber Academy, whose courses are accredited by GCHQ. "Our business is constantly expanding and as well as developing cyber security we are training others to the highest standards." Somehow the future seems more secure in that knowledge.

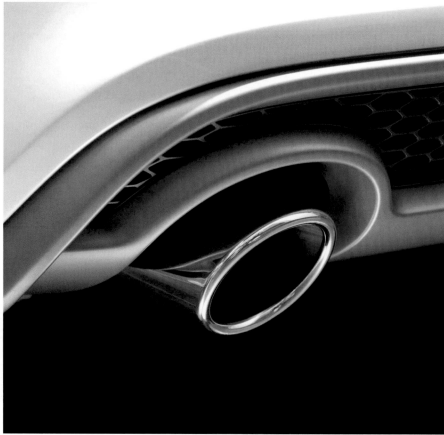

Sustained science

For over 200 years, British firm Johnson Matthey has applied its science to create solutions that enable a cleaner, healthier world

www.matthey.com

The motor car has revolutionised the world, and the internal combustion engine at its heart is both powerful and efficient. However, burning petrol or diesel in a confined space produces toxic gases such as carbon monoxide and nitrogen oxide. It's why most engines are fitted with catalytic converters, which use precious metals to transform these emissions into harmless carbon dioxide and water. What's more, a third of all these catalytic converters are produced by one company: Johnson Matthey. "Our catalytic converters remove about 40 tonnes of pollutants from the air every minute of every day," explains Corporate Communications Director Sally Jones. "And we're using our science to develop the next generation of high-tech products that will power emission-free electric cars as well."

For a firm with an annual operating profit of around £0.5 billion, Johnson Matthey keeps a relatively low profile. Since 1817 it has specialised in delivering products that draw on its expertise in chemistry to deliver startling efficiencies in science and engineering that quietly and invisibly benefit people's lives.

"As well as using precious metals and other chemical elements in our products, we are also the world's largest recycler of platinum group metals," says Jones. "Our ability to refine and reuse those metals set the stage for a whole range of different products and industries that we take for granted today, including emission reduction technologies, pharmaceuticals and electronics."

The 75th anniversary of VE Day is a reminder of how the firm helped Britain prevail in the Second World War. Platinum from Johnson Matthey was used in everything from electrically heated jackets for airmen to laboratory apparatus in munitions factories and water purification devices. "As a British company, we played our part in the war effort where we could, and sadly lost part of the Johnson Matthey family as a result," says Jones. "That commitment is very much retained in our values today, in protecting people and the planet."

Johnson Matthey's work isn't just confined to the petrol car. Its scientists are developing a range of technologies that will help the world transition to a low-carbon future — from new materials to power the next generation of electric vehicles to technologies that convert household waste into fuels. "Sustainable technologies are a hallmark of what we do," says Jones. "So we're applying our expertise to today's challenges and evolving our business that way."

Adapt to thrive

To connect with the people it serves, the Chartered Institute of Legal Executives (CILEx) prioritises diversity and flexibility

www.cilex.org.uk

Society is constantly evolving. To remain relevant and reflective of the community in which they exist, organisations must change, too. It's a concept that one of the three professional bodies covering the legal profession, the Chartered Institute of Legal Executives (CILEx), has long stood for.

"The strength of CILEx is that it has always evolved to reflect society," says Linda Ford, CEO of the organisation, founded in 1892. "We've always recognised that it's not just about the needs of today, but the needs of the future — and that's very much our direction of travel."

According to Ford, CILEx's primary role is to enhance the standing of Chartered Legal Executives and its 20,000 members, who include paralegals, other legal professionals and those studying to be lawyers. One of its key aims is to provide an accessible and flexible route into the profession. Regardless of members' backgrounds and previous academic achievements, CILEx offers training and education and develops people all the way through their careers.

"A key agenda for us is ensuring that the legal profession is diverse and reflective of society," says Ford, "that there is opportunity for everyone based on merit rather than background and without barriers." Accordingly, three-quarters of CILEx members are women, while 11 per cent come from a BAME (black and minority ethnic) background.

It has some notable high-profile and inspirational success stories. After taking part in its Judicial Development Programme in 2017, Elizabeth Johnson became the first female Chartered Legal Executive to be appointed to the Judiciary in 2019. And earlier this year, CILEx board member and its former president Millicent Grant became the first Chartered Legal Executive to be appointed an Honorary Queen's Counsel.

"They are both fantastic role models," says Ford. "Elizabeth comes from a non-traditional legal background, while Millicent was the first person from a BAME background to hold a leadership position in a professional membership body when she became our president in 2017."

These concepts of inclusion and representation are driving CILEx into the future — something that Ford recognises will lead to a better legal profession for society as a whole. "The diversity of our membership is critical," she says. "It's made up of people who are recognisable across the general population. Which means the compassion and the understanding of the consumer experience is much greater."

Data perfection

Minesoft's international database of patent information is the go-to resource for investigating and managing intellectual property

www.minesoft.com

"When we started working in the industry, the internet was nonexistent," says Ann Chapman-Daniel, Co-Founder and Director of Minesoft. "Nobody had ever even heard of it. It was just for the military." How times have changed since Chapman-Daniel and her husband, Ophir Daniel, set up their intellectual property search engine company in 1996.

Today, thanks to the internet, Minesoft enables anyone — but particularly innovative companies, investors and specialist law firms — to access a vast library of patent information research. And all the company's products handle huge quantities of data much faster than they did when the company started out.

Minesoft provides access to a searchable database of more than 125 million patent documents, including innovations that go back hundreds of years, which are updated every week with new publications. The company also offers an array of 14 different products for the intellectual property (IP) industry. These specialise in patent searching, intellectual property document retrieval, patent analytics and different legal and competitive intelligence systems.

Minesoft serves around 70,000 patent information professionals around the world and its database it constantly being accessed by major companies who need the very latest data on intellectual property industrial designs. "Our customers are the blue-chip companies around the world," says Chapman-Daniel. "Whether clients are patent attorneys or patent engineers who know their area of technology very well, they still need to be able to search for patents in more detail than is achievable from an internet search engine." And over the years Minesoft has honed its indexing down to a very fine level of detail indeed.

The company, which is based in Richmond, south-west London, has become an international business with offices in the USA, Germany and Japan. It also employs further staff in smaller operations in countries where there is advanced manufacturing technology, such as Israel and India.

Minesoft has incorporated many other languages into its database through collaboration with RWS Group: international specialists in science intellectual property translation and life sciences language services. This has helped the company reach into all major global markets to the point where around 90 per cent of its turnover now comes from outside the UK. The company won the Queen's Award for Enterprise in International Trade in 2009 and again in 2015.

What makes Minesoft stand out in this highly competitive market is its complete dedication to the world of patents. For many of its rivals, patents are just one part of an information-provision operation. "So we are seen very much as a niche player and are very close to our customer base," says Chapman-Daniel.

Minesoft also carries out bespoke product development with some of its larger clients. It is developing a patent-knowledge management product; and it uses customised software to host the patent archives for some of the best-known technology manufacturing companies.

With almost a quarter of a century under its belt, Minesoft is looking to expand further over the coming years. Ahead of Brexit, it has consolidated its operation in Germany to launch Minesoft GmbH. It has also expanded its operation in the USA, with offices now in New York, Washington and San Francisco. "We developed a suite of products last year that are going down very well in America," says Chapman-Daniel. "We anticipate that the USA is going to be a really good growth area for us."

A fine balance

JBW Group balances the need to fulfil its duty to society while protecting vulnerable individuals when collecting fines and overdue payments

www.jbwgroup.co.uk

Fairness sits at the heart of everything the JBW Group does. Fairness for society, and for the individuals that exist within that society. The company, which is owned by Outsourcing UK, is responsible for collecting fines and overdue payments owed to the UK government and local authorities, and endeavours to do so in a way that is both fair and highly effective.

"Everybody has the right to be treated fairly as an individual," says Nick Tubbs, JBW's Chief Executive. "We have to be fair to society and also to the people who do pay for the services they receive from local authorities. It's a balance, and the way to get it right is to understand people's circumstances while focusing on returning the optimum amount of money to our clients."

Since being acquired by Outsourcing in 2016, JBW has expanded from a single company, returning £26 million per annum to its clients, into a national collections group which now reclaims up to £250 million in unpaid debts and fines per annum on behalf of the government and public sector organisations. Its sister company is Liberata UK, itself a public services veteran, which was also acquired by Outsourcing in 2016, and like Liberata, the JBW Group continues to grow.

Given the nature of its service, JBW regularly has to work with vulnerable individuals. To ensure that its work is done in the most responsible manner possible, an independent advisory group led by Sir Martin Narey provides independent and objective scrutiny. "His role is to support and challenge the JBW Group to deliver improvements across our strategic, business and operational activities," says Tubbs. Sir Martin was previously Director-General of the Prison Service of England and Wales and CEO of the charity Barnardo's,

and was knighted in 2013 for his services to vulnerable people.

On the frontline, JBW's approach is designed to ensure that people receive equitable treatment. "Our approach is to deal with everybody as an individual so we can understand their unique circumstances and provide them with a solution that works for them," says Tubbs. "Our staff are trained to deal with people as individuals. All the information for a case is presented to them in an operating system that centres on the person themselves. Inherently, the whole system is constructed so we are treating people fairly in accordance with our key principles of accountability, respect and governance."

This includes a set of guidelines that helps JBW teams to identify both vulnerable and potentially vulnerable people. Accompanying this is a flexibility regarding the ability of debtors to make their payments. JBW sees its role as returning much-needed money to local authorities — something that is essential for society to function — while acknowledging that sometimes people can find themselves in difficult situations. In such cases, there is often a complex balance to be struck regarding the individual and the wider interests of a civilised society.

"As well as investing significantly in the way we deal with vulnerable people, we make sure that people have the opportunity to pay the debt if they are able to," says Tubbs. "It is all about identifying if people have the ability to pay and helping individuals to free themselves from the burden of debt. We are looking forward to delivering our new contracts with Her Majesty's Courts And Tribunals Service and developing our services to ensure we remain a first-class partner to the UK government."

Checks and balances

Bureau Veritas is the trusted safety inspector of hundreds of thousands of companies in Britain and overseas

www.bureauveritas.co.uk

"What we do every day comes down to asking one simple question," says Ken Smith, UK CEO of international testing, inspection and certification partner Bureau Veritas. "How can we make this world a safer place?" The company has been doing just that for nearly 200 years, and it has developed a wide portfolio of services to support clients in all sectors.

With more than 400,000 clients across 140 countries, Bureau Veritas applies this model to every sector imaginable, from nuclear waste and chemical management through construction and transport to food production. Its services improve safety, reduce risk and create more sustainable businesses.

The company motto is "Leave your mark". This applies to the work it carries out for clients and also to the employees it recruits. "When you're with us, you're ensuring health and safety, guaranteeing quality, improving performance and working towards environmental protection, sustainability and compliance," says Smith. "You truly leave your mark on society."

At one end of the scale, Bureau Veritas might carry out workplace health and safety inspections for clients, including a major retail banking organisation. "This particular client has nearly 2,000 properties across the UK and Ireland," says Smith. "We make sure that each building has a clear assessment of the way it is used and occupied. For instance, this can range from legionella and asbestos management to fire-risk assessments where we can offer combined compliance solutions to the client."

At the other end, Bureau Veritas might need to check, say, that a manufacturer's production facilities are safe and compliant. BV's services help to protect brand reputation, improve efficiency and enhance corporate responsibility. "We enable clients to manage those wider risks beyond simple compliance," says Smith. "For instance, we might inspect guarding on equipment which can help to ensure the management of safety risks in order to become a much more effective and sustainable organisation in its widest context."

The company works with the Ministry of Defence and has developed a successful programme to recruit ex-military personnel, for which it has been awarded an Armed Forces Employer Recognition Gold Award. The programme offers training with career opportunities in a supporting, rewarding work environment. Bureau Veritas appreciates the transferrable skills and attributes that those leaving the Armed Forces can bring. All helping to make the world a safer place.

Keeping Britain on the move

Logistics specialist Maritime Transport ensures that the nation's shops and businesses are fully stocked – and we can get on with our lives

www.maritimetransport.com

Although they wouldn't say it themselves, Britain's logistics businesses are the country's de facto fifth emergency service. Without the likes of Maritime Transport delivering cargo nationwide, the country would soon grind to a halt.

"We're a link," says Tom Williams, the son of Maritime Transport founder John Williams and the company's Managing Director of Container Transport. "People might not think about where their sofa or can of Coke came from, but the importance of logistics and transport can't be underestimated."

Operating over road and rail, Maritime Transport moves cargo from ports to distribution centres, and from there on to retailers. "We deliver anything, as long as it's in a container or a trailer," says Williams. "Major food retailers, drinks, online retailers, furniture… If you see it advertised on TV on a daily basis then it's likely that we move it."

The business was founded in 2001 with five depots and 130 trucks. It now has 33 depots across Britain and some 1,500 trucks on the road on a daily basis. It employs more than 2,500 people and has a turnover of over £330 million.

For one of the biggest privately owned logistics businesses, Maritime Transport manages to remain nimble and efficient. When the country's buying habits suddenly change – when the weather improves or around the time of a major sporting event, for instance – it has to be ready. "If it's a national celebration people might be buying barbecues and soft drinks," Williams explains. "If there's a national emergency we might be making sure that medical supplies are being dispatched. We've got to be flexible."

Last year, it diversified its operations by cementing its rail relationship with DB Cargo UK. This recently led to the opening of a new strategic rail freight interchange at SEGRO Logistics Park East Midlands Gateway. Capable of handling 16 trains a day and storing 5,000 20 ft containers on site, the move is significant because it opens up another part of the country for the movement of freight.

"Customers already on the site such as Nestlé, Amazon and The Very Group can benefit dramatically," says Williams. "Their cargo can arrive at a port, be put on one of our trains and delivered straight into the East Midlands as opposed to central Birmingham. This also helps to significantly reduce our carbon footprint." It's safe to say that Maritime Transport is one of the vital unseen arteries that keeps British businesses moving.

Aiming higher

The all-round skills training offered by Leading Edge Aviation ensures that all its students become more than just high-flyers

www.leadingedgeaviation.com

Leading Edge Aviation is a rising star in the commercial flight-training sector, drawing on many years of industry experience to provide accessible, inspirational and innovative aviation training. The academy was founded in 2018 when Andy McFarlane, a former RAF Wing Commander, brought together a team of like-minded individuals from the industry, including some former RAF colleagues.

"We had the same values and beliefs," he says. "We knew that there was a better way to provide high-quality aviation training." The senior team of six, along with their growing staff, take great pride in seeing their students graduate and take up First Officer roles with their chosen airlines.

Based at London Oxford Airport, Leading Edge Aviation uses a variety of training methods, including a Virtual Learning Environment and Neurotracker, virtual and augmented reality, not to mention its ALSIM AL42 simulator and a fleet of Diamond DA40 and DA42 aircraft. There is a modular course, for students who might be transitioning from their Private Pilot's Licence (PPL) to complete a Commercial Pilot's Licence, and an integrated course with a BSc degree which offers students the opportunity to go from zero experience to achieving a frozen Air Transport Pilot's Licence (fATPL) in as little as 18 months.

The school's success is in part down to a belief that being a successful First Officer is about more than flying skills. "Airlines have been saying for years that they don't just want somebody who flies an aeroplane," says McFarlane. "Most airlines have around nine core competencies and only two or three are actually flying related. It's about skills such as teamwork, leadership and communication, which we teach. It's an example of how we think about things differently."

Well-being plays a significant role in the training offered by Leading Edge. "Students are taught right from the very beginning about mental health along with fitness, diet, hydration and stress management so they have all the tools to deal with anything that might occur further down the line in their career," says McFarlane. "We do this from the first day and every couple of months we run well-being sessions with students and staff. Our aim is to nurture a family atmosphere, and people say they like the way it feels here. That comes from recruiting the right people with the right values and then passing the benefits on to the students."

Victory in its sites

Ridge offers an expansive range of property and construction services, creating better places for people to live, learn and work

www.ridge.co.uk

From motor racing facilities to the RAF Museum in Hendon (pictured above), Ridge and Partners LLP delivers prestigious projects worldwide. One example is in the world of Formula 1 racing, where the path to victory begins not on the track but in the laboratory. Night and day, Formula 1 teams put all their energies into overtaking the opposition by boosting engines and building lighter, sleeker chassis. All this work is done in highly serviced, technical buildings that enable these engineers to realise their goals reliably and safely.

"In such a highly charged environment, unless you're absolutely top of your game in what you deliver, you're not going to be invited to build the next project," says Adrian O'Hickey, Senior Partner. "In the last decade, every Formula 1 team that's won the championship has operated out of a Ridge building."

Founded in 1946, Ridge has become one of the UK's leading multidiscipline property and construction consultancies, assisting clients in everything from project and cost management, town and country planning, architecture, surveying, design and engineering to specialist consultancy services. "The cross-section of disciplines that we offer is unsurpassed," says O'Hickey. "And employing around 700 people, we are large enough to work on any development, but retain an agility that allows us to collaborate on a partner-led, individual level with our clients."

This approach enables Ridge to deliver intricate and prestigious projects to a wide range of clients. These include the Ministry of Defence, for whom Ridge is building a new facility with Boeing for the P-8A Poseidon Maritime Patrol Aircraft at RAF Lossiemouth. Ridge has also worked on the RAF Museum at Hendon and on over 40 British embassies around the world. "We've got an excellent track record in delivering work that supports the British government," says O'Hickey "and strong relationships with international business overseas."

Fittingly, Ridge regards the celebrations around the 75th anniversary of VE Day as an opportunity to reflect on its own 75-year history and further ways it might enhance the reputation of British design, engineering and consultancy around the world.

"We've grown significantly over the past 75 years, from beginning as a quantity surveyor in the postwar period to delivering new and exciting projects on a global scale," says O'Hickey. "We see ourselves as a true British success story."

Growing with the flow

Today's challenges mean that the UK Warehousing Association is busier than ever, keeping everything moving behind the scenes

www.ukwa.org.uk

Established in 1944 to help keep the nation fed and clothed during wartime, the UK Warehousing Association (UKWA) is now busier than ever, keeping everything moving behind the scenes. It supports more than 800 corporate members of Britain's warehousing and logistics sector, offering technical advice and support on government affairs to big operators such as DHL, UPS and Eddie Stobart as well as hundreds of smaller companies. It acts as a single voice for them all, advocating to government and giving members the chance to participate in shaping policy.

For its CEO Peter Ward, UKWA's peer-to-peer network is its most crucial asset. "We marry traders to logistics service providers and suppliers of specialist products and services, including technology and automation. We introduce supply and demand across the whole network."

For Ward, UKWA's 75th anniversary in 2019 was an opportunity to reflect on parallels between now and 1944. "Now here we are 76 years later," says Ward, "helping to make sure there is minimal disruption to essential supply of food, materials and manufacturing at this fresh time of political uncertainty. There's definitely a symmetry."

UKWA's growing membership attests to its important role in taking on the challenges posed by Brexit. But while the association offers support and advice in matters ranging from customs paperwork to stockpiling and supply chains, it presses members to adapt to the demands of today's digital economy.

"We're now in a situation where an increasing percentage of goods are delivered direct to consumers," says Ward. "Our biggest thing is educating members. We remind them that this industry is presenting them with unprecedented levels of opportunity, but they need to embrace and transform to the digital age, and not get left behind."

Despite the challenges, Ward remains optimistic about continued growth, prosperity and opportunity for an industry that most of us don't even think about until something goes wrong. "It will require different sets of skills from the past, but it's a fantastic career opportunity. I'd love to spread the word and share some of my passion for this industry — an industry that is understated but so essential to people's lives."

Brand and deliver

Focus7 is a brand-led business growth agency that enjoys a special relationship with the military

www.focus7.co.uk

Leona Barr-Jones recalls her time in the British Army with pride. It was there that she learned courage, discipline, integrity, loyalty, selfless commitment and respect for others – qualities that have carried over to her work as Chief Operating Officer at Focus7.

"People ask me how I've changed from being an army officer for 30 years, serving in Whitehall for six years, to co-founding a brand and marketing agency," says Barr-Jones. "And the answer is, 'Not a great deal has changed, really.' I've used the same model of values and standards as a basis for everything we do at Focus7."

Focus7 has a strong connection with the Armed Forces. Like Barr-Jones, both the CEO and Chief Marketing Officer at Focus7 have military family backgrounds; and the company runs a guaranteed interview scheme for all servicemen and women. "We're one of the smallest companies to have been given the gold award on the Ministry of Defence's Employer Recognition Scheme," she says. "It's the highest badge of honour to be given to any business that supports our forces."

Focus7 blends military efficiency and clarity of purpose with its brand and marketing strategies. "We run a two-day 'Brand School' to help businesses identify their Brand DNA," says Barr-Jones. "We help change their growth mindset to secure the long-term value of their asset and identify who they are talking to and what they want to be known for. We help them transition from a traditional business model to a brand-led business model which is all about an emotional connection of shared values."

From there, Focus7 generates a multi-media strategy that stays true to each client's core purpose. Take Anglo, a London-based solutions provider that needed to reposition itself after undergoing a merger. Focus7 came up with a new corporate narrative that drew on the history of both the merged companies while highlighting Anglo's recent ecological initiatives. "It makes such a big difference when you start thinking about your business as brand-led," says Barr-Jones, "instead of just looking for new sales."

Focus7 is proud to have supported the marketing effort for the Ministry of Defence's Armed Forces Day, further proof of its commitment to supporting Britain's servicemen and women. This year's VE Day celebrations hold a special significance for the company. "It's hugely important that we articulate our debt of gratitude to those who gave their lives for the freedom that we have now," says Barr-Jones. "We should never take that for granted."

Changing the world of work for good

Shaping the future

Community – a trade union representing a broad range of sectors – is changing the face of labour and industrial relations across the UK

www.community-tu.org

"As the world of work has changed, we have changed with it," says Roy Rickhuss CBE, General Secretary of Community, a trade union with a 100-year history but a clear focus on the future. Community has its roots in assorted venerable trade unions, in particular the Iron and Steel Trades Confederation (ISTC), which was founded in 1917. As the industrial landscape changed, the ISTC began to broaden its remit beyond steel and, in 2004, joined forces with the Knitwear, Footwear and Apparel Trade Union to become Community – a name that evokes Rickhuss's belief that "trade unionism doesn't only serve the workplace but families and the wider community, too."

Alongside its core membership in the steel and textile industries, Community also represents workers in sectors as diverse as social care, justice, finance and charity, including the self-employed. "Community has adapted to new ways of working by meeting the needs of the modern worker," says Rickhuss, who last year was invited to join the government's Industrial Strategy Council. "Our vision is rooted in the best traditions of the trade union movement, while understanding changes in the labour market. We work with good employers who value good industrial relationships, and, in doing so, hope to provide a blueprint for modern trade unionism." It is this belief in working in partnership with good employers that makes Community unique.

Campaigning is also at the heart of Community; last year members voted for a new campaign to help homeless veterans of the armed forces. Among Community's successes was the 2007 case brought to the European Court of Justice (ECJ) regarding the Pension Protection Fund. The ECJ ruled that the government had breached the law by not offering sufficient protection, which led to the creation of the Financial Assistance Scheme, benefiting thousands of workers and ex-workers. More recently, Community is developing a vision for the future of work through its Commission on Workers and Technology, dedicated to assisting workers in dealing with changing technology.

"It's about making sure workers are part of shaping how technology is used in the workplace to make their jobs better," says Rickhuss. "Technology should be an opportunity for workers rather than a threat. Ultimately, our aim is to help members direct their own future."

Stay connected

Energy pioneer Centrica, the owner of British Gas, is honouring its workers and its roots as the company that maintained Britain's energy supply during the war

www.centrica.com

"Keep the home fires burning" was more than just a morale-boosting wartime song lyric for some. Through Centrica's origins as the 1812 Gas Light and Coke Company, from which the entire industry developed, its people played a central role in the war effort, maintaining energy supplies to homes, businesses and communities — a crucial comfort at a time when lives were turned upside down.

At the outbreak of the Second World War, many employees — from lamp-fitters to stokers and meter readers — gallantly enrolled on active service, 402 of whom made the ultimate sacrifice. "Our company was deliberately attacked in an attempt to cripple production," says Centrica's Corporate Affairs Director Alan McLaughlin. "Our engineers worked tirelessly to repair those plants targeted by bombs, and repair thousands of miles of pipes. Our workers also installed lights in hospitals, refrigerators in submarines and cookers in evacuee homes and barracks. To this day, our people are our greatest asset."

Maintaining connection was primarily the responsibility of fast-response repair gangs, who faced grave danger during the worst of the aerial conflict. "When St Paul's Cathedral was bombed in 1940, our people fought flames and fire to stop the flow of gas from a burning main right next to the device," says McLaughlin. Thanks to these courageous men, the landmark remains standing today. The repair gangs lived up to the company's motto to "not let London down", and in total, attended 20,500 incidents throughout the war, earning 20 George Medals, alongside many other awards.

With many male workers in action, women eagerly adopted important, often dangerous responsibilities, paving the way for the increasingly valuable role of women in the energy sector. "To this day we are building a pipeline of female talent at all levels for a diverse and inclusive workforce that reflects society," says McLaughlin of Centrica's current workforce. "We seek to inspire the next generation of engineers by showcasing strong female roles to tackle gender stereotypes, and demonstrate how exciting a career in energy can be."

Such challenging times inspired both comradeship and innovation, as the industry underwent rapid transformation to feed war's appetite for energy, driven by efficiency and collaboration. For their courage and service, Centrica today honours the pivotal role in Britain's history of its wartime employees, and the legacy of their contribution to the company, the gas industry and the entire nation.

Love is the rug

The Afghan Rug Shop in West Yorkshire is helping to spread a unique and beautiful craft, as well as helping communities in Afghanistan

www.theafghanrugshop.co.uk

"We are the only company outside Afghanistan, anywhere in the world, selling purely Afghan rugs and kilims," says James Wilthew, owner of The Afghan Rug Shop. Wilthew is often asked by his customers just how fairtrade, handmade Afghan rugs have found their way from the Hindu Kush to Hebden Bridge in West Yorkshire. The answer is intriguing.

Wilthew (pictured, left), an RAF veteran of four operational campaigns, spent six months serving in Afghanistan in late 2003, based in Mazar-e-Sharif in the Northern Provinces. Part of his role was to engage with local elders in the towns and villages in order to monitor the security situation. "Whenever time allowed we'd drop into the rug shops, drink tea and chat to the locals," he says. "This is where my love for their rugs started."

Having bonded with one of the rug traders, his interest in the rugs and traditional methods grew. "I sent about 40 rugs back during my time in Mazar-e-Sharif," he recalls. "I thought it would be my only chance. It was 2003, there were no smartphones and the internet was unstable, and I never thought I could buy any again once I'd left. I sold several in the mess and to friends, which helped pay for my wedding, but I didn't give it much thought after that, as I was still serving and busy on other operations."

About 12 years later, Wilthew's circumstances had changed. He'd left the RAF, been diagnosed with PTSD and moved to Hebden Bridge with his family, when the rug in his home started to attract attention. When a friend asked if he could track down the maker of his rug and order one for himself, Wilthew accepted the challenge and the idea for the business was born. "It took a few months of cold-calls to Afghanistan,

social-media searches, emails to strangers and lots of Facebook messages," he says, "but ultimately I tracked down my old friend Rafi, the rug seller I hadn't seen or spoken to since the spring of 2004."

After an online reunion, Wilthew quickly acquired premises in the centre of Hebden Bridge. "We had to establish imports from a very rural and remote part of the world, establish money exchanges, import tax and banking issues, but we eventually figured it all out," he says. "There are no middle-men — these rugs come direct from the weavers' markets. We can supply any size of rug, to suit a canal boat or a stately home. People don't mind waiting if it's a bespoke order either." The Afghan Rug Shop also uses its extensive stock of "kilim" tapestries unique to this part of the world to create bespoke kilim-covered furniture, along with beautiful handmade glass from Herat and pottery from Istalif.

Now in its fifth year, The Afghan Rug Shop is proudly partnered with Turquoise Mountain, an NGO that helps the local craft industry in Afghanistan. The shop is a registered Living Wage employer and a corporate sponsor of Afghanaid, putting money directly into projects in the communities their rugs come from. Having won Highly Commended in the 2019 Soldiering On Awards for its positive impact on Afghan communities, The Afghan Rug Shop is currently a regional finalist in the FSB International Business of the Year Awards. Wilthew recently became an ambassador for X-Forces Enterprise, and is helping other veterans take their first steps in starting businesses of their own. "We are a growing business," he says, "with a remarkable story."

The future is clear

Clearly Drinks takes advantage of a natural resource while giving plenty back to the local community

www.clearlydrinks.co.uk

Bottled drinks company Clearly Drinks is a sparkling example of what it means to be a modern British business. It combines decades of tradition with a focus on the future, not only for the brand but also for its employees and out of respect for the planet. "We have a 135-year heritage," says Marcus Hudson, Sales Director. "But we're also about renewal and investing in our people up in Sunderland. We put the environment at the front, and we think local."

Formerly called Villa Drinks and recently relaunched, Clearly Drinks knows it's on to a winner. "We have our own spring water source on-site in Sunderland," says Hudson. "It comes down from the Cheviot Hills, direct from Hadrian's Well, and we make sure it's the best taste and the best flavour it can be. We're improving our existing drinks and launching new flavours. The response has been really positive."

This regional pride isn't confined to the water. "We've got people who've worked for the business for over 40 years," says Hudson, "and 95 per cent of our employees are local to Sunderland. We work with local primary schools, put on family days in the summer and hold monthly awards. We're all about building the team and the people." And it's clear the feeling is mutual. "We used to be known as Villa Drinks," he says, "and everyone in the North East of England knows and loves Villa Pop!"

Looking out for the environment plays an important part, too. "It's one of our core values," says Hudson. "We employ a sustainability officer and we recycle every single bit of waste on-site. Plus we reduced our use of plastic by 140 tons last year and reduced our carbon footprint by 8 per cent."

Clearly Drinks is a heritage brand that represents the very best of British values going forward. It is inventing new products all the time and using some of the eco-friendliest packaging in the field of bottled drinks. And perhaps most important of all, it is an essential part of the local community, as supportive and proud of its workforce as the workers are proud of their employer.

Bags of style

London bag brand Knomo has a handle on the needs of style-conscious commuters the world over

www.uk.knomo.com

"We make bags to prepare people for their everyday journey," says Knomo's Managing Director Marco Hackstein. "They are practical, distinctive, beautiful designs that make our customers feel confident about the way they look and about their organisation for the day."

Knomo set out 15 years ago with the desire to support people to make things happen with a commuting bag that wasn't the same as everyone else's. "Our customers are style conscious and have to manage numerous tasks," says Hackstein. "but often that attention to detail doesn't extend to luggage. You have particular needs when commuting and Knomo aimed to meet those needs."

Today the company is synonymous with beautifully designed but affordable bags that are comfortable to carry and also eminently practical. Their memorable exteriors disguise numerous handy pockets and sleeves for devices, gadgets, wallets and travel essentials like passports. Little wonder that Knomo enjoys such international appeal, with its bags sold in more than 600 offline and online points across 32 countries worldwide.

"We're making an impact across the world with exquisite workmanship that is a delight to look at but which also makes our customers' lives so much easier," says Hackstein. "However, Knomo is rooted in its British heritage and is proud to be a London brand." The company has its own shops in London's Fitzrovia and Covent Garden and the collection is also stocked in numerous other outlets in the capital including Harrods, Selfridges and John Lewis.

The very British-sounding Beauchamp — pronounced Beecham — is the company's signature backpack and one of its bestsellers. "The original bag, in black, was made for women," says Hackstein. "But it quickly became apparent that its classic lines and timeless appeal are both unisex and ageless. It complements many lifestyles."

Alongside the Beauchamp are numerous styles for men and women in a range of seasonal colours, sizes and materials. As well as several different backpacks there are elegant totes, briefcases, laptop and cross-body bags and a range of carry-ons with wheels. They all contain space for a Knomad personal organiser. "Our Knomads have proved equally popular," says Hackstein, "helping people to keep everything in an easily accessible place. Knomo is becoming ever-more aspirational while reflecting the functionality needed to span work/life challenges with ease." Knomo's future, like its past, would seem to be in the bag.

A good yarn

Steeped in tradition and driven by creativity, tartan design innovator Prickly Thistle prides itself on its "flock-to-frock" vision

www.pricklythistlescotland.com

No other company weaves together tradition with forward-thinking business practices like Prickly Thistle. An independent tartan designer and weaver based in the Scottish Highlands, it has established a global brand by making products using traditional artisan methods while incorporating strong green credentials.

"We're using very old equipment that was abandoned some time ago for faster looms," explains Clare Campbell, the owner of Prickly Thistle. "We invested in skills, people and this equipment to bring weaving back to life in the Highland region — its ancestral home." All the looms used to create the tartan are made from cast iron, with no computer involvement at any stage. "They're engineering works of art," she says. "In 300 years, these looms will still be going, while all modern ones will have been scrapped."

The yarn used is purchased from Scottish spinners and dyers, in response to the damaging effects of fast fashion and polyester-based clothing. The aim is to create a "flock-to-frock" scenario that keeps its ecological footprint as small as possible. "We're trying to play a role in the fabric of the planet," says Campbell. "People may never fly, drive a fossil-fuel car or drink from a plastic bottle, but they will be wearing clothes."

They combine this commitment to the Scottish supply chain with charitable work and spreading environmentally conscious information on social media. "We're selling our beliefs respectfully," says Campbell. "When people buy our products, they're wearing our values - they believe in the same things as us."

This mindset has struck a chord with people all over the world, leading to sales as far afield as Hawaii, Japan, Russia, New Zealand, America and beyond. "There's a huge Scottish diaspora of support, plus a lot of people who aren't Scots who want to be Scots," says Campbell. Plenty of high-profile names are fans of Prickly Thistle, including fellow Scot Sam Heughan — star of *Outlander* and tipped to be a future James Bond. But Campbell is as humbled by every customer who endorses and supports the brand.

Prickly Thistle is a modern Scottish business in every sense of the word. It makes long-lasting products that stand out from the crowd, while maintaining its integrity at every stage. "We want to be thought-provoking," says Campbell. "And we want to deal with the fabric 'elephant in the room' — but with Scottish style, by creating cloths and collections that embody our principles."

"We shall have failed and the blood of our dearests will have flowed in vain if the victory which they died to win does not lead to a lasting peace, founded on justice and goodwill"

King George VI, Victory in Europe Day 1945

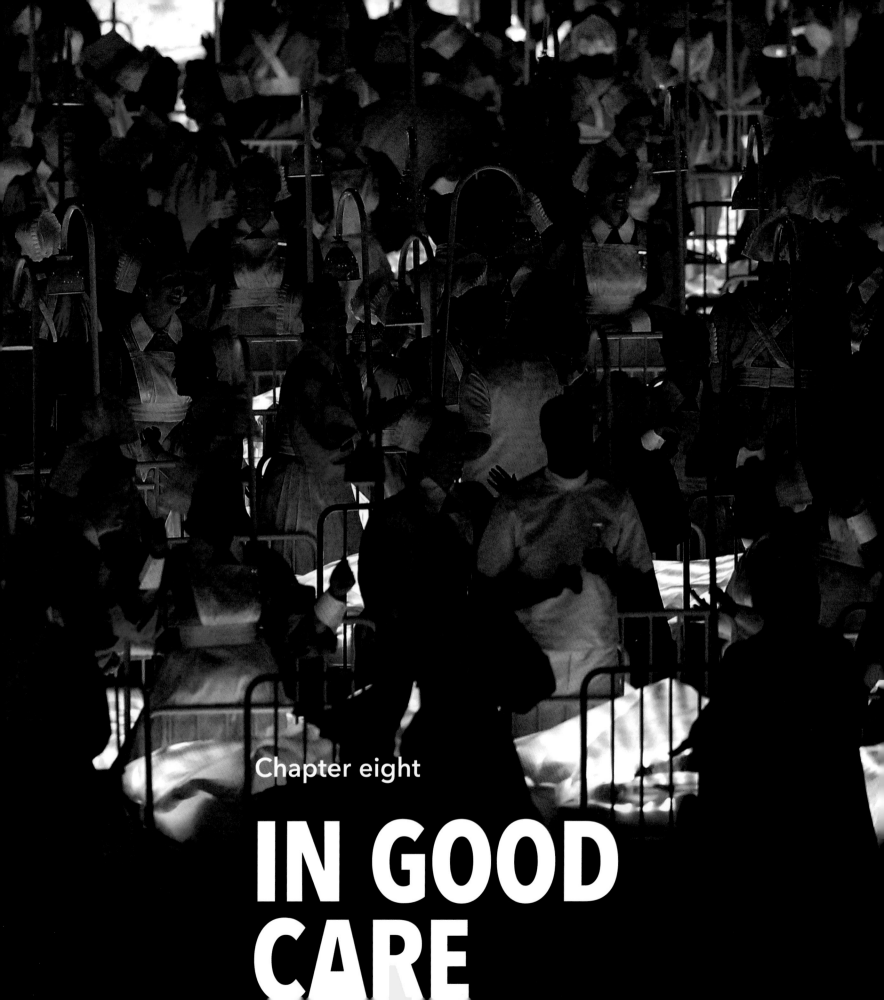

Chapter eight

IN GOOD
CARE

Charity, at home and abroad

Following VE Day, SSAFA's mission to support the welfare of Britain's military personnel and their dependants was never more vital

On VE Day, the nation's thoughts were not just on celebration: thanksgiving, charity and the future were also on people's minds. In the days, weeks and months that followed, the goal of reconstruction were paramount; of rebuilding a better world out of the rubble of war. Both at home and overseas, ordinary citizens, military personnel, politicians and community leaders were focussed on defeating the enemy in the Far East, and also, in the words of Field Marshall Montgomery, on "winning the peace" in Europe.

At home, with daily reminders of the losses sustained during the war, people wanted to express their thanksgiving for a hard-won peace by supporting others. One way they did this was through fundraising. In Chesterfield, a gaily decorated Chesterfield Corporation Bus bore banners with Churchill's face on it and the words "Victory in Europe: Well done Allied Nations" in big bold letters down the side. It ran on various routes in the town throughout VE Day for free, but the bus conductor carried a collection box in aid of SSAFA, the Armed Forces charity, taking donations from the passengers.

Established in 1885, SSAFA had been supporting military personnel and their families for more than half a century when the Second World War broke out. Prior to the Munich Agreement of September 1938, SSAFA was receiving around 980 letters and requests for help a month. By September 1939 — just one month into a war that Neville Chamberlain's agreement had failed to prevent — these letters asking for help had increased to well over 3,000. These requests for support would only increase as the devastation of the Blitz, the frontline losses and the prisoner of war captures escalated.

Throughout the war, SSAFA had been providing support to service personnel and their families. The association had 20,000 voluntary workers, 200 of whom were deployed overseas in all theatres of the war. Each of these volunteers upheld the duty to eliminate the words "trouble, worry and anxiety" from the minds of all serving men and women about their families. They helped to solve domestic and financial problems, often giving immediate grants in cases of hardship not covered by government welfare schemes.

On 27 April, 11 days before VE Day, SSAFA launched a national £1 million appeal in The Times. Even with peace in sight, the charity predicted that the cost of its welfare support programmes would rise, as more soldiers, sailors and airmen returned home needing support. The appeal sought to raise £500,000 for their emergency Children's Homes. SSAFA had opened its first Children's Home in 1941 in response to the Blitz and, by the end of the war, was operating 13 such homes, with more to follow. A quarter of the appeal's £1 million was to relieve Armed Forces personnel of home worries, supporting those military personnel still deployed, including those in the Far East, prisoners of war, and their families. The remaining £250,000 was to help returning service personnel re-establish themselves in civilian life. Around five million men and women in the Armed Forces had to be integrated back into civilian life. The government had developed a plan for demobilisation, its chief architect being the coalition's Minister of Labour, Ernest Bevin. Military personnel were released in order, based on the length of their service and age. However, for many the process was slow and anger grew, with a number of disciplinary incidents breaking out in protest.

Former service personnel encountered a variety of problems as they returned to civilian life. Those who went off to war did not come back the same, nor did they return to the same world that they had left. The differences weren't just due to property damage, but also the social and cultural changes

that had occurred. Many women had achieved a degree of independence and autonomy during the war. Couples who had effectively been apart for years had to now live together again and settling back into normal family life was a challenge. Many couples who had married in wartime were now living together for the first time. The tensions and associated issues that arose are reflected in the high post-war divorce rate, with over 60,000 applications processed in 1947 alone.

As it had always done since its inception, SSAFA provided support to military families readjusting to the new order. "His Home is His Castle" was the strapline for the £1 million SSAFA appeal aimed at relieving the pressures. "Home — that is the picture that rises before his eyes as he goes into action. Home — that's what he's fighting for; what he dreams of returning to. SSAFA is his link with home. Despite improved government provisions, the need still exists for that personal touch which only an organisation like SSAFA can give at times of domestic crisis. SSAFA needs £1,000,000 to look after his family."

SSAFA's Bristol branch held an AGM on 11 May 1945 and heard that, by VE Day, 7,000 families were on the charity's case books in Bristol alone, with more than 200 fresh applications for aid coming in every week. Expenditure during the year had totalled £8,152. Gifts had been made to 531 mothers, 803 girls and 916 boys. The emergency hostel on the Downs in Bristol had looked after 164 children and 16 mothers over the course of the year. Major-General EO Lewin asked for more volunteers, stating that SSAFA's workload would become heavier, not lighter, in the coming years.

On 13 May 1945 — the day of official thanksgiving for peace that followed VE Day —

SSAFA chairman Air Vice-Marshall Sir Norman McEwen made a wireless appeal to the nation. He asked the people of the United Kingdom to remember the soldiers and their families in their thanksgiving by donating to the SSAFA Appeal. Tewkesbury Abbey held thanksgiving services that afternoon, with a parade assembling outside the Town Hall beforehand. A collection was taken at the service and was divided between the Tewkesbury and District Nursing Association and SSAFA, while a Victory Service at Deerhurst parish church in Gloucestershire also took donations for SSAFA.

Six days later, the Stirlingshire Branch held a Forces Families Day on Flag Day, in aid of branch funds. Over the course of the war the branch had distributed grants amounting to £2,600 towards the relief of distress among servicemen's wives and dependents. "The need is greater than ever," ran the advertising. "Please give generously." All SSAFA branches made similar appeals — essential for the welfare of those soldiers, sailors, airmen and their families who had made such great sacrifices to secure victory in Europe.

As predicted by Major-General Lewin and SSAFA, the welfare work of the charity became more urgent in the years that followed the war. The Ministry of Labour's Resettlement Service Offices referred all cases affecting family welfare to local SSAFA branches. By November 1945, SSAFA was running 15 emergency homes for children, caring for 6,000 a year. By 1946, 258,000 men who were still based overseas had used the SSAFA bureaux, with enquiries about their loved ones at home coming in at a rate of 1,500 a week. By 1947, the charity comprised 1,540 branches in the UK and had some 30,000

Opposite A SSAFA
volunteer sorts through
a stack of POW letters

voluntary workers, working across every county, city and town, and in thousands of villages in Britain and Ireland. In addition, 150 representatives were working overseas in the 60 enquiry bureaux that had been set up to support deployed troops. That year alone, more than 1,250,000 garments were distributed by SSAFA Central Clothes Depot, overseen by Mrs Seary Mercer OBE, who had been managing the charity's clothing distribution depot since 1942.

In light of the growing demands placed on the charity by both the public and the state, a fundraising appeal for a further £1 million was launched in 1947. At a press conference to launch the Scottish share of the appeal (£40,000), Her Grace the Duchess of Montrose, then chairman of the West of Scotland branch, delivered a speech. "SSAFA does not usurp the functions of the state," she said. "Rather it supplements them in cases of proved individual need, and also provides a body of well-disposed persons; men and women, who by their personal human touch can bring sympathy and understanding to those who are in trouble… When demobilisation commenced, great numbers of cases arose of illness at home or other special features containing a compassionate element, and SSAFA has carried out a considerable part of the enquiry work."

These "great numbers of cases" were similar across the UK, where SSAFA branches were dealing with the fall-out of demobilisation. The main work of the branches was recorded as: financial assistance, clothing provisions, housing issues, assisting with applications for compassionate leave for personnel in active service in the UK, appeals for premature release from service and matrimonial discord.

In 1947, SSAFA ran the following appeal in many local and national newspapers, telling the story of a mother who struggles to support a family of four, with her invalided husband unable to work. The editorial ran as follows:

"When her husband was invalided out of the army after D-Day, it took all Mrs X's strength and devotion to keep the little family of six together.

"For two years she struggled on bravely, making do with the children's allowance and her husband's disability pension. Then suddenly her husband's pension was suspended until he could undergo a further medical examination.

But the rent alone was 23/6 a week, and the family must eat. Besides, a fifth child was on the way. The anxiety began to tell on Mrs X's health.

Very sensibly she came to SSAFA for help. SSAFA went into the case, paid her rent for two weeks in advance, promised further help when the baby arrived. There were tears of gratitude in Mrs X's eyes when she left — an intolerable load had been taken off her shoulders.

What is this Association that is so ready to help a mother in distress? It is an Association whose sole aim is to help the families of service and ex-service men. SSAFA (rhymes with JAFFA) stands for Soldiers, Sailors and Airmen's Families Association. Its patrons are their Majesties the King and Queen, and Queen Mary.

SSAFA Children and Homes Department provides emergency care for children and a Nursing Branch cares for families at important Service Stations. Clothing, bedding, prams, layettes — furniture, even — are supplied in genuine cases of need."

A similar editorial told the story of Agnes and her family, who were all living in just one room. Pregnant Agnes was caring for her five children and nursing her husband. After approaching SSAFA, she received much-needed support including respite from child-care, with her four younger children taking up temporary places at SSAFA Emergency Children's Homes until their baby sibling was born.

By 1947, SSAFA had launched a Welfare of the Children Plan in a bid to tackle the increasing child abandonment, neglect, malnutrition and other poverty-associated diseases such as tuberculosis (TB). British children needed SSAFA more than ever. Janet Humphries worked as a nursery nurse at SSAFA's Grangemuir Children's Home in Wimbledon. The home had been opened by the Duchess of Gloucester

"So vital was the post-war work of the charity that donations came from far and wide. Field Marshal Bernard Montgomery sent a cheque for £10,000"

in 1947, and Janet had begun working there as a student nurse as soon as it opened. She describes Grangemuir as "a lovely Victorian home with turrets overlooking the common, where we used to push the babies in big Silver Cross prams."

Grangemuir was a short-stay home. "Some children only stayed a little while," recalls Janet, "while their mothers had an operation or a baby, many fathers were away in the Forces then." Other children, who had been abandoned, were taken in until a more permanent home could be found. One such child was David John, who Janet recalls was named after the policeman who found him in the marshes on Wimbledon Common. On days when the weather was good, Janet would take David John home to her parents' house, where he would be spoilt by her family and played in the garden.

The beautiful gardens at the home, the fresh air of the common and the places they were taken to visit, including local allotments and the staff's own homes, were a far cry from where many of the children had been living previously.

The positive impact that the SSAFA Children's Homes and the Rest Homes provided for families were recorded in the newspapers of the day and letters and correspondence sent to the charity. One such letter was from a young sailor's wife, who had TB and whose two young children were placed into a SSAFA Children's Home until she recovered. She wrote of the great benefit felt by herself and how delighted she was at the condition of the children when they returned home.

In another case, a five-year-old child, who had been left severely traumatised by bombing raids, was taken to SSAFA's Nettleden Lodge, Hampshire for a two-month stay while he waited for a place at the Mental After Care Association. Following his stay, SSAFA received a letter commenting on the Mental After Care Association team's amazement at

the child's improvement as a result of his time at Nettleden Lodge.

The work of these Children's Homes was well known and well supported, with fundraising efforts held regularly throughout the year specifically to raise money to create new homes or support those already in existence. The Royal Family, as patrons of the charity, were strong supporters of SSAFA's Children's Homes, with Princess Elizabeth even sending a gift of honey to SSAFA, which was shared among the SSAFA emergency Children's Homes in England, Wales and Scotland.

So vital was the post-war work of the charity that donations came from far and wide. Field Marshal Bernard Montgomery — the hero of El-Alamein and North Africa, known to all as "Monty" — sent a welfare cheque for £10,000 to SSAFA in 1947. And he sponsored a further appeal that year held in the British Zone of Germany, which raised an additional £25,000 for the charity.

Monty had long been an advocate for the welfare work that SSAFA provided to military personnel and their families. He was the military leader that requested that SSAFA open its first bureau, which was embedded with the British Army. This SSAFA bureau travelled with his own British Liberation Army, which after the war became the British Army of the Rhine (BAOR). Monty's insistence that SSAFA should operate alongside him in the theatre of war continued into the post-war period. SSAFA volunteers and welfare workers had been with the British Army as it advanced through Germany both in the lead up to the surrender and in its aftermath.

"We have won the war, now let us win the peace," Field Marshall Montgomery said to his troops immediately after VE Day. He was referring to what he would later describe as the eradication of Nazism from Germany. This was the sweeping clean of the nation that had been under Nazi rule

for 12 years, the six years of war that had "resulted in more than material destruction" and the reconstruction of the society in accordance with "the principles that we hold to be right".

At the end of the Second World War, Germany was divided into four zones of occupation, with each of the major Allied powers – the United States, Britain, Russia and France – taking control of a zone. Within months, the American, British and French zones had joined to form West Germany (including the enclave of West Berlin) and the Russian zone became East Germany. The British ruled an area half the size of their own country, containing a population that was starved, homeless, destitute and, in many cases, displaced. The military governor of the British zone was Field Marshal Montgomery,

who had received the German surrender at Luneburg Heath, near Hamburg. "I had suddenly become responsible for the government and well-being of about 20 million Germans," wrote Monty in his memoirs. "Tremendous problems would be required to be handled and if they were not solved before the winter began, many Germans would die of starvation, exposure and disease."

Conditions in the country for the Germany population, the displaced and the occupiers were difficult and dangerous. Articles published in the British Zone Review, a fortnightly review of the activities of the Control Commission for Germany in the British Zone, painted a bleak picture. There was no gas, no electricity, the water was impure, the local industries at a standstill, homes

Above SSAFA supported dependents as well as military personnel during and after the war, as it does to this day

Opposite SSAFA's Children
Homes provided infant and
adolescent welfare support
to those in vital need

in rubble. These were towns and cities with no operating or functioning infrastructure, no amenities, no transport and no food supplies.

Living in these conditions were not only the soldiers of Monty's BAOR and the German population that they now governed, but also the families of the British troops deployed to the area. Just 15 months after VE Day, wives and children were joining their husbands serving in the BAOR. It was announced in June 1946 that 9,000 British families would be heading to Germany, with the first wave expected to arrival in August of that year. Known as Operation Union, this deployment of British families was supported by SSAFA, with the charity living up to its motto of "We'll look after them".

An article published in the *Eastbourne Herald* in 1946 describes the scene at Tilbury Docks, where troops and their families boarded ships to travel to their new life in the British Zone of Germany. "No ship carrying troops' families leaves or enters Tilbury Docks without SSAFA's travel officer being there to see that this stage in their journey goes smoothly," reads the paper. "Nurses wearing SSAFA armlets are there to help mothers with feeding their children and to see that they get aboard comfortably. Blankets are often supplied and even clothing provided by SSAFA's clothing depot is distributed in needy cases."

SSAFA Sisters was the nursing branch of SSAFA. It was set up in 1892 and officially known as SSAFA Alexandra Nurses after the charity's first president, Queen Alexandra, the wife of King Edward VII. Long before the start of the Second World War, SSAFA nurses had become an integral part of the British Army, but they gained international recognition when the war brought Allied Forces into a truly global theatre, and this international activity continues to this day. Their nursing practices were so successful that, when the National Health Service came into being in 1948, the SSAFA Sisters were used as the model for the District Nursing Service.

Queen Alexandra's association with nursing can be traced back to the Boer War. While still the Princess of Wales, she had raised funds to fit out a hospital ship to bring back the wounded from the conflict in South Africa. She became queen-empress consort in 1901 when her husband ascended to the throne, and Queen Alexandra's Imperial Military Nursing Service — QAIMNS — was established by Royal Warrant in 1902. Queen

Alexandra remained President of the service until her death in 1925. Her dedicated patronage of both Army nursing and SSAFA ensured that her association with the service would long outlive her, with QAIMNS retaining her title when they were incorporated into the Army Medical Corp and rebranded Queen Alexandra's Royal Army Nursing Corps in 1949, 24 years after the queen had passed away. The SSAFA nurses also retained their royal patron's name, bearing the official title, SSAFA Alexandra Nurses throughout the Second World War and into the post-war period.

The SSAFA Sisters had served during the war, both at home and aboard, and their involvement with the British Zone of Germany was not to be limited to Tilbury Docks. As the conditions in Germany were fully realised, thoughts turned to limiting the threat that starvation and disease of an entire population could pose to the wider world.

Monty was well aware of this threat. In the very first edition of the *British Zone Review*, he observed that "epidemics need no passports". He asserted that the economic and social collapse of Germany would be "as disastrous for Western Europe as a whole as it would be for Germany". His sentiments were perhaps informed by the pandemic that had ravaged the world at the end of the First World War. The so-called "Spanish Flu" is thought to have infected up to a third of the world's population between 1918 and 1920, and historians estimate that it claimed somewhere between 20 million and 100 million lives. Equally, the Allies were aware that the hardships faced by Germany after the First World War had given rise to Hitler and the popularity of the Third Reich. Reconstruction was the most important means of preventing such disasters, and the British Army's work to rebuild Germany began in earnest.

In 1946, as the reconstruction began, the War Office asked SSAFA for nurses. It was intended that a nursing service be established for the families finding themselves stationed in the British zone. The nurses would not only provide healthcare but also, working with the SSAFA in-service committees of wives, they would teach vital first-aid and health courses to those living in the British zone.

The SSAFA nurses, all qualified nurses or midwives, were based out of Bad Oeynhausen, a spa town in the North Rhine-Westphalia region of Germany. Following the German surrender, this became the seat for the British division of the

Control Commission for Germany and headquarters for the military government run by the BAOR. The town, fabled for its thermal salt waters and 19th century architecture, had been heavily bombed towards the end of the war. Those stationed there were left with the same impression as other international visitors and workers to Germany — that of "a once beautiful country now blown to pieces".

Required to be where the British troops were, the SSAFA nurses did not remain in Bad Oeynhausen but were posted to key areas such as Hamburg, Berlin and Luneburg — where half a million Germans were homeless. From these key BAOR postings, the SSAFA Sisters provided health care and welfare services to the Armed Forces families. Wearing khaki uniforms with SSAFA flashes, the first group of six nurses was sent out to the British Zone in August 1946. Leading the SSAFA Sisters was Miss AM Elliott, a veteran of overseas nursing deployments and the first member of her profession to be selected for the BAOR health-care scheme. Originally from Derby, Miss Elliot trained at the Leicester Royal Infirmary and had served as a SSAFA nurse in Malta and Gibraltar for six years before this appointment.

An article in her home-town newspaper, the *Derby Evening Telegraph*, quoted Miss Elliott as she embarked on her new posting to Germany. "I am terribly keen on this new job," she told the paper, "and we are determined to make it a real health service — as good as anything the families would have at home in England, complete with a school, nursing services, pre-natal and welfare clinics."

In September, a second contingent of SSAFA nurses was sent to other areas of the British zone, including Luneburg, and by the end of 1946 there was a total of 25 SSAFA nurses operating in the country. Time in the British Zone was difficult, fraught with deprivations and dangers. In October 1946, it was reported in the *Hull Daily Mail* that one of the first SSAFA nurses posted to Hamburg, Miss Elsie Johnson, had been seriously injured in a motor accident and had been admitted to hospital.

Establishing hospitals and health services in a country that had been brought to its knees was an uphill battle. There were also the mounting tensions between the Allied nations, as the Soviet Union become more opposed to the British, French and Americans. By 1949, Germany was divided into two separate countries — the Federal Republic of Germany (West Germany) run by three western Allies and the German Democratic Republic (East Germany) run by the Soviet Union. The ensuing Cold War, which would last until 1991, placed Germany at the epicentre of geopolitical tensions, with those in the west living with the threat of Soviet expansion and aggression, and the ominous spectre of nuclear armament. The Cold War saw the rule of the British Army in Germany change over the years from one of post-war reconstruction to Cold War defence and protection.

Throughout, SSAFA — in the form of its nurses, the growing number of in-service committees of military wives and the increasing number of West German SSAFA branches — continued to provide health, welfare and personal support to the serving personnel of the BAOR and their families. As they did for the Armed Forces community back in the UK and elsewhere in the world, operating wherever the British military was deployed, as they still do to this very day.

A national treasure

One of the most significant decisions in the aftermath of the Second World War was the creation of the National Health Service, which is proving as essential today as ever

The National Health Service was launched three years after VE Day in a society weary but disciplined by war. Its foundation can be seen as perhaps the most lasting achievement of postwar regeneration – a grim determination to take the lessons learned by war and use them as a force for positive change.

For much of the first half of the 20th century, the vast majority of British people did not have access to healthcare. Aside from a small number who could afford private healthcare, most people were reliant on hospital charities, funded by philanthropists. As far back as the 19th century, some municipalities – such as the London County Council and Middlesex County Council – tried to run hospitals as well as utilities, but GPs were funded by Friendly Societies that paid them as little as possible. Some bigger teaching hospitals (such as St Bart's, Guy's and St Thomas's) received private investment, while others were developed in conjunction with universities. But each voluntary hospital was a law unto itself, raising funds and deciding its own admission policies. Patients were usually charged and many hospitals were nearly bankrupt.

In 1920, a report was commissioned by the government on the possibility of a systematised provision of medical services. Lord Dawson,

physician to the Royal Family and chairman of the Consultative Council on Medical and Allied Services, provided a hugely forward-thinking report on how a health service might be organised, using primary and secondary health centres. In 1929, Local Government Act forced local authorities to take over poor law hospitals that now became municipal hospitals serving ratepayers, not paupers. But quality varied from town to town, and many needed huge upgrading and investment. By the 1930s, reports by the British Medical Association, the King's Fund and the Nuffield Provincial Hospitals Trust attempted to bring about a standardisation of care.

The experience of the Second World War, during which an emergency medical service was created as the country came under command and control, provided an example of what could be achieved. William Beveridge, later a Liberal MP and peer, wrote a report on social welfare in 1942. This report appealed to Conservatives who might oppose a health service by arguing that strong welfare institutions would increase the competitiveness of British industry and create healthier and more motivated workers. After Labour's election victory in 1945, Health Secretary Aneurin Bevan presented to the cabinet a plan that favoured the nationalisation

Previous pages Health Secretary Aneurin Bevan meets nurses on the day the National Health Service came into being, 5 July 1948

Left An NHS mobile immunisation unit goes to work in the fight against diphtheria, 1951

Right Nurses appear in NHS uniforms from each of the past eight decades of the service's existence

of all hospitals, voluntary or council, and a regional framework.

The National Health Service was launched on 5 July 1948. In a country that was rebuilding itself from the rubble of war and dealing with austerity, rationing, a dollar crisis and a fuel shortage, the NHS had to compete for resources with other priorities. New hospitals had little claim on the few building materials available — housing and schools came first. This was also a time of massive innovation in medicine, which put further pressure on healthcare costs. The pharmaceutical industry was creating a flood of new drugs. Antibiotics, better anaesthetics, cortisone, drugs for the treatment of mental illness such as schizophrenia and depression, good diuretics for heart failure and antihistamines all became available. In addition, ultrasound was developed from wartime electronics expertise. These developments, while improving the lot of the patient, raised the cost of the NHS.

Its funding system was unique. The NHS was almost entirely financed from central taxation. The rich paid more than the poor. Everyone was eligible for care, even people temporarily resident or visiting the country. Initially, care was free at the point of use — when prescription charges of one shilling were suggested, it split the Labour party.

Many prominent Conservatives opposed the NHS but, when the party was returned to government in 1951, it pragmatically maintained a commitment to the service. Throughout the 1960s and 1970s, the elderly, the mentally ill and handicapped, children's services and the disabled were the subjects of reports, sometimes following scandals. Changes in abortion law in 1968 led to new pressures on gynaecological services. Medical advances included the increasingly wide application of endoscopy and the advent of CAT scanning. Transplant surgery was becoming increasingly successful and genetic engineering slowly began to influence medicine. Intensive care units became widely available and new drugs appeared, including non-steroidal anti-inflammatory treatments. Kidney dialysis became more widely available and surgery established a place in the care of coronary heart disease.

By the start of the 1980s there was greater emphasis on the financial limits within which the NHS operated. With the introduction of MRI scans, minimal-access surgery, increasing heart and liver transplants, and a huge increase in the number of hip and femur replacements, the NHS could no longer even pretend to do everything medically possible.

Following the 1990 Community Care Act, the government started to introduce the "internal

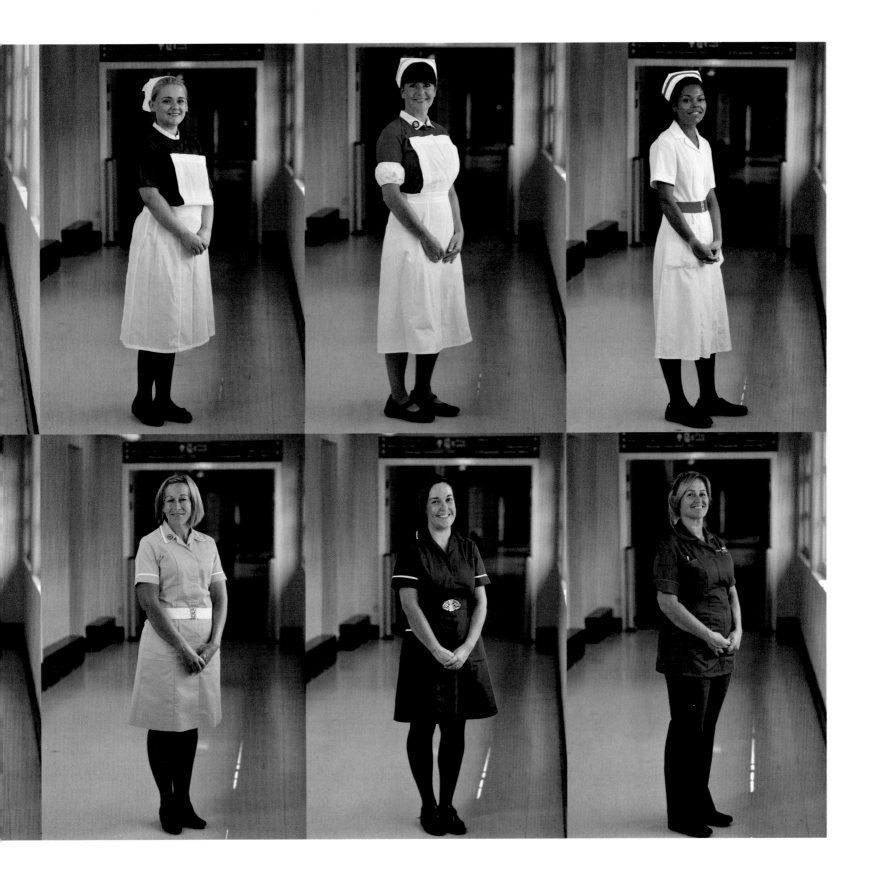

market" in the NHS. It divided sections of the NHS into "purchasers" (health authorities and some family doctors) who were given budgets to buy healthcare from "providers" (acute hospitals, ambulance services, organisations providing care for the mentally ill and people with learning disabilities and the elderly). That internal market has been maintained under successive changes in government since then, with NHS Trusts turning into Primary Care Trusts and Strategic Health Authorities, which in turn have mutated into Clinical Commissioning Groups. Regulation came in the form of the National Institute for Health and Care Excellence (NICE, established in 1999), which assessed the cost-effectiveness of new drugs and technologies, and the Healthcare Commission (established 2004, and reformulated as the Care Quality Commission in 2009), which looked at the quality, governance and financial management of trusts.

When the Health and Social Care Act 2012 became fully operational on 1 April 2013, it highlighted one of the Department of Health's major policies: to increase the integration between health care and social care. This joining up of services is fundamental in view of the UK's ageing population, with the percentage of people over the age of 85 set to double in the next two decades. Politicians and healthcare professionals are still engaged in a debate about how care for the elderly can best be funded and allocated, with many victims of Alzheimer's and dementia finding that their care needs are not provided by the NHS.

Seventy-five years since VE Day, many features of the post-war consensus have fallen by the wayside. But, in its eighth decade, the NHS still finds itself being fiercely defended by the British people, its very existence and the principles upon which it was founded becoming sacrosanct to most voters, regardless of their political stripe. Whatever the future holds for the NHS, one thing remains certain, and was summed up perfectly by Bevan: "We shall never have all we need," he said. "Expectations will always exceed capacity. The service must always be changing, growing and improving — it must always appear inadequate."

Left A London bus drives past the Cenotaph bearing a message of thanks to the NHS, May 2020

You'll never walk alone

War veteran and modern-day fundraising champion
Captain Tom Moore's fortitude and goodwill in the face
of adversity encapsulate the VE Day spirit

With the nation in lockdown due to Covid-19, plans to mark VE Day 75 have been significantly restricted. And yet the courage, bravery and optimism of the wartime generation have never been more present in the nation's minds, nor more pertinent. Just eight days before the 75th anniversary, one former Army captain has come to epitomise that generation.

In April 2020, Captain Thomas Moore, a Yorkshireman living in the Bedfordshire village of Marston Moretaine with his daughter Hannah and her family, become a national treasure and fundraising hero. Honoured by the Queen and the Royal Family, the Prime Minister and the British Army, Captain Tom became the oldest holder of a chart-topping single, the face of resilience at a time of a global crisis and, not least, the man who raised more than £32 million for the National Health Service in less than a month.

What started out as a "little family joke" — walking 100 laps of his garden before his 100th birthday to raise "a little bit of money" — turned into the biggest ever fundraising effort in the history of the donation platform JustGiving. Initially aiming to raise £1,000 for NHS Charities Together by 30 April 2020, neither Tom nor his family could have envisioned how such a simple idea would capture the nation's attention and see people digging deep into their pockets.

Spurred on by growing national and international support, Captain Tom completed his 100th lap on 16 April, two weeks before his birthday. As he crossed the "finish line" — flanked by a guard of honour provided by the 1st Battalion of the Yorkshire Regiment (the modern-day incarnation of Tom's old regiment) — his fundraising total stood at £13 million; an extraordinary sum, but less than half of what he'd ultimately raise. When his donation page closed at midnight on Thursday 30 April, he had raised a grand total of £32,794,701 from more than 1.5 million supporters for NHS Charities Together.

Tom was born in Keighley, West Yorkshire. After having completed an apprenticeship as a civil engineer, he enlisted into the 8th Battalion of the Duke of Wellington's Regiment (145th Regiment Royal Armoured Corps) as the Second World War broke out. Ambitious from the start, Tom was not content to remain a private. "Once I started I thought I am not going to stop as a private soldier," Tom told fellow former soldier Michael Coates on his Declassified podcast. "I set out to do my very best so that I got a commission, and I became a captain by the end."

Tom was selected for officer training in 1940. He gained a commission for the 9th Battalion of the Duke of Wellington Regiment just as they were being re-equipped to be sent out to India to, in Tom's words, "do battle with the Japanese in Burma". Often described as "the forgotten war", the Burma campaign saw 100,000 British fight alongside 340,000 Indian and 80,000 African troops. For many the greatest threat they faced was not the Japanese, but the Burmese jungle — its climate, terrain and attendant diseases. During the Arakan campaign of 1943, of which Tom was a part, 50 troops were being evacuated each day from one British brigade, all suffering from malaria.

On VE Day, Tom was back in the UK. He had returned from India to be an instructor at Bovington Camp, Dorset, where he was helping soldiers learn to use armoured warfare as they prepared to join the fight in the Far East. Granted a day off from instruction, Tom travelled north to spend VE Day with his parents. He recalls the "joy and pleasure" in his father's eyes upon seeing him return home. But Tom's own thoughts ran to those still fighting in the Far East. As he says, "I was having mixed thoughts, remembering all my friends still fighting the Japanese."

Despite the challenges of his Far East deployment, Tom speaks with great warmth of his time in the Army. "Was I proud of my service?" he says. "Yes I was. Every minute of it. I am proud of all the people in the Army now and all those who were in the Army before. They are so essential."

After being decommissioned in 1946, Tom — as the only Yorkshire officer in his regiment — was tasked with organising an annual regimental reunion dinner. "From 1947, 180 ex-Duke of Wellingtons gathered each year," says Tom. "We continued that for 65 years, when it had whittled down to just me." Eight years after the last of his regimental dinners, and just a month away from his 100th birthday, Captain Tom's cheerfulness in adversity would galvanise a whole nation.

Previous pages Captain Tom Moore completes the 100th lap of his incredible fundraising challenge

Left A birthday message for centenarian Captain Tom Moore is displayed in Piccadilly Circus on 30 April

Right Tom served in Burma during the Second World War and is rightly proud of his years in the Army

"What Captain Tom Moore is doing for our NHS and country is brilliant," said Joel Chamberlin, a registered nurse at Brighton's Royal Sussex County Hospital, working on a 'Covid Red' A&E ward. "He is bringing so much positivity at a time of negativity and tragedy. I've had difficult shifts, having to tell two sons that wanted to be with their dying mother that they couldn't go in together and then coming off shift and reading in the news about spikes in deaths and that the NHS hasn't got enough PPE to go around. So, reading about Captain Tom has been something good. With him and the clapping on a Thursday at 8pm, it keeps you going. But there is also another message here. It shouldn't take a 100-year-old man to raise cash for the NHS. Now, more than ever, it is clear that the NHS should be well funded, and we must invest in its future, especially care for the elderly. Captain Tom is an example of why our older generations deserve access to the best care possible."

For General Surgery Senior Registrar Dr Ellen Murgitroyd, who is also an RAF Squadron Leader, Tom is not only an exemplar of the military spirit of perseverance in adversity but also a much-needed advocate for the NHS. "Captain Tom lived in a world before free healthcare," she says. "He fought for his country's freedom and returned home to see the formation of the NHS. Veterans

like Tom remember what it was like before the NHS existed, and value it more highly because of that. I hope the people follow his example and continue to protect the NHS so it stays free for all at point of access."

In his interview for the Declassified podcast, Captain Tom recalled the NHS being established. "It was an eye opener for so many people, who up to then if they had been poorly, would have trouble to get anyone to deal with them, because they had to pay," he said. "People who complain about our health service, they should have been there when it wasn't there at all. Nobody pays, the service we get now is absolutely phenomenal. I have such a high regard for the NHS. I am glad for every penny they get. They did so well for me when I broke my hip and had cancer. I am absolutely delighted and thrilled the nation is taking part in the defence against this unknown foe."

When the Covid-19 pandemic took hold — claiming 233,792 lives around the world by the end of April 2020, and 26,711 in the UK alone — comparisons were quickly made with the Second World War. Prime Minister Boris Johnson, himself hospitalised by the virus, described the virus as the single biggest challenge Britain had faced since the war, and singled out Captain Tom as an example to all. "If we as a country can show the same spirit of optimism and energy shown by Captain Tom

Right Just some of the thousands of birthday cards sent to Captain Tom, displayed in a local school hall

Moore — who turns 100 this week — if we can show the same spirit of unity and determination as we have all shown in the past six weeks, then I have absolutely no doubt that we will beat it together, we will come through this all the faster and the United Kingdom will emerge stronger than ever before."

Three days later, the Prime Minister would again speak of Tom's actions. "Your heroic efforts have lifted the spirits of the entire nation," he said, in a birthday address. "You've created a channel to enable millions to say a heartfelt thank you to the remarkable men and women in our NHS who are doing the most astounding job. There is a tradition going back some years now where the Prime Minister takes a moment each day to thank someone for their service to others, by recognising them as a point of light. Captain Tom — that is exactly what you are, a point of light in all our lives."

These sentiments were echoed by others. The RAF performed a flypast over his home and Captain Tom, having seen Hurricanes and Spitfires flying "in anger" during the war, said he was pleased to see them now "flying peacefully". Captain Tom was also appointed the first Honorary Colonel of the Army Foundation College in Harrogate — a particularly poignant appointment for a former instructor at the Armoured Fighting Vehicle School. He was also given the annual Regimental Medal by the Yorkshire Regiment.

A school in Bedfordshire — attended by Captain Tom's grandson Benjie — was inundated with 140,000 birthday cards, sent from all around the world. So many cards were sent directly to Captain Tom that his local mail centre in Northampton had to set up a dedicated collection box. "None of the team have ever known one person receive so much mail," the South Midlands Mail Centre manager told the *i* newspaper.

The Queen sent a 100th birthday card with the addition of a special message stating: "I was also most interested to hear of your recent fundraising efforts for NHS Charities Together at this difficult time." Tom described the card as "very special".

Prince William referred to Tom as "an absolute legend", while Prince Harry said his efforts were "utterly amazing".

Royal Mail marked all post sent in the UK on the week of Captain Tom's birthday with a special postmark that read: "Happy 100th Birthday Captain Thomas Moore. NHS fundraising hero. 30 April 2020". Tom's local postbox, in Marston Moretaine, was painted NHS Blue in his honour, and local villagers decorated the streets with bunting, handmade cards and pictures to honour their resident fundraising hero. "On behalf of the whole family, thank you all so much," said Captain Tom's grandson Benjie Ingram-Moore to *Forces News*. "I think this is a snapshot in history that we really can't look past, it is something we will hold in our hearts forever as a nation, and I am really glad that we could share it."

NHS workers across the country also marked the centenary of their champion. Dr Sophie Stevens, a GP in Bath, took part in celebrations for Captain Tom's birthday at her surgery, and explained that her own grandfather, Captain John Smith, would also have turned 100 the same week as Tom if he had still been alive. "Captain Tom Moore is an inspiring man, and his fundraising efforts are without comparison," said Dr Stevens. "Those of us working in the NHS have been touched by his endeavour and it has given us all a dose of joy and optimism in what are challenging days. His actions have caused me to reflect on the actions of all our veterans and how important they are to this country still."

Captain Tom Moore gave a humble message of thanks to all his supporters. "Thank you very much all of you throughout the world," he said. "I am absolutely enthralled by the kindness of all you people giving so much money to this fund. My legs may be tired, but my mind is racing and I'm hoping to be back very soon with other ways in which I can help people, help others. I would like to say to people, do remember things will get better, as the song says the sun will shine and we will never walk alone. I believe that to be true. Things will get better."

Care at home for life

Consultus Care and Nursing continues its time-honoured, traditional values well into the digital age

www.consultuscare.com

"My aunt was one of a number of formidable women starting care businesses back in the 1960s," says Peter Seldon. "She was a great example of self-reliance and making things happen."

Seldon is remembering Anne Stevens, a housewife with two young children, who started a home help service in 1962 from a lean-to in her back garden after she was left with very little money. She provided local home help, gardeners and, increasingly, carers. "It very quickly grew into a dedicated care provision service," says Seldon. "Nearly 60 years later, here we are." "Here" is Tonbridge, Kent, from where Seldon, previously a software entrepreneur, has been the CEO of Consultus Care and Nursing since 1998 when, with his existing business experience, he was asked to pick up the reins of his aunt's business on her retirement.

Consultus offers two principal services: an introductory agency for 24/7 live-in carers contracted directly by clients; and fully managed, regulated, 24/7 live-in care and nursing services. While the former covers the UK and the Channel Islands, Consultus continues to expand the latter from established regions across southern England and further north. "Our growth partly reflects the increasing demand for care," says Seldon. "According to the Office of National Statistics many more people are now living longer in the UK: more than 15 million people aged between 60 and 89 in the UK, and many want to stay in their own homes rather than move into residential care or a nursing home."

The key to the company's success is investment in staff. "We offer all carers initial residential training, plus supplementary courses up to diploma level," Seldon explains. "Our Skills-for-Care 'Centre of Excellence' accreditation reflects both the high standard of our training and our carers. We're focused on setting an example to

the whole care sector by fully professionalising existing carers as well as those from outside the sector with the necessary life skills."

Consultus's priorities are to provide the support that makes a real difference to clients and enables them to stay in their own homes for as long as possible. Ideally they will do this for life, enjoying familiar surroundings, family, friends, pets and the continued personal interaction and companionship from a 24/7 live-in carer.

Carers and nurses must be capable, reliable and kind-hearted, and able to build a rapport with clients. "It is a factor we consider very carefully," says Seldon. "We try to find a match between client and carer so they can share life experiences, which is the key to real companionship. I oversaw the care of my own mother for nine years, and witnessed what matters first hand."

Looking to the future with his technology business background, Seldon is now introducing the complementary support of machine learning and artificial intelligence technology which identifies small but significant changes in behaviour patterns that could be significant for predicting health conditions before they fully develop. This technology promises to transform the industry, but Seldon is emphatic that it will support, not replace, Consultus's personalised live-in care.

"My biggest challenge has been expanding our business in a competitive market while retaining the family ethos that is and has been at the core of Consultus since its inception in 1962," says Seldon. "I'm most proud of my own people and those who work with us, and who typically demonstrate tireless energy and commitment in looking after older people. Most of us appreciate what they have done for our own families and, in many cases, for our country too."

Home advantage

Since launching in the US 27 years ago,
Home Instead has become the world's biggest
provider of home care for the elderly

www.homeinstead.co.uk

When Home Instead Senior Care co-founders Paul and Lori Hogan were looking for personalised care that would suit the needs of Paul's grandmother in Omaha, Nebraska, they were very clear that her wish was to stay at home rather than go into a facility. "I suppose the rest is history," says Martin Jones, the company's UK CEO. "Like any great business, they started around the kitchen table."

Twenty-five years on from that experience of having to seek out home-based care, Paul and his wife Lori still run the company, which now operates as a franchise across 14 countries, including the UK, where it was set up in 2005. As a franchise business, Home Instead has more than 215 locally owned and operated offices across the UK, employing over 13,000 people who together delivered in excess of 6 million hours of quality care last year to more than 21,000 clients. Each Home Instead franchisee benefits from high-quality training and efficient processes that enable them to focus on delivering outstanding care to the client in their own home.

According to Jones, there are two reasons why Home Instead has been so successful in such a highly competitive market. "The first is that we put the client at the heart of every single thing that we do — that's why we're here," he explains. He points to figures showing that 98 per cent of over-65s said it was important for them to stay living independently at home.

The second, he explains, is that the company's franchise model means that the owner of a Home Instead franchise — each of which is based in a distinct geographic region — is buying a business to make a difference. "The roll call of people who have taken on franchises includes footballers, pop stars, doctors and retailers, rather than only those with a career in social care," says Jones. "Often this is because they have been inspired by personal experience to make a difference to the care of the older generation."

Another thing that makes Home Instead stand out from the competition is that it matches its clients with its carers — known as CAREGivers — to ensure they are mutually compatible and the

right fit for happy home care. "It's this process that makes us very, very different," says Jones. In one case, Home Instead matched a client who used a mobility scooter with a CAREGiver who was training to run the London Marathon. The CAREGiver would go on a run as part of his training and his client would ride alongside him. "That typifies exactly what Home Instead is all about as it provided the wonderful companionship the client needed," says Jones.

The company's belief in the benefits of relationship-led care ensures that its clients see the same familiar faces at every visit. This means that not only do they build trust and establish a friendly relationship, but also the CAREGiver is able to monitor changes that might affect a specific client's health and can help prevent worsening health conditions.

More than two thirds of Home Instead's CAREGivers are over the age of 50, which often ensures a greater personal connection between them and the client. While social care providers have traditionally focused on the tasks that need to be done, such as getting the client dressed or ensuring that they have taken their medications, Home Instead also understands the value of conversation and personal connection. This is why its CAREGivers visit for at least an hour rather than the sector's standard 20 minutes. This ensures plenty of time for quality care while still leaving time to chat and build a genuine relationship. It also means that CAREGivers can take clients out on trips to, say, shops or the local park or garden centre.

"We understand that people's needs change over time," says Jones, "which is why a dedicated care manager continues to monitor and reassess their plan to make sure it is suited to their individual requirements."

A growing challenge for those helping care for the elderly is the rising occurrence of dementia and Alzheimer's. There are an estimated 940,000 people with dementia in the UK at present — a figure that is set to soar to 1.7 million by 2050. All CAREGivers undergo accredited Alzheimer's training that has been recognised with both a Princess Royal Training Award and City & Guilds. Home Instead also offers family and friends training and advice to support people living with dementia that has seen more than 40,000 people trained free of charge.

A common trend among older people is a tendency to not eat healthily and fall into bad food habits and eat comfort foods — which is why Home Instead also has a focus on nutrition. To this end it has launched a campaign that aims

to help families that are providing care for their loved ones themselves to be aware of an older person's risk of becoming malnourished.

Sixty two of its offices have received an "outstanding" rating from the Care Quality Commission, with offices in Scotland and Wales meeting or exceeding the standards of their regulators. In 2016, the company received the Queen's Award for Innovation — the UK's highest accolade for business success. "One of the reasons is that we invest in the social well-being of our clients," says Jones. "Our CAREGivers are there not just to cook and clean; they are there as a friend, to spend time getting to know the client." Home Instead was also voted as one of the most recommended home-care companies in the Top 20 Home Care Group awards 2019 across England, Scotland and Wales.

Looking ahead, Home Instead and its franchise teams are eager to embrace innovation in an effort to find ways to enhance the person-centred care they deliver. While technology will never replace the human touch, it can enhance peoples' lives. It can help to keep clients connected and engaged with their family, loved ones and the world, as well as ensuring they are safe in their homes 24 hours a day.

"We describe it as high-tech, high-touch," says Jones. "You have got to marry the two elements together to deliver the best results. Technology can provide a valuable safety net, but it will never replace the personal touch that we provide."

Respect for our elders

The Abbeyfield Society offers a variety of residential choices worldwide to meet the diverse needs of an ageing population

www.abbeyfield.com

The Abbeyfield Society — a charity that believes in always "Making time for older people" — started life back in 1956. Its founder, Officer Richard Carr-Gomm had left the army and undertaken voluntary work as a home help for underprivileged and lonely older people. In the course of this work he realised these people needed more than just practical help; that in many cases they wanted company and connection to a community. He decided to spend his army gratuity on a house in Bermondsey and moved four local, lonely older people into it.

"Our organisation has always been about combating loneliness," says David McCullough, Chief Executive. Today Abbeyfield runs 900 houses across seven countries and offers a supportive living community to over 9,500 older residents. It employs a combination of trained managers and staff; and a staggering 4,500 local volunteers, who are key to the family atmosphere. "When you go to an Abbeyfield house," says McCullough, "you find volunteers chatting to residents about so-and-so, the greengrocer in the town. It's a very different feel to an area manager coming down from 40 or 50 miles away and only visiting once a fortnight."

Carr-Gomm's founding vision was to give residents a home in which to make friends, eat together, take part in activities and generally continue to enjoy a sense of community. This remains the basis of all Abbeyfield's houses today; residences not just in the UK but in Jersey, Belgium, Canada, South Africa, New Zealand and Australia.

The houses are typically small-scale converted dwellings in central residential areas. The objective is that residents can then stay well connected to their surrounding community — just as the first Bermondsey residents did 64 years ago. Today, Abbeyfield's many dwellings are varied, to cater for the different requirements of prospective residents. For example, one house in the North West of England is built on the first and second floors above a row of shops. That doesn't necessarily sound ideal but, says McCullough, "You can take a lift down to the front door; and when you come out of the exit you're right on the street, where there are cafés, museums and parks."

Abbeyfield's supported houses offer older people their own space to live a fulfilling life but with the peace of mind of having someone on hand to support them with daily activities, and communal areas where they can meet and mingle with other residents or meet friends and other visitors from the wider community.

Looking ahead, McCullough says that Abbeyfield plans to expand its sites both at home and abroad. In the UK this will include looking at towns and areas where the charity does not already have a presence. Overseas, there are plans to open an Abbeyfield home in Malawi in east Africa, where there is no state provision for older people. A local chief there has set aside a large enough plot of land for Abbeyfield to build a home on and also grow its own cash crops to generate revenue.

"I think once that is up and running," says McCullough, "there will be a lot of countries in the global South that will see the simplicity of how the model works and realise they should have one of those too."

Ahead of its time

The Cardiff and Vale University Health Board has seized the initiative to start addressing the problems of the future

www.cardiffandvaleuhb.wales.nhs.uk

A nation's health never stands still. New factors and trends — such as a growing, ever-more diverse and ageing population — pose multiple challenges for healthcare organisations. That's why the Cardiff and Vale University Health Board (CVUHB), one of the largest NHS bodies in the country, is continually reviewing and evolving its health and wellbeing services.

To that end, the CVUHB recently put in place a 10-year transformation and improvement plan. Len Richards, its CEO, says this strategy — Shaping Our Future Wellbeing — is a chance to work collaboratively with its workforce and the public to make itself more sustainable. "Together, we can improve equity for all of our patients," he says, "both today and tomorrow."

Founded in 2009 and comprised of a teaching health board, a centre of excellence and 11 hospital sites, CVUHB employs approximately 14,500 staff and spends around £1.4 billion every year bringing health and well-being services to around 472,400 people living in Cardiff and the Vale of Glamorgan. "As the busiest health board in Wales," says Richards, "we recognise that we are best able to deliver services that matter to people through partnerships. We are working with two local authorities, local universities and a whole host of charity and third sector organisations and the Welsh Assembly."

The local population is set to increase in the next 10 years, and with it problems arising from long-term health issues, unhealthy lifestyles and poverty. "We have made significant steps this year in tackling health inequalities," says Richards. "We've also developed health services that focus on keeping people well and in their own homes, living independently for as long as possible."

Richards is rightly proud of the work the Health Board is pioneering for military veterans suffering from psychological trauma, including PTSD. He enthuses about virtual reality therapy, which has been shown to improve and speed up rehabilitation for those who have suffered from neurological and physical injuries.

"The Cardiff and Vale University Health Board is proud to provide specialist support to veterans," he says. "We hope that by using cutting-edge technology and the latest treatment methods we can address some of the physical and mental health challenges of those who have served their country."

Military aids

UK Veterans Hearing Foundation is on a mission to find the right equipment for ex-servicemen whose hearing has been damaged

www.uk-veterans-hearing-help.co.uk

It's easy to assume that most service veterans suffering hearing loss are elderly. However, as Sam Bennett, founder of UK Veterans Hearing Foundation, explains, this is a condition that spans all ages. She first became aware of it on a personal level when her husband Ben started to struggle with his hearing aged just 43, after 13 years in the Royal Artillery.

As a hearing aid audiologist, Sam quickly diagnosed what was happening and had her husband fitted with the correct hearing aids. At his next Royal Artillery reunion, many of Ben's colleagues commented on his hearing aids and their own issues, and the Bennetts decided to start a community interest company (CIC) called UK Veterans Hearing Help. As of this March, the company received approved charity status and it is now called UK Veterans Hearing Foundation.

"We deal with people aged 26 to 97," says Colin Baker, a retired RAF squadron leader who, until recently, worked as a Business Development Manager for the charity. "Lots of youngsters return to civilian life with hearing loss and it's very isolating, especially in social and work situations. Often, they're trying to move into a new career and it can trigger anxiety and depression. I'm a veteran and I struggled with my hearing, but the NHS aids couldn't improve it. The ones I got through UK Veterans Hearing Foundation are set to my personal hearing loss and have made such a difference."

Colin and Sam have spent much time building relations to secure funding for these hearing aids, having previously accessed The Royal British Legion's Veterans Hearing Fund, which provided support to ex-service personnel who have developed hearing loss as a result of military service. "We work together with other veterans' associations helping veterans access the funding," says Sam. "We ensure the hearing aids provided are of the highest quality and the service offered is first class by using stringently vetted audiologists across the country. This is a life-changing fund and the support it provides is second to none, with audiologists seeing people in their homes, if necessary. We also offer support with mental health issues caused by hearing loss and associated conditions such as tinnitus.

"We help get assistive listening devices when needed, for use with television, telephone and meetings. Even tinnitus can be treated with top-of-the-range hearing aids. UK Veterans Hearing Foundation is now inundated with enquiries as our service becomes well known; and we are always delighted to help veterans get the best-quality service available."

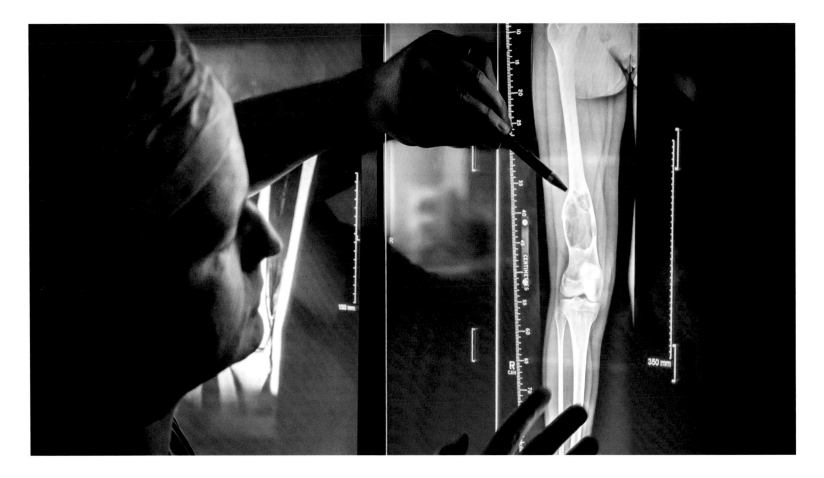

Joint effort

Given the challenges of an ageing population and new technology, the British Orthopaedic Association's work is more essential than ever

www.boa.ac.uk/joint-action

As a medical student, Don McBride was inspired, somewhat surprisingly, by a particularly cantankerous surgeon. "Despite his mood," he says, "he made orthopaedics interesting. He showed how much we could do to rehabilitate patients and get them back on their feet. Unlike many other fields, it's a really hopeful branch of medicine."

Nearly three decades later and now President of the British Orthopaedic Association, McBride is grateful for his teacher's foresight. With people living longer and needing more medical care, one out of every four surgical patients in the UK is undergoing an orthopaedic procedure. In recent years, total hip and knee replacements have helped McBride and his peers restore patients' mobility and transform their lives.

Such demand is reflected in the growth of the British Orthopaedic Association, a charity that provides training, education and research opportunities as well as benevolent funds. Its 5,000 members range from medical students and trainees to consultants. "I'm delighted that we're now seeing a growing number of women surgeons operating at senior levels, says McBride. "It's a very diverse group."

The decision to found the association was made in November 1917. Fifteen surgeons, most of them recently returned from their experience of military hospitals in the First World War, met to discuss the need for an association tailored to their specialist branch of medicine. Considered a controversial breakaway group at the time, this new network enabled sharing of best practice across the UK, and also forging strong links with American and European surgeons to develop and share vital ideas.

Over a century later, these strong ties continue to bear fruit with British surgeons emulating American colleagues by building trauma centres across the country. In return, British pioneers have shared their renowned expertise in randomised control trials.

This field of medicine is still evolving, with the treatment of children's illnesses, research into bio-engineering and the use of virtual reality procedures all coming to the fore. The British Orthopaedic Association continues to take a central role in embracing this technology, expanding learning and seeking to provide international assistance, through training, for lower-income countries.

So 30 years after Don McBride was first inspired by orthopaedics, his branch of medicine is looking more hopeful than ever.

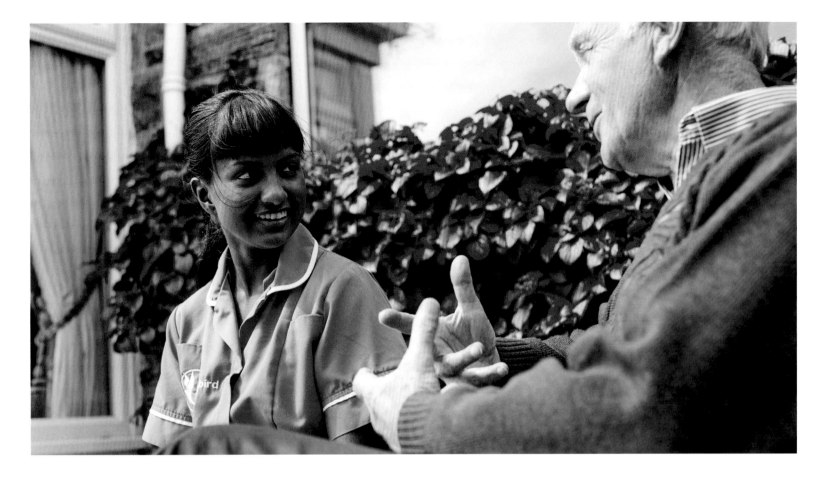

Care tactics

Bluebird Care believes that our ageing population deserves to enjoy their very best life while living in their own homes

www.bluebirdcare.co.uk

"Our later years in life should be spent doing the things we love," says Yvonne Hignell, Managing Director of Bluebird Care. "We've got one Second World War veteran that we look after who used to love dancing the lindy hop in his youth. Now he loves going along to watch local swing jazz dances and remembering those times."

These people, says Hignell, deserve to be enjoying life and doing the things they love. But, when age-related ill-health hits, some people think that their only option is to move into a residential care home and subsequently lose the ability to enjoy these beloved moments. "The fact of the matter is that our ageing population can stay at home, surrounded by the things they love — be that family, pets or familiar belongings," says Hignell. "Being at home is where we are happiest, and the health benefits associated with this are remarkable."

Bluebird Care is a leading provider of care and support at home and prides itself on keeping people happy and safe in their own homes. Services range from a 30-minute visit through to full live-in care services and everything in between, and the company helps people live their best lives no matter their age, ability, health or state of mind. It offers specialist services such as dementia care as well as providing companionship.

Ranked 16th in the Elite Franchise top 100 and with 200 offices nationwide, the company has a strong focus on creating bespoke packages, tailored to individual needs. "Every person is unique and has unique needs," says Hignell. "We work with families to truly understand individual requirements and tailor a care package to suit."

Bluebird Care's compassionate and highly trained care team ensures that every customer is listened to and cared for, and continues to be the person they were. "Our employee training programme far exceeds industry requirements," says Hignell. "We want each and every one of our care assistants to have extensive knowledge in order to be compliant and feel confident to deliver on all levels of care and companionship."

It means that Bluebird Care customers, who include many war veterans, feel safe, loved and respected. "We treat our customers with upmost respect and dignity as well as bringing a smile to their faces," says Hignell. "Our customers often describe our visits as the highlight of their day. After all, our exceptional care assistants love to listen to an old war-time story."

Fit for a king

King Edward VII's Hospital may be a private
hospital but it has treated wounded soldiers
since the second Boer War

www.kingedwardvii.co.uk

Behind a grand pair of front doors in London's Harley Street medical
district stands a hospital distinct in two impressive ways. As well as
its proud history of royal patronage, the independent King Edward VII's
Hospital is a charity and offers charitable treatment for veterans,
inspired by its remarkable wartime legacy.

The hospital was established in 1899 in the home of two sisters,
Agnes and Fanny Keyser. "They devoted themselves to caring for
wounded soldiers, beginning with those returning from the second
Boer War," says Chief Executive Lindsey Condron. "King Edward VII
was one of 24 original donors and later became our patron."

In its present location since 1948, the hospital extended by
40 more beds when it took over a neighbouring bombed site. This
history has inspired the hospital's mission, both in its quality of
service and its continuing benevolence to military veterans.

Today King Edward VII's is a modern, private hospital offering
a range of surgical procedures and a high standard of medical care
to self-paying and insured patients. It houses three operating theatres
— soon to be four — and 300 highly trained staff. Thousands of surgeries
are performed here annually across a range of specialties that include
orthopaedics, urology, colorectal surgery and women's health.

Aside from surgery, state-of-the-art facilities and even first-rate
food, the hospital guarantees a top-level quality of service recently
recognised with an Innovation in Care Award. "Our patients have
come to expect the highest quality when they come to King Edward
VII's Hospital," says Condron.

Private patients can relax in the knowledge that they are receiving
the best possible care but, thanks to the hospital's charitable foundations,
those who have served have a chance to benefit from the hospital's
high standards. "We can offer means-tested grants to veterans and
discounted prices to any serving or ex-serving military personnel,"
says Director of Veterans' Health Tim Brawn, "giving them access
to exceptional medical care."

The hospital's Centre for Veterans' Health also offers a Pain
Management Programme, free of charge to veterans from all
services, to help improve their quality of life in all respects.

While King Edward VII's Hospital maintains high standards
of care for all patients, its charitable work continues to set it apart,
helping transform the lives of veterans of the Armed Forces.

"Neither the long years, nor the dangers have in any way weakened the unbending resolve of the British nation"

Winston Churchill, Victory in Europe Day 1945

Chapter nine

A FRESH PERSPECTIVE

Forging a new cultural identity

In the wake of victory in Europe, a resurgence in the arts saw Britain establish itself as one of the world's great cultural superpowers

There is a famous wartime quote that is often attributed to Winston Churchill where, when asked to cut funding for the arts to support the war effort, he is said to have angrily responded "Then what would we be fighting for?" Historians have never been able to verify that this conversation ever took place, but there is plenty of evidence of Churchill espousing similar opinions. "The arts are essential to any complete national life," he said, while addressing the Royal Academy in 1938. "The State owes it to itself to sustain and encourage them."

As a painter, writer and historian himself, Churchill was well aware of the centrality of art and culture to a sense of national identity. "It is by art man gets nearest to the angels and farthest from the animals," he said. "It lights the path and links the thought of one generation with another, and in the realm of price holds its own in intrinsic value with an ingot of gold." Not long after the end of the war, one of the last acts of Churchill's wartime coalition was to form the Arts Council of Great Britain and launch the BBC Light Programme.

This might have been a country ravaged by six years of war, but much of the art premiered in the months after VE Day had a timeless and progressive quality. George Orwell's *Animal Farm*, Evelyn Waugh's *Brideshead Revisited* and Nancy Mitford's *The Pursuit Of Love* have not been out of print since; JB Priestley's timeless agitprop play *An Inspector Calls* was premiered in September 1945 and remains on the school syllabuses 75 years on, while David Lean's classic romantic drama *Brief Encounter* — regarded as one of the greatest British films — was released in November 1945.

In the months after VE Day, a new Labour administration entered office and maintained and expanded the wartime cabinet's commitment to the arts. By 1947, Deputy Prime Minister Herbert Morrison started to plan the Festival of Britain, a nationwide celebration in the summer of 1951, designed to give people a feeling of successful recovery from the devastation of the war, as well as promoting British technology, design and the arts. The Festival resulted in a string of modernist venues along the South Bank of the Thames in London, which all became symbols of postwar artistic regeneration. They included the Royal Festival Hall and the National Film Theatre (both built in 1951), the Hayward Gallery (1968), the Queen Elizabeth Hall (1969) and the relocation of the National Theatre (1976), while the Royal Shakespeare Company was established in Stratford in 1961 to maintain the centrality of the Bard to British cultural life.

Throughout the 1950s, theatre was one of the first art forms to undergo a true post-war transformation. With hubs of creativity based around the Royal Court in Chelsea (an early home of the National Theatre), the Theatre Royal, Stratford East (home of Joan Littlewood's Theatre Workshop), the Edinburgh Festival Fringe (started in 1947) and later the Chichester Festival Theatre, the British stage started to chime with a new egalitarian spirit, one in which people of all classes were starting to get a voice. Plays like John Osborne's *Look Back In Anger* (1956) and Shelagh Delaney's *A Taste Of Honey* (1958), along with work by other "angry young men", including Arnold Wesker and Neil Dunn, ushered in a new British social realism.

Above and opposite
The British cinema classic
Brief Encounter was
released just six months
after victory in Europe
was announced

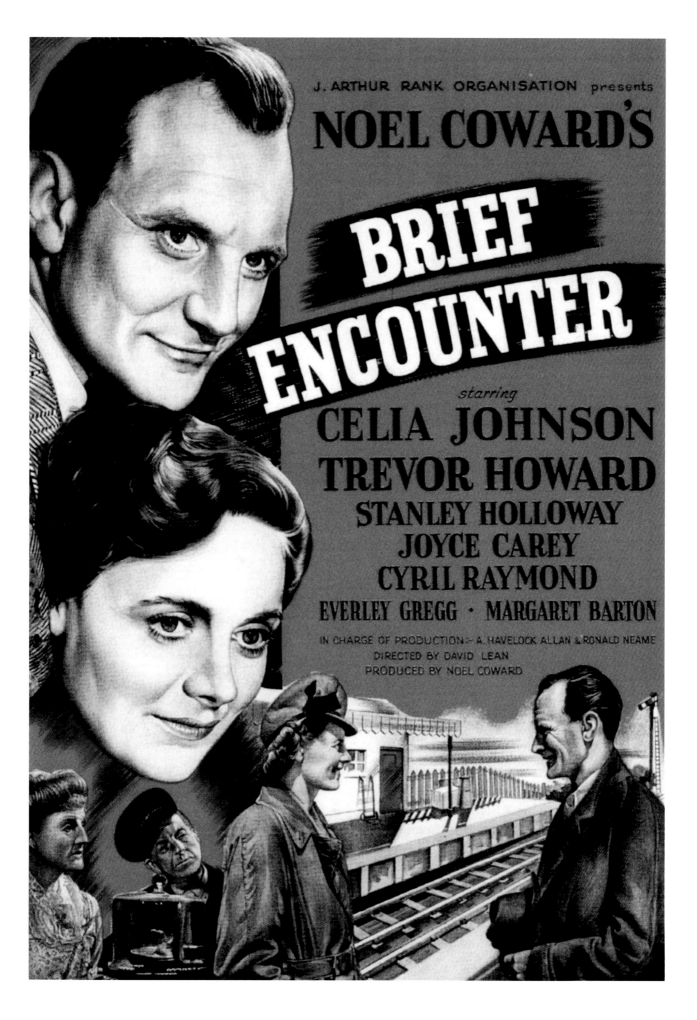

Left The Festival of
Britain in 1951 showcased
an optimistic and future-
facing country

Right The launch of
such television shows
as Coronation Street
chimed with the emerging
egalitarian spirit of the
post-war years

It started to find a home on television in the form of theatrical presentations like *Armchair Theatre* (launched 1956) and *The Wednesday Play* (from 1964), and heavily influencing soap operas such as *Coronation Street* (launched 1960) and the situation comedies of Galton and Simpson, and Johnny Speight.

This egalitarian spirit had a knock-on effect on other art forms too, with bright working-class Britons starting to find a voice in everything from painting and photography to film and literature. The most dramatic medium in which this occurred was popular music, where a generation of Brits born around VE-Day started to have an immeasurable effect on the cultural landscape. The Beatles, born during the war, ended up transforming both popular music and British culture in the mid-1960s, incorporating elements from the music hall, the art school and the avant garde to create a distinctly English-accented pop music. When they reached huge success in America in 1964, it opened the floodgates for a new generation of British musicians, all born in the mid 1940s, who would transform British society beyond recognition. The year 1945 heralded the births

of Eric Clapton, Rod Stewart, Pete Townshend, Van Morrison, Bryan Ferry, Fleetwood Mac's John McVie, Lemmy from Motorhead and Davy Jones from the Monkees; while in 1946 and 1947 came the births of David Bowie, Elton John and most of Pink Floyd, Queen, Led Zeppelin and Deep Purple.

All helped turn rock 'n' roll music into a truly transatlantic conversation — one in which Britain would prove to be just as important as America — and helped to transform the UK itself, whose place in the world became defined by "Swinging London". At the same time that Britain's political and economic influence was in decline, Britain transformed itself into what the historian Dominic Sandbrook has described as "a cultural superpower". It became the home of world-straddling superstars, from James Bond to Doctor Who, from JRR Tolkien to JK Rowling, from Agatha Christie to Adele, from Monty Python to Harry Potter. Culture has become Britain's greatest gift to the world. It is art that draws from the past while forging into the future. As Churchill himself once wrote: "Without tradition, art is a flock of sheep without a shepherd. Without innovation, it is a corpse."

World class

UNESCO was established in 1945 to help heal a war-torn world. Seventy-five years on, the challenges it faces may be different but they are no less urgent

The United Nations Educational, Scientific and Cultural Organization, or UNESCO as its better known, grew out of the ravages of conflict — a symbol, like so many organisations established in the wake of VE Day, that humankind would never again descend to the depths witnessed in the Second World War.

The international organisation saw itself as the UN's "intellectual agency", its core belief being that "political and economic agreements are not enough to build a lasting peace". Its stated mission was instead to build peace on the basis of humanity's moral and intellectual solidarity — "in full and equal opportunities for education for all, in the unrestricted pursuit of objective truth, and in the free exchange of ideas and knowledge ... for the purposes of mutual understanding and a truer and more perfect knowledge of each other's lives".

How did it plan to achieve this? By creating a series of links between nations. These would variously be based on education, the protection of national heritage, the promotion of cultural diversity, and — increasingly in recent years — the spreading of scientific knowledge to help build crucial defences against global warming.

UNESCO has its roots in the International Committee on Intellectual Cooperation (ICIC), which was established in Geneva in 1922 as part of the League of Nations under the leadership of Japanese scholar Inazo Nitobe, and featured such stellar scholars as Albert Einstein and Marie Curie. In 1926, this informed the creation of the International Institute of Intellectual Cooperation (IIIC) — a Paris-based institution that united areas as diverse as universities, libraries, arts, information, media and intellectual property. Its activities were suspended due to the outbreak of the Second World War, but some of its roles were continued by CAME (the Conference of Allied Ministers of Education), which was launched in London in 1942. In November 1945, CAME met in London and agreed to revive the principles of ICIC under the banner of a new organisation: UNESCO.

Seventy-five years on from its formation, UNESCO's mission to "reaffirm the humanist missions of education, science and culture" seems — if possible — even more relevant than when it was first founded. Today, it has 199 National Commissions across the world, ranging from Albania to Zimbabwe. As conflicts rage in member states in Africa and the Middle East, while tensions between the world's superpowers escalate, the pressing question remains: how can UNESCO address the global crisis in the years ahead?

"This is a fundamental issue for UNESCO," says Dr Qian Tang, the Canada-schooled Chinese educationalist who has served as the organisation's Assistant Director-General for Education since 2010. "We want to go back to the basic question: what is education for? Today, of course, many people say education is for people to learn to read and write, to gain knowledge and skills — they even talk about it in terms of its economic value. But, at UNESCO, we think the basic mandate of education should be to teach a new generation to grow up to become responsible citizens of society."

So what exactly does it mean to become a responsible global citizen? UNESCO has been promoting the concept since the 1990s. Educational initiatives have included everything from morality lessons in Japan to a pupils' parliament in Lithuania. Dr Tang elaborates. "We want to create a young generation that is against violence, tolerates other people, different civilisations, different religions," he says.

But the challenge of bringing up young people who reject violence and tolerate other cultures involves the education of more than one generation. In certain countries, no matter how persuasive schoolteachers are, the influence of parents and grandparents counts for more than a few lessons. "In recent years we've had requests for assistance in this area from the ministers of education from certain Arab countries," says Dr Tang. "Since the Arab Spring, the young generation has been expressing its views more strongly. They want to know what democracy means, what human rights mean, and how to tolerate co-existence with other religions and cultures."

"The basic mandate of education should be to teach a new generation to grow up to become responsible citizens of society"

How do you teach tolerance and co-existence to children who have experienced life in war zones? "Our statistics say that more than 50 per cent of children out of school — that means not attending any school — live in conflict-affected countries," says Dr Tang. "This is one of the major obstacles to education for all. Firstly, we are working to ensure access to education for children like Syrian refugees in Jordan. Secondly we want to teach these same children how to live with others without hatred."

His remark picks up on an initiative launched by UNESCO's former Director General Irina Bokova titled "Youth Education for Stability". This emphasised how the problems of Syrian refugees needed to be addressed in part by making sure that young people in Jordan and Lebanon would be welcoming and sympathetic to their plight. "We are deeply convinced," she said, "that tackling the problem of Syrian refugees separate from the development issues of the host country is not a good strategy."

A challenge that faces all schoolchildren today, regardless of whether or not they are affected by conflict, is the growing threat of climate change. "This is a vast subject," says Dr Tang, "so we focus on three areas. These are climate change, biodiversity and the prevention of crisis." UNESCO's multifaceted approach clearly illustrates the breadth of the challenges, asking students to focus on problems ranging

from the links between water pollution in Uzbekistan and birth defects, to the issues surrounding growing coffee in the Amazon. The stated aim — "to improve the quality of life now without damaging the planet of the future" — is a daunting task.

The internet has obviously had a huge impact on the way UNESCO can conduct its educational initiatives. "At the beginning, connectivity was a huge challenge," says Dr Tang, "but now even poor countries have more or less solved their connectivity problems, so access to education is much easier." UNESCO has backed schemes to help as many children in developing countries as possible own their own laptop.

However, new stumbling blocks have emerged. "Kids in primary schools in developing countries are much more advanced at using the internet than their teachers," he says. "So now we have to train the teachers so they can properly guide the pupils."

The challenge of delivering equal educational opportunities to all — especially those in areas of conflict — is daunting. But if the words of King George VI on VE Day are to be heeded, to "Resolve, as a people, to do nothing unworthy of those who died for us and to make the world such a world as they would have desired for their children, and for ours", then the work of UNESCO isn't just an aspiration, it is essential.

Previous pages Students study as part of a UNESCO initiative to increase literacy in Haiti, 1949

Right A classroom in Syria — just one of the areas of conflict where UNESCO is striving to help children gain a quality education

Tours de force

Leger Holidays' burgeoning portfolio of fully escorted battlefield tours reflects a growing interest in the experience of war

www.legerbattlefields.co.uk

"The very first tour I did, the chap sitting behind me asked me about a particular cemetery near Ypres and said his dad was buried there," says Paul Reed, Head Battlefield Guide at Leger Holidays. "As soon as we walked in, he peeled off and walked straight to his father's grave. He said, 'I didn't know if I'd remember where my dad was; but I had this feeling.'"

Since Leger Holidays recruited Reed in 1997 to add battlefield tours to its portfolio of fully escorted holidays, the business has expanded to include 80 such destinations. It helps to supply what is evidently a growing demand from the general public, as well as the relatives of veterans — who are interested in the history, experience and sacrifice of war. First and Second World War battlefields are popular but so too are the locations of other significant conflicts, including Waterloo, the American Civil War and the Boer and Zulu wars of South Africa.

A specialist battlefield guide, whose in-depth knowledge of warfare and key events inspires and enhances the visitor experience and brings the history to life, accompanies each coach or air tour. "As guides we're storytellers, really," says Reed. "We try to bring that war alive through the research we've done — in my case interviewing hundreds of First World War veterans."

Leger's 30 full-time guides and 60 seasonal guides — who are available to meet demand for the most popular tours at the busiest times — all share a passion for, and expertise in, their subject. The impressive breadth and depth of these excursions is one thing that sets the company apart from other operators. Another is its range of convenient local coach joining points.

Collecting customers from hundreds of pick up points across the UK, they are delivered to Folkestone to meet their tour coach, allowing for a smooth and relaxing journey.

Leger offers tours of varied duration as well as destination. The shortest ones, by coach, start on a Friday and allow for two days of visits to European battlefields before returning on Monday. Longer tours, some by air, can be of 13 days' duration or even longer. These include trips to the United States for a tour of the American Civil War battlefields. Or there's Vietnam, where visitors can take in stunning scenery from locations such as Ha Long Bay, Hanoi and Ho Chi Minh City, as well as the Vinh Moc tunnels and the site of the My Lai Massacre.

Two of Leger's most popular packages are introductory tours to the First and Second World War sites. One of those, All Quiet on the Western Front, entails a visit to Ypres and the Somme that gives an insight into what the Great War was really like from an ordinary soldier's point of view. The other, the D-Day Landings in Normandy tour, commemorates a decisive turning point in the defeat of Nazi Germany and serves as an excellent introduction to the Second World War.

Reed says that, since the centenary of the end of the First World War in 2018, the company has seen an increase in numbers coming on its tours. "The centenary was not the end but a beginning in that more and more people want to understand this and they want to remember it," he says. "It's part of their family's story, it's part of our nation's story and I think it's something that people think is worthwhile to continue to remember and understand."

Incredible journey

A uniquely storied Victorian mansion, Palé Hall Hotel has been restored and transformed into an iconic five-star hotel

palehall.co.uk

Today, the Palé Hall Hotel is the only five-red-star hotel in North Wales, thanks to the vision of husband-and-wife team Alan and Angela Harper, who bought the Grade II* listed venue back in 2015. Despite having no experience in the hospitality industry, the couple transformed a run-down, three-star hotel outside Bala, on the edge of Snowdonia, into an exquisite space befitting its impressive past.

"Palé is a very special place with an equally special history," explains Angela Harper. "It was built in 1870 by the railway magnate Henry Robertson as a statement of arrival, without reference to expense." Since then, it has hosted some of the greats of British history, including Queen Victoria and Winston Churchill; it was used as a hospital in the First World War, and as a home for evacuated children in the Second World War.

The Harpers embarked on an extensive but sympathetic renovation to restore this Victorian mansion to its former glory, receiving five red stars from the AA after just 18 months. "It's full of our own antiques," notes Harper, "and it's different from other five-star hotels in that it's very relaxed and friendly. It's a beautiful home first, and a hotel second. She has her own magic."

The restaurant currently holds three AA rosettes for its food, thanks to its high calibre of staff, including head chef, rising star Gareth Stevenson. "We also had two pastry chefs who reached the semi-finals of last year's *Bake Off: The Professionals*, including Sam Widnall, who is profoundly deaf," says Harper, clearly proud of her team. "He's a fine young man who did brilliantly."

The green credentials of Palé Hall Hotel are exceptional. The venue has its own hydro-electric plant, dating back to 1920, which has received a £300,000 upgrade. "We now produce all our own electricity in an ecologically sound way, and you can charge your electric car here — which means that you'll have a car that effectively runs on water," says Harper. "Plus, we use organic toiletries and local produce. We do as much as we can to ensure that our footprint is as small as possible."

All this has been achieved in just four years. "Our philosophy is to combine the best possible quality, with the friendliest possible atmosphere, says Harper. "It's been an adventure, it's safe to say!"

Heritage and modernisation

The Royal and Ancient Golf Club of St Andrews and The R&A draw from a rich 266-year history to make golf a more inclusive and welcoming sport

www.randa.org

On 9 October 1946, a round of golf was played on The Old Course at St Andrews, home to The Royal and Ancient Golf Club of St Andrews, one of the oldest and most prestigious golf clubs in the world. Just over 17 months after VE Day, General Eisenhower (pictured below, right) took to the course as hundreds watched on. He was there to accept an honorary life membership from the club. "I had thought that Scotland had already exhausted every possibility of further kindness to me," wrote Eisenhower in a letter of acceptance. "Your letter shows me my mistake." Winston Churchill was also gifted membership but politely declined, as he no longer played golf.

It is but one landmark in this revered club's extensive history, one that harks back to its founding on 14 May 1754. In 2004, the club's governance role was taken on by a separate but related entity, The R&A, which, together with the USGA in its own jurisdiction of the US and Mexico, governs the sport worldwide. It also supports golf's growth and development globally and is the organiser of The Open, The AIG Women's Open, The Senior Open and a series of amateur championships and matches.

"We continue to honour our past while looking to the future," says Martin Slumbers,

Chief Executive of The R&A and Secretary of The Royal and Ancient Golf Club. "We work with 159 global affiliates, including national associations and other organisations, to further the sport. One example is the On Course Foundation, which champions the recovery of injured service personnel by introducing them to golf through nationwide events and industry representation." Afghanistan veteran Stewart Harris, who had sustained multiple injuries and, later, PTSD, when an IED exploded under his vehicle, credits golf as a key part of his recovery process. Harris has become an ambassador for Wales Golf, regularly competes in national championships and, for those wondering, plays off a 17 handicap.

Further initiatives have seen The R&A introduce the Women In Golf Charter, an industry-wide campaign. The project aims to increase women and girls' participation in golf and encourage more women to work within the wider golf industry.

"The heritage of the club gives The R&A as a governing body the opportunity to lead the sport on a global stage," says Slumbers. "Our purpose is to ensure that, in becoming more diverse, welcoming and sustainable, golf is thriving 50 years from now."

Taking the natural course

On The Green CBD is pioneering the use of natural hemp extracts to improve performance on the golf course

www.onthegreencbd.com
www.onthegreencbd.co.uk

Golf is a sport of fine margins. Every small improvement in performance will help a player knock one or two strokes off their round. The products made by On The Green CBD can offer that improvement. The company was the brainchild of Nick Fishenden, a golf lover from England who moved to the US in 2008 to attend the Golf Academy of America, where he obtained his degree in Golf Management. Fishenden turned pro before a back injury ended his dream of a professional career, and he started working in the fledgling cannabidiol (CBD) industry. This takes cannabidiol, a compound extracted from hemp, and uses it to treat a wide range of conditions, from chronic pain to anxiety. In 2019, Fishenden put his two interests together and created On The Green CBD, a company that makes CBD products tailored specifically to meet the needs of golfers.

"With my background in golf and CBD, I was able to figure out what would be useful for the golfer," says Fishenden. "Among our unique product range, we have three lines of tinctures - Focus, Recovery and Sleep. I use our products myself on a daily basis. The sleep tincture helps me get restful sleep every night and the roll-on cooling gel with menthol is within arm's reach at all times as I constantly use that for my back pain. It has an immediate effect."

Other popular products include sunblock, vegan gummies, soft gel capsules, hand sanitiser and an arnica and turmeric relief cream. All have been created to either aid players when they are on the course by helping their mind relax, or to assist their post-round recovery by improving sleep or reducing inflammation, allowing them to return to the course. Nick has teamed up with his father, Neil, an experienced entrepreneur, and the pair have already made inroads into the US and UK

markets through specialist golf shops and online direct-to-consumer sales.

On The Green CBD has been established as a prestige brand, with products endorsed by professionals such as Phil Golding, who plays on the senior tour and Scott Drummond, former winner of the Volvo PGA Championship at Wentworth. "We are a premium product with real authenticity," says Fishenden. "We are being stocked ahead of larger CBD brands in specialist golf shops because we have a reputation of being exclusive and unique to golf."

The Fishendens stress that On The Green CBD products do not contain THC, the cannabinoid that induces the psychoactive high associated with cannabis. Instead they mix high-quality CBD with other terpenes - the naturally occurring chemicals in plants used to manufacture essential oils. As a result, CBD was removed from the World Anti-Doping Agency (WADA) banned substances list in early 2018, allowing its use by PGA tour players and Olympic athletes. Bubba Watson, Charley Hoffman, Lucas Glover and Scott Piercy are among the high-profile PGA Tour names actively promoting the use of CBD, along with senior players such as Scott McCarron and Fred Couples. Between them they have cited CBD's anti-inflammatory properties, its role in pain and anxiety relief, and in improved sleep.

While On The Green CBD's range is currently targeted at golfers, the founders have had discussions with representatives of other sports, including cricket, cycling and racket sports. But, for now, golf remains the singular focus. "We know our CBD source is very good but we also triple lab-test every single one of our products independently of our suppliers to make sure it is compliant for a professional," says Fishenden. "That means it is suitable for anybody."

La dolce vita

Life really is sweet at the Baglioni Hotel London, where guests are pampered in singularly Italian style

www.baglionihotels.com

It's often said that Italian is the most musical and passionate language in the world, and speaking to Ambra Gallo, Head of Media for Baglioni Hotels & Resorts, it's hard to disagree.

"The warmth from the staff is the first thing you'll notice," she says, describing the five-star Baglioni Hotel London, which opened in 2004. "The Italian touch can immediately be seen through gestures," she continues, with a laugh. "We're well known for the way we gesture while talking — as I'm doing to you right now!"

The spirit of Italy is conveyed throughout every aspect of this luxury hotel, with countless little touches designed to bring a piece of this beautiful Mediterranean country into the heart of London.

"The majority of our staff are Italian and we observe many Italian customs," says Gallo. "For example, we offer the Italian aperitivo — Italian drinks like Campari, Aperol or prosecco — and we pride ourselves on the Italian art of welcoming from the staff. Every night in the turndown service we leave Italian treats as gifts, rather than common chocolate, as well as an Italian phrasebook that looks at the most popular Italian words used around the world, such as ciao, arrivederci, and so on."

Food and drink are among the Italian rituals that play an important role at the hotel's Brunello Bar and Restaurant, an eatery inspired by the Milanese trattorias of the 1950s. "And then there's the coffee: not only espresso, but lungo, corto, macchiato and literally hundreds of types of Italian coffee," says Gallo. "And we have an Italian chef, of course, who uses as much seasonal produce as possible, plus a traditional afternoon tea with an Italian twist, serving sweets such as cannoli, which are popular in the south of Italy."

It's the search for the essence of Italy that has made this prestigious London hotel so popular with guests from around the world, particularly with Americans, visitors from the Middle East, people from the UK and of course, Italians. Location plays a part in this, as Gallo explains: "We're in Kensington facing Hyde Park, a very prestigious location. It's elegant but discreet at the same time.

"We aim to enrich the guest's stay with unique experiences that are based around all things Italian," says Gallo. With plans underway to team up with high-profile Italian brands, it looks like a stay at Baglioni's London hotel is set to be more bello than ever.

Pool of talent

Students at Cornwall's Pool Academy benefit from a culture where aiming high is just one part of the process

www.poolacademy.co.uk

When Claire Meakin took over as Principal of Cornwall's Pool Academy two years ago, she had a very clear plan in mind. It was based on three keywords: aspiration, belonging and respect.

Meakin feels that one vital step to help students achieve their best is to guide them to have strong goals. "For the students, aspiration is a major focus," she says. "We help them believe they can achieve their dreams, that they can make a positive impact on the world. Aspiration celebrates that every one of them is unique — and each one a responsible, active British citizen."

Instilling a sense of belonging starts early. Pool Academy nurtures strong links with its local partner primaries, sending its student leadership team as ambassadors to make those vital connections. "The students see those same faces when they come to the school and as they grow up there," says Meakin. "We have effective peer mentoring and a strong anti-bullying strategy so the students have confidence that someone is listening to them and will act to support them."

Respect is an important feature of pastoral care. "Emotional support takes various forms," she says, "including our support dog Rufus, who has proved a huge hit with staff and students alike. Our cadets and citizenship awards play a large part in giving students confidence in themselves. And, with just over 620 pupils, we know each student individually. Personalised postcards for each Year 11 or new Year 7, to encourage them with their revision or welcome them to the school, are just a few of our supportive strategies."

Pool Academy has high academic expectations, driven by excellent teachers. But at the same time it is committed to helping individuals recognise their strengths and possibilities, with an emphasis on creative enrichment.

"Digital involvement, music, drama and art — including our own art gallery — are very important," says Meakin. "So is working with parents and locals, who see us as being at the heart of the local community. This is such a rewarding job and I feel that pride every time I see a student switching on to something and realising that their future is brighter and better as a result."

Screen saviours

Impero Software aims to improve digital learning by combining learner wellbeing with device management

www.imperosoftware.com

A few months ago, Impero CEO Justin Reilly found himself addressing a teaching conference about the changing landscape of social media. "I asked the audience how many had heard of TikTok," he says. "Everyone put their hand up. I said, 'How many of you knew of it last year?' One person put their hand up."

Reilly knew, of course, that teenagers around the world had known about TikTok for a lot longer than all the adults in the room. That delay in awareness still concerns him, given the profound influence children's use of the internet has in shaping their understanding of the world around them. If teachers don't know what their pupils are doing online, how can their learning strategies keep pace?

The solution, Reilly says, comes in the holistic approach to student safeguarding and device management that Impero offers to education authorities across the UK, the USA and the Middle East. Installed on devices using Windows, iOS and Google Chrome, Impero's EducationPro allows teachers to monitor when and how their students are using computers during lessons and across the school network, while its digital concern tracking solution EdAware provides a comprehensive view of student wellbeing.

"Our products give teachers the opportunity to see, in real time through a series of thumbnails, everything that's happening within the classroom on all devices," says Reilly. Impero's software also incorporates a number of classroom engagement tools, including live chat functionality, permitting conversations between the teacher and individual students. "It takes away the barriers to entry for education technology in the classroom."

Enhancing pupil safety online is also a high priority for Impero. That includes using a database of over 24,000 keywords to ensure that children are not succumbing to bullying, eating disorders or even extremist influence, no matter what device the company's software is installed on. Reilly recalls one case of Impero's software detecting depressive tendencies in a pupil at a British school. "That student was really struggling, even thinking about suicide," he says. "And it would have remained completely undetected otherwise."

For Reilly, that imperative to safeguard students online makes the celebration of the 75th anniversary of VE Day all the more important. "Our work is about protecting the values of the schools and, beyond that, of the country at large," he says. "To keep people safe and invest in their futures."

Welcoming foundation

London Metropolitan University has always been about improving the life opportunities of its students

www.londonmet.ac.uk

London Metropolitan University has a long and varied history, but today its focus is on the future and how it can improve the lives of under-represented and disadvantaged groups, both in London and around the world. According to Head of Marketing Demetria Maratheftis, it's all down to one person.

"Our Vice-Chancellor, Professor Lynn Dobbs, is a true change-maker," says Maratheftis. "Her vision is to give back to the whole of London by supporting students and empowering the labour market, as well as internationalising the university by building partnerships with others across the globe." This means providing opportunities for students to access the university's high-quality provision in their own countries and to graduate under the London Met badge. More locally, the university works with schools and colleges and sets up summer schools in neighbouring boroughs like Islington and Tower Hamlets to help underprivileged students with their GCSEs.

Equality is central to the ethos here, perhaps best exemplified by one of its most famous alumni: Mayor of London Sadiq Khan. "Sadiq came from humble upbringings — his father was a bus driver," says Maratheftis. "He read law at the University of North London, a predecessor institution to London Met, and he's now one of Europe's most important politicians." That story is similar to many of the university's students, including Professor Dobbs herself, who was a mature student and mother of two taking on a politics degree while working around her children's schedules. Now she's the Vice-Chancellor of a major university and the *Evening Standard* has named her one of London's most influential people for her contribution to advancing social equality.

Back in 1848, when the Bishop of London and the Reverend Charles Mackenzie set up the university's earliest incarnation, they did so to provide vocational work for unskilled people. "Social mobility has always been the aim of the university," says Maratheftis. "It was always a very forward-thinking, progressive and welcoming place to be."

More than just turning out graduates, the university aspires to betterment for all, particularly those members of society who tend to be overlooked. "The beating heart of all this," says Maratheftis, "is about making sure people from disadvantaged areas have a chance to grow, from an educational point of view, improve their lives and get themselves into great careers."

Coast with the most

A sweeping coastline, a remarkable history and a flourishing contemporary culture all make Norfolk the place to be

www.norfolk.gov.uk

Norfolk has always been a county that embraces opportunity and never more so than at the present time, combining tradition with the latest technologies. Little wonder that the county has an enviable reputation as a desirable place to live and work in, as well as to visit. "We have a population of nearly 900,000 people and a significant history in our varied thriving economy and good homes," says Andrew Proctor, Leader of Norfolk County Council.

Part of Norfolk's draw as a holiday destination is the sheer variety of attractions on offer. "We have a lovely coastline and renowned seaside resorts," says Proctor, "as well as beautiful countryside, picturesque market towns and excellent shopping, plus fascinating heritage and cultural activities."

Norfolk undoubtedly has a lot to offer in economic terms, with an impressive 37,000 businesses based in the county. The Energy Coast and Norwich Research Park support a range of exciting careers in tech, while the care industry also provides a great many important jobs. "There's a good balance here between traditional industries such as farming, tourism, the caring professions and the new technologies," says Proctor. "We're creating new and stronger communities, and crucially providing the support needed to sustain these — so Norfolk becomes an increasingly appealing place to live and work for all ages." Good housing at reasonable prices is also key to the county's success: "Lots of quality new homes are being planned and built over the next 10 to 15 years."

Excellent schools and improving infrastructure add to the county's allure, as do the renowned universities and colleges, not to mention The Forum — one of the biggest libraries in Britain. Those looking to cultivate a healthy lifestyle can enjoy a wide range of outdoor activities, and there's a fantastic variety of family theme parks and attractions, as well as historical sites, including medieval castles.

"Norfolk is for families, for young professionals, older people enjoying retirement and young people just starting their careers," says Proctor. "It's always been a great tourist attraction and now we want to make sure people realise that it's so much more than that. We want to encourage them to enjoy the benefits of living here year-round. Norfolk is a county of opportunity and strong communities, working together to get the best from life."

Licensed to learn

With its roots in the brewing industry, LVS Ascot is an independent school in Berkshire that focuses on the happiness and resilience of its students

www.lvs.ascot.sch.uk

It's an unusual school that offers its pupils half a pint of ale at lunchtime, but that was what happened at LVS Ascot when it first opened its doors back in 1803. Its founders were publicans - Licensed Victuallers who gave the school its name — and they were appalled by the dirty water at its original site in Kennington, south London. "The water in this part of Berkshire is fine, so that's no longer the case," Principal Christine Cunniffe quickly explains, with a laugh.

What hasn't changed in over two centuries is the school's focus on providing pupils with an all-round education. On its 26-acre site in Ascot, a mile away from the racecourse, 300 staff are dedicated to creating a unique start in life for 830 co-educational pupils aged 4 to 18.

The Queen is the school's patron, and bursaries are offered through the Licensed Trade Charity. But there are no entrance exams, nor any other barriers to an education at a school where pupils' wellbeing is paramount.

"Our exam results are very impressive considering we're non-selective," says Cunniffe, "but we pride ourselves on our pupils' happiness, their resilience and balanced perspective on life. It's not all about league tables."

Cunniffe's passion is inspired by her negative personal memories of education. "No child will go through what I went through. No child will be unhappy here and bullying isn't tolerated. Morale is very high and we are an incredibly tight, happy community."

She has worked at the school for 17 years, the last 10 as head. "Being Principal is a privilege, and I know the way I act, people will follow," she says. "And maintaining the school's unique approach is key to recruiting staff. Qualifications are paramount, but the first question I ask everyone is, 'Why do you want to work here?' I'm not your typical headmistress. I love to have fun as well as work hard, and I want my staff to share that same feeling, and so pass it onto the children in our care.

"We don't know what the world is going to look like in a few years, but I know that our pupils will have the tools, the skillset and the resilience to take on this world."

Leagues ahead

With exemplary ratings, eco-activities and emphasis on students' growth and learning, St Mary's Shaftesbury in Dorset is a hothouse of happiness

www.stmshaftesbury.uk

The history of St Mary's Shaftesbury School in North Dorset is inextricably linked to the Second World War. The school shares a 75th anniversary with VE Day, and the building in which it was housed played an important role in the war. Founded as St Mary's Convent, it was set up by Mary Ward nuns for evacuees from St Mary's in Hampstead who remained in the West Country after the war. The building served as a small hotel before the war, but was requisitioned for the US Air Force, who rechristened it the "flak shack". It was also used by the Red Cross as a house of recuperation, with a butler serving drinks to recovering air crews from a bar. To celebrate VE Day 2020, the school is recreating that original wartime bar.

It is now a Catholic boarding and day school for 190 girls aged between 9 and 18. One thing that hasn't changed is the idyllic rural setting. Gold Hill in Shaftesbury was the setting for the famous Hovis ads of the 1970s, and is still used for the annual cheese-running competition. Nearby Cranborne Chase provides the perfect opportunity for cross-country running and adventure training. The school hosts a regional games competition, and the girls have a fully equipped gym, a year-round tennis academy and a swimming pool..

St Mary's Shaftesbury has onsite chickens, sheep and alpacas, plus a walled garden in which pupils keep bees and raise seedlings in a greenhouse built out of recycled bottles. The school has its own solar panels and is working towards power self-sufficiency. Headmistress Maria Young is a lay head, but the ethos of St Mary's Shaftesbury has not changed since the nuns left in 1998. "The heart of the school, its faith, its kindness, its inclusivity and its sense of joy and wonder remain undimmed," she says. The school is in the top 10 of smaller independent schools for its academic results. A recent inspector said that each girl is "individually known and individually nurtured".

"Pupils in girls' schools step up into the limelight and become leaders," says Young. "They are free of pressures to be or look a certain way, and can be themselves." There are plans to reintroduce horse-riding and a vibrant sixth-form Global Citizenship programme. More immediately, the school will celebrate VE Day — and its 75th anniversary — with a giant street party, and has invited old girls back to take part in a 1940s-style tennis match. As the Headmistress says, "St Mary's girls are friends for life."

Extra special forces

Evolve Military College has developed a traineeship for potential Armed Forces recruits, emphasising the core values and morals of the military

www.evolvemilitarycollege.co.uk

Adapting to military life is not easy. The first time Andrew Emmett was allowed home during his basic training for the Royal Marines, he found the experience so challenging that he was in tears as his train pulled into Leeds station. Some years later, after a successful military career followed by more than a decade working as an instructor at military training colleges, Emmett wanted to ensure that young people would not experience similar problems. In 2016, he founded Evolve Military College to provide a supportive physical, academic and pastoral environment for those intending to make a career in the forces.

"I was working for a larger training provider and I didn't believe their core values and morals so I set the college up with a desire to support the military community," he says. "That includes finding employment opportunities for veterans so they can pass on their experiences to ensure young people are prepared for what lies ahead."

The course is free for 16 to 24 year olds and lasts a maximum of 26 weeks, with facilities in Bury and at several sites in Lancashire. It is designed to raise aspirations, skills and qualities, both physical and academic, for those hoping to join the Armed Forces, bringing them to the level required by the military. Some of the students may require additional pastoral care and therapy, while instructors can give advice and guidance for those applying to join the military. "We don't sugar-coat the reality of what they are signing up to but we can give an insight into what life in the Armed Forces will be like," says Emmett. "We are trying to prepare young people for all these emotions and let them know it is okay to feel that way. People are often turned down because of lack of fitness, lack of confidence or their responsiveness to discipline. Our course is designed to help them overcome those barriers."

Evolve extends its offering to younger schoolchildren, providing alternative provision for those who struggle with the classroom environment. "It's a similar programme for young people who might have issues with attendance, discipline or the academic side," says Emmett. "The classroom isn't always the right place for young people and we offer courses to give them a bit of relief from that environment."

A force for education

With many of its pupils being the children of servicemen, Stanchester Academy in Somerset has developed strong links with the military

www.stanchester-academy.co.uk

For Amy Joynes, the Headteacher of Stanchester Academy in Stoke-sub-Hamdon, Somerset, the Armed Forces are "a large part of our community". The school's catchment area includes Royal Naval Air Station Yeovilton, so it contains many pupils whose parents are serving either in the Royal Navy or the British Army. This provides occasional challenges but also unique opportunities.

"We attend their Remembrance Day service which is always a very emotional experience and we bring members of the forces into the school to talk about the huge range of careers available," she says. "We regularly go to Sandhurst for experience days. They run a STEM (science, technology, engineering, maths) course for girls and offer experience of officer training for those interested in military careers at a high level."

Children whose parents are in the forces, particularly the Army, can move schools regularly. Some may have lived abroad so need to adapt to the UK system. Others will have experienced trauma. These pressures have allowed Stanchester to develop exceptionally high standards of pastoral care as well as the ability to build strong relationships with families to understand children's needs.

The school has a family network group that meets regularly, consisting of forces' children from across years 7 to 11. "It's run by someone whose husband is in the forces," says Joynes. "It is about bringing together children who have had similar experiences and background, and trying to support their needs. They have their own room in the school to meet when they need to. It's a safe space."

The emphasis on pastoral care benefits all the school's pupils, as does being in such close proximity of the base. Joynes says that the school's relationship with the base allows pupils to access numerous possible careers and many children go on to have jobs in the forces. Being close to the military also enhances the children's understanding of the national story.

"Seeing the Armed Forces around on a daily basis lets the pupils understand a bit more about our national history," says Joynes. "Our youngsters have a great deal of respect for the forces and also a better understanding of our history and the reasons we hold the forces in such respect. We are a school that focuses very heavily on personal development as much as academic attainment and having the base nearby allows us to teach tolerance and respect, beyond which children will usually experience."

"Resolve, as a people, to do nothing unworthy of those who died for us and to make the world such a world as they would have desired for their children, and for ours"

King George VI, Victory in Europe Day 1945

Chapter ten

FOR QUEEN AND COUNTRY

Leading by example

Her Majesty The Queen's close relationship with the
Armed Forces is the most enduring of any monarch
in British history

When newly recruited British conscripts to
Her Majesty's Armed Forces perform their
"attestation" by pledging allegiance to the
monarch, they are paying tribute to the special
relationship that their branch of the military
shares with its ultimate boss. Indeed, the Queen's
reign has endured for so long that most current
and ex-servicemen and women alive today have
named her personally in their oath. They have
sworn that, "I will be faithful and bear true
allegiance to Her Majesty Queen Elizabeth the
Second, her heirs and successors, and that I will,
as in duty bound, honestly and faithfully defend
Her Majesty, her heirs and successors, in person,
crown and dignity against all enemies."

As Princess Elizabeth, the Queen herself
donned a uniform in the Second World War when
she served in the Auxiliary Territorial Service
(ATS) as an engine mechanic and driver. And
since she became monarch, and thus head of the
military, she has doubled up as the wife, mother
and grandmother of a succession of princes who
have served with distinction in the forces.

It is a tradition of long standing that the
reigning monarch and members of the Royal
Family are closely associated with the Armed
Forces. They have been proud to serve in all three
branches. Her husband and consort the Duke of
Edinburgh served in the Royal Navy and achieved
a distinguished record. He was mentioned in
dispatches for his actions during the Battle of
Cape Matapan in March 1941, when he spotted
an enemy vessel while operating the searchlights.
Prince Philip went on to attain the rank of
Commander and seemed destined for even higher
rank; but his naval career was cut short in 1952
when his wife became Queen.

The monarch's direct heir, the Prince of
Wales, who holds the highest honorary rank
in all three Armed Forces, commanded a
minesweeper in the Royal Navy and also passed
out with his wings after RAF training. He has
received numerous titles, decorations and
honorary appointments during his adult life and
carries out hundreds of engagements linked to
the military every year.

Her Majesty's grandsons, Prince William
and Prince Harry, both graduates of the Royal
Military Academy Sandhurst, joined the
Household Cavalry (Blues and Royals) as second
lieutenants. William later served with "C" Flight
22 Squadron at RAF Valley, Anglesey as a
search and rescue pilot. Harry served two tours
of duty on the frontline in Afghanistan, the
second as an Apache attack helicopter pilot.
He also established the Invictus Games, an
international adaptive multisport event in
which wounded, injured or sick military
personnel compete for medals.

Since serving in the ATS, the Queen
has maintained a close relationship with the
Armed Forces through regular visits to service
establishments and ships. She holds many
military appointments and honorary ranks.
Possibly the most visible demonstration of
this is the ceremony of Trooping the Colour:
a celebration that has taken place on the
monarch's official birthday for 260 years.
Every June, around 1,400 soldiers from British
and Commonwealth regiments parade with
200 horses and 400 musicians for a spectacular
display of military precision in Horse Guards
Parade. The Royal Family, in attendance on
horseback or in carriages, return to Buckingham

Previous pages Princess
Elizabeth inspects
a parade of Grenadier
Guards at the Wellington
Barracks in London,
7 May 1945

Left Her Majesty smiles
as she looks on at her
grandson, Prince William,
at Trooping the Colour,
June 2018

Right The Queen attends
the military event in 1981,
at which six blank shots
were fired

Palace afterwards to watch a Royal Air Force fly-past from the balcony.

For many years the Queen attended Trooping the Colour on horseback herself, dressed in a biretta and bright red Guards Regiment uniform decorated with the medals she was awarded before becoming Queen. For 18 of these years she rode Burmese, a black mare gifted to her by the Royal Canadian Mounted Police. In 1981, the Queen and mount were on their way to Trooping the Colour when six blank shots were fired. Although Burmese was startled, the Queen was able to bring her under control with characteristic composure and dignity. She continued to attend the event on horseback until Burmese was retired in 1986. Since then, Her Majesty has ridden in an open carriage and worn a Brigade of Guards badge instead of a uniform.

Her Majesty is the Patron of SSAFA, the Armed Forces charity, following in the footsteps of her parents, grandparents and great-grandmother, Queen Alexandra, the charity's first ever president. The Queen has supported SSAFA throughout her life; from donating honey to its children's homes and gifting £500 to the charity on the occasion of her wedding in 1947, to officially opening the current SSAFA headquarters, Elizabeth House, in 2013. Throughout her working year, she spends time meeting servicemen and women of all ranks, and their families, as well as those who have retired from active service.

The Queen also presents various military honours at investitures, including the highest and most prestigious medal, the Victoria Cross (for valour in combat) and the George Cross (for valour other than in combat). The monarch also instituted the Elizabeth Cross — the first medal to which she put her name — in 2009. This gave special recognition to the families of those who have died on military operations, or as a result of terrorism, since 1948. The Queen said she hoped it would add further weight to the nation's debt of gratitude to the families and loved ones of those who had died in the service of our country.

There is no doubt that our Queen feels a sincere attachment to her Armed Forces and to those who serve and who have served. That loyalty is returned and, indeed, is implicit in the term "to fight for Queen and country". It is not just her formal role that makes Her Majesty a natural leader for the military but the way she has led her life. She has faced extremely challenging times throughout her long reign, and understands what it means to fight for her country.

Queen Elizabeth II remains today a beacon of stability and a world leader of whom our military continues to be exceptionally proud.

Hire power

Pertemps prides itself on
a more supportive approach
to recruitment than that found
in today's corporate culture

www.pertemps.co.uk

Pertemps Recruitment Partnership was launched
from a single Birmingham office in 1961 and,
guided by Lifetime President Tim Watts, has
grown to become the UK's largest privately
owned recruitment business.

Despite having more than 200 branches
across Britain, Pertemps maintains a strong
local feel. "Community has always been at the
heart of our business," says Watts, "and was
part of the original ethos created by our founder,
my mother Constance. That family feel extends
to our military personnel."

Pertemps has established a strong and
lasting relationship with the Armed Forces.
"We were one of the first companies in the UK
to sign up to the Armed Forces Covenant," says
Managing Director and ex-REME mechanic,
Kent Thompson. "We also created a Pertemps
Armed Forces support programme to offer
clear paths for progression for service leavers,
veterans, reservists and the wider military
community, their spouses and families."

"A large number of personnel leave the British
Armed Forces each year and we recognise
the value that veterans and reservists bring to
employers. However, they do sometimes face
challenges. Our Armed Forces support programme

trains and provides military personnel with
the necessary skills and support required
to transfer into regular jobs."

In 2016, in a ceremony officiated by
Prince William, the Ministry of Defence
awarded Pertemps gold status in recognition
of its work with reservists and ex-services
personnel. That accolade shone a spotlight
on the company's achievements to date. "We
have a dedicated forces liaison team, involving
former and serving military and reservist
personnel," says Tim Watts. "They not only
work tirelessly for candidates but partner
with numerous military charities to ensure
that Pertemps makes a lifelong difference
to the Armed Forces community."

As well as its military work, Pertemps
offers solutions for all manner of recruitment
needs. "If a company requires a couple of
drivers once a week, we'll provide that," says
Kent Thompson. "But if a large-scale business
is looking to recruit 1,000 extra call handlers,
we can source that too. With our managed
services model and branch network, businesses
can flexibly outsource all or part of their
recruitment needs and leave Pertemps to
deliver efficiencies for them."

Canine-do attitude

How might a detection dog do its bit to conserve
the great crested newt? Wagtail UK is finding out

www.wagtailuk.com

When it comes to protecting life, preventing crime and detecting
danger, Wagtail UK's highly trained canines have some of the best
noses in the business.

The company, launched in 2003 by former Royal Air Force Police
dog handler Collin Singer (pictured, right), has dogs and handlers
working around the world. Tasks include hunting for trafficked exotic
pets and endangered species in Hong Kong and Africa, working at
airports and seaports, sniffing out people, drugs, cash and tobacco
and keeping public venues clear of explosives.

"The skills I learned during 23 years in the RAF have been crucial
to the success of the company," says Singer, "not just as a dog handler,
but in building a business." And that business is constantly expanding.
Wagtail UK currently has a number of dogs based in northern France,
working as "live body" detection dogs with the UK Border Force,
operating around the clock, 365 days a year.

"We also have many dogs based at our headquarters in North
Wales," says Singer. "They are used to detect substances such
as explosives, drugs, cash and illegal tobacco, as well as being
employed in conservation-related roles."

A recent contract in conservation saw Wagtail work on the HS2
project with Atkins Ecology and train one dog, Rocky, to identify
a protected species called the great crested newt at several large
construction sites. A feature on the BBC's *The One Show* saw Rocky
undergoing a series of practical and scientific tests to verify that he
was "the first scientifically proven great crested newt detection dog".

Among Wagtail's British government clients are the Ministry
of Defence, Border Force, HMRC, the Police and Trading Standards.
Its private clients include Boeing, Airbus, GE, Lockheed, the Sultan
of Oman and 22 UK stadiums such as Lord's and Wembley. The
company has won a Home Office Supplier of the Year award and has
recently achieved the Armed Forces Covenant Gold Status, among
many other awards and accolades. It has been approved by the MoD
to train service leavers to become dog handlers, with the result that
many of its 77 staff are ex-military.

"Many years ago I searched the Royal Albert Hall as an RAF dog
handler," says Singer, "so it's great to be supporting the VE Day 75th
Anniversary celebrations at this iconic venue." Life — for both man
and dog — has come full circle.

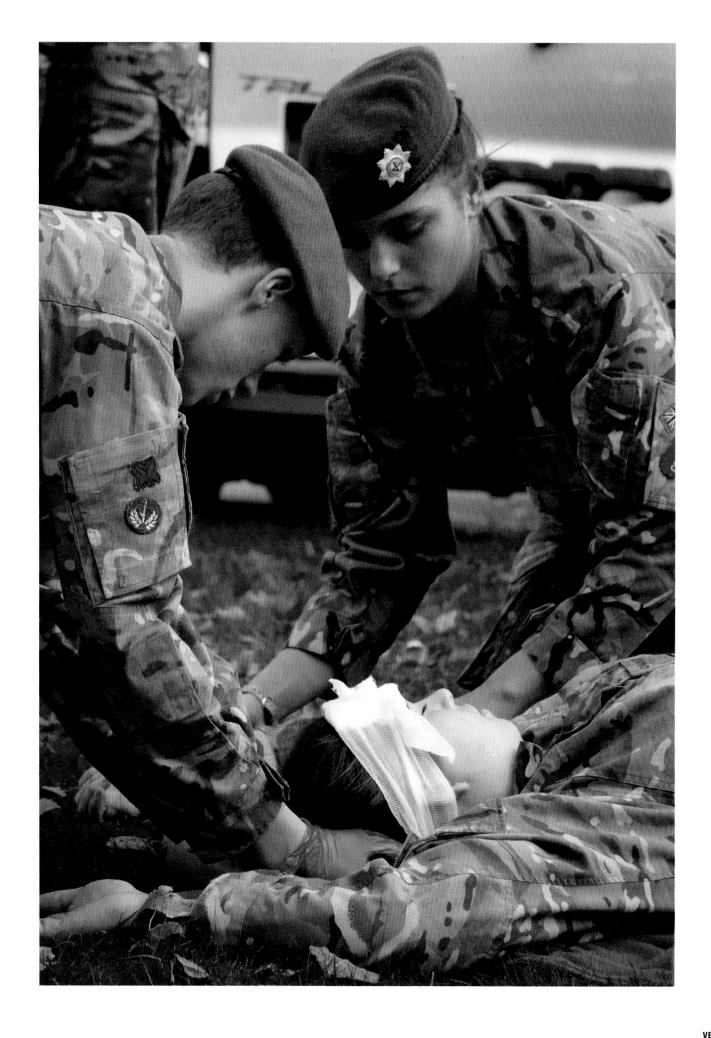

Inspiring a generation

The Army Cadets is determined to move with the times while staying true to much of its initial purpose

www.armycadets.com

"The big four words for us are fun, friendship, action and adventure," says Army Cadet Volunteer Dr Richard Crawford. "The Army Cadets represent an opportunity for young people to step outside their comfort zone and try something new." The organisation was formed in 1859, albeit initially with less emphasis on the fun. The country was under threat of invasion by France and it was felt that internal volunteer militias might be needed to counter that possibility. Even in its infancy, though, the Army Cadets were motivated by an earnest sense of social mission.

In 1889, the social reformer Octavia Hill formed London's first battalion in the hope of socialising deprived urban youngsters searching for direction. "If such ideals can be brought before the young lad before he gets in with a gang of loafers," she said, "it may make all the difference to his life." Hill's language might sound archaic to modern ears (and girls are welcomed into the Cadets now too), but her principles remain intact and the Army Cadets has adapted to changes in society without ever losing sight of its foundational purpose.

Now with around 69,000 young people actively involved in the organisation across 2,000 UK locations, the Army Cadets (Army Cadet Force and Combined Cadet Force Army) have a clear direction, as Deputy Commander Cadets, Brigadier Mark Christie OBE explains. "Our vision is to inspire young people to achieve success in life through a spirit of service to our Queen, their country and their local community and to develop in them the qualities of good citizens. We do this through a progressive, military-themed training syllabus and broader developmental activities, all designed to be challenging, adventurous and above all fun.

"This activity is underpinned by the Army's core values and standards — courage, discipline, respect for others, integrity, loyalty and selfless commitment. There's also a values-based inclusive leadership code, which provides a blueprint for life, regardless of whether the individual cadet ultimately decides to apply to join the Army."

In 2019, a Censuswide poll found that children below the age of 14 were spending an average of 23 hours a week using smartphones and other screen devices — twice as long as they spent conversing with their parents. "I once saw two new cadets texting each other while sat next to each other," says Dr Crawford. "They had no confidence to have face-to-face conversations. But within six months, these two were at our annual camp, shouting instructions across a valley to each other without a mobile phone in sight. Once they've got their uniforms on, they're part of one team and there's no looking down on anyone because they haven't got the latest gadget. Cadets is great for social mobility."

Senior Volunteer Leader Colonel Clinton Riley, one of many adult volunteers who keep the organisation running, describes a cycle that nurtures those involved on an ongoing basis. "I was a cadet myself before I volunteered so I've seen it from both sides," he says. "We provide key skills for life, and watching our cadets flourish reinforces our motto — inspire to achieve."

Colonel Riley and Dr Crawford are not alone in their enthusiasm. Around 11,000 others have been inspired to become Adult Volunteers, with the desire to support young people, enabling the Army Cadets to function and continue to be one of the leading youth organisations in the country.

Soldiering on

Faced with ex-military personnel trying to adjust to Civvy Street, Trafford Council is dedicated and committed to help veterans move on with their lives

www.trafford.gov.uk

For military veterans returning to civilian life, the challenges can be overwhelming. Trafford Council — which recently received a Gold Award from the Ministry of Defence and the Armed Forces Covenant for its outstanding support for members of the Armed Forces and their families — aims to lighten that load.

"We owe anybody who serves a debt of gratitude," says Armed Services Lead Officer Sue Wright. "They signed on a dotted line to say they're prepared to serve their country and give their life if necessary. When they come home it's my job to recognise that and support them on their journey back into civilian life."

Wright considers homelessness the biggest problem. "Sometimes a veteran can have a Queen's Commendation for bravery and end up sleeping in his or her car. Not all veterans qualify for a pension when they leave the service, so I'm able to provide the help and support they need from the council at what is often a difficult time."

Trafford Council has a strong history of supporting the military; the image on the right is a "Salute the Soldier Parade" which took place in Sale in 1944. "We continue to provide support, but it isn't only young service leavers who need Trafford Council's help," says Wright. "Veterans who left the service 30 years ago can suddenly be triggered and diagnosed with PTSD. It can happen overnight or decades later."

There are several veterans employed by Trafford Council, which provides additional paid leave for reservists, helps to secure employment and education for veterans and encourages local businesses to do the same. "Partnerships are key to my success," says Wright. "I'm now being asked by other organisations to support their efforts.

"Going the extra mile for veterans can be challenging and upsetting," says Wright. "I need to be able to make sure these brave people know that they're not alone. Together with Trafford Council I am committed to providing all the help and support they need when they need it most."

It's a job that Wright finds immensely rewarding. "Success is seeing veterans who came to me in pain, at rock bottom, gradually become settled, able to function, employed and independent," she says. "When they tell me they don't need to see me any more, I'm sad to see them go, but I'm happy they are healing and moving forward."

Aero dynamics

As a specialist in providing technical engineering services for safety-critical environments, AACE recognises the importance of getting it right

www.aace.co.uk

AACE was founded by former RAF officer Rick Hussey in 1996 out of the family's spare bedroom, to provide specialist consultancy services into the Ministry of Defence. Since then the business has grown into the AACE Group, consisting of three companies. AACE provides specialist technical services across air, land and maritime environments, both into the MOD and industry. Allyance is a technical recruitment company which places skilled individuals on temporary and permanent roles across government departments and into industry; while Clearwater is a managed IT services company which specialises in providing IT and security support into businesses working within defence.

The group is still owned by the Hussey family, with Rick's daughter, Lynette Hussey, now the Managing Director, ensuring that it continues to promote the family values on which it was founded. AACE specialises in airworthiness, system safety engineering, integrated logistics, training, technical publications and IT services. "Our pedigree in aviation engineering and highly technical areas such as airworthiness and system safety engineering are still core to what we do," says Lynette. "But we've broadened those specialist services to include maritime and land domains. We are finding a wider demand for the skills and knowledge we offer around technical, regulatory and governance issues. For example, we now provide training services into other sectors, such as healthcare, as we have developed and applied our 'human factors' compliance and awareness training from aviation into other safety-critical environments."

For the Hussey family, the company's military ethos is key to its success. "The majority of our employees come from a military background," says Lynette, "and with that comes an incredible work ethic and quiet determination, with talented individuals working as part of a team to get the job done, no matter what. This is of great value to our customers who can rely on us to deliver the highest quality output, time after time and without exception. The value of the military culture that is instilled within AACE, thanks to most of our employees being ex-military personnel, cannot be underestimated and is one of the core strengths of the company."

With a strong team ethos and commitment to quality service, Lynette Hussey and the AACE staff are sure to deliver benefits to military and non-military customers well into the future.

Where IT's at

Sopra Steria remains a pioneer in designing and delivering digital tech solutions to a multitude of weighty clients

www.soprasteria.co.uk

Whenever Sopra Steria's Sue-Ellen Wright sees police constables on a London street, she wants to shake them by the hand. "I like to think we've recruited them," she says. "We've been responsible for their pay, organised their uniform and done everything we can to enable them to do a good job."

Wright is Managing Director for Aerospace, Defence and Security at Sopra Steria. Prior to this role, she led its SSCL Police business, which handles all the Metropolitan Police Service's business support and administrative needs. SSCL (Shared Services Connected Ltd) is a joint venture between Sopra Steria and the UK government and it sees members of the police force through from attraction and recruitment to retirement. Recently, it received a fresh call to action.

"When the prime minister promised 20,000 more police on the street, that was a big challenge for the Met," says Wright. "We needed to transform the recruitment process and the ways in which we engage with potential candidates so that we can deliver."

The Met is just one of hundreds of Sopra Steria clients worldwide, including substantial government and defence contracts. It has built black boxes for Concorde and the French company Airbus has long been a client. It also devises innovative commercial solutions in the private sector for multinationals ranging from HSBC to Tesco and McDonalds.

As a market leader in digital transformation and a specialist in consulting, digital services and software, Sopra Steria stands out from the competition. "We help guide our customers, partners and employees to make bold choices," says Wright, "leveraging digital technology and building a positive future for all of us."

Sopra Steria has a distinguished heritage. It dates back to the FI Group, the company that IT pioneer and mathematician Dame Stephanie "Steve" Shirley started in 1962 to create career IT job opportunities for women with dependants and caring responsibilities. Following a series of mergers with Xansa, Steria and then Sopra Steria, Steve Shirley's influence continues today with many women in senior roles.

Sopra Steria needs to adapt as quickly to evolving markets as its clients. It has created a number of "Digilabs", environments designed to encourage creative working and thinking, attracting not only bright graduates full of ideas but specialist consultants and highly expert ex-service personnel as well as clients and partners.

Yet despite its huge and diverse client-base, Sopra Steria is about more than just IT. "Our people have a sense of common purpose and pride, a real public-sector ethos related to helping every citizen," says Wright. Sopra Steria maintains many charity links, including a recent partnership with the Armed Forces charity SSAFA. "We are incredibly proud to support them," says Wright. "Many of our colleagues are ex-Armed Forces and we know how important SSAFA's role is."

Wright sees her company's work in action every day. "When my friends need to apply for leave to remain, or my own children are applying for passports, that's Sopra," she says. "When I meet any member of the Armed Forces, I think, 'We paid you last week'."

One of the company's biggest gains last year was the contract to manage human resources and payroll services for British military personnel. It has also been tasked with providing an MoD logistics system accessible inside the UK and overseas, and is undertaking further work in logistics and biometrics.

With many more contracts coming up, Wright is proud of her company's role in supporting the country's defence and national security. "When I'm walking down the street," she says, "I feel proud that we are contributing in many ways to helping keep our country safe."

Going with the territory

G3 Systems provides a wide range of deployable systems, fixed infrastructure and associated support services to the military, public and private sectors

www.g3-systems.co.uk

From building UK and NATO hospitals in Afghanistan to manufacturing deployable command-and-control facilities, G3 Systems is a key player in the military arena. The company, based in Dorset, has been designing, delivering and supporting fixed and deployable infrastructure systems to the Armed Forces for almost 20 years. In that time, it has grown to cover multiple lines of business across the world including the UK, the Middle East, Africa and the Falkland Islands, and support military operations in a variety of theatres, including Afghanistan, the Balkans and the Gulf.

"Our core military activities are an essential part of what G3 does," says Managing Director Mike Puckett. "But we're also an outward-looking company, working with numerous government and commercial partners both here and overseas. For example, we've developed emergency response systems and capabilities for the nuclear energy sector, which is a difficult environment. But we enjoy working in these challenging areas."

G3 Systems was set up in 2001, initially delivering deployable facilities and systems for the British Army. Once the company had played a crucial part in equipping the UK and NATO missions in Afghanistan and Iraq, it made sense to start delivering all manner of critical support services. "NATO liked the way we delivered our services," says Puckett, "so they asked us to look at other areas for them. That's how we moved into providing airfield fire and rescue services, which have become one of our major business streams."

G3 continues to deliver services around the world; 350 of the company's 410 employees, drawn from 25 nations, are deployed overseas. It is also a Silver Member of the Armed Forces Covenant scheme. More than a third of its workforce is made up of military veterans, and many others have family links to the Armed Forces.

"As a company with close ties to the UK, US and allied armed forces, we're delighted to support VE Day 75," says Puckett. "And not simply as a business, but through the veterans who are part of the G3 Systems family. It's important that we continue to recognise and remember the extraordinary achievement and sacrifices of our forebears, who fought and sacrificed so much to secure victory and freedom in the Second World War."

Built to last

Innovative technology and four decades of expertise combine in Drumgrange Ltd's steadfast, singular approach

www.drumgrange.com

When George Howe set up Drumgrange Ltd in November 1979, it was inspired by his own service in the RAF. "I know first-hand that, alongside great service personnel, the equipment and support provided is essential to the success of defence operations," he explains. More than 40 years later it has developed into a thriving independent UK engineering-system house, specialising in the design, development, integration and through-life in-house support of military equipment, with focus on both the maritime and land domains.

Howe, as Managing Director, has worked hard to establish Drumgrange's enviable reputation as an expert in its field. With a proven track record for the rapid realisation of demanding design tasks manufactured to the highest quality, Drumgrange provides products and capability services for the UK Armed Forces, NATO forces and foreign militaries.

"Since the 1980s, Drumgrange has been actively involved within the maritime sector including VLF (Very Low Frequency) submarine broadcast communications supplying transmitter, platform and HQ equipment," says Howe. "We have worked closely with the Royal Navy, specialising in niche areas where high performance and levels of reliability are mandatory to establish efficient intercept and high efficiency passive sonars and trusted communication systems." Drumgrange has worked with warships, submarines, survey vessels and offshore patrol vessels to provide complementary technologies that support highly resilient position, frequency and timing systems.

Drumgrange specialises in the integration of navigation, communication, tracking and situational awareness systems for military, security and rescue platforms, providing a wide range of experience in computer-based training systems and equipment simulators. "In recent years we were delighted to deliver the Mercury Radio Project to the Army Cadet Force," says Howe. "It provides a communications solution that allows them to train effectively and enable a key safety communications network for support on exercises and other activities. We hope it helps to inspire young people within the unique life-learning environment of the Cadets."

A new IT system will allow the company to focus on the development of its processes and products, and as a company itself. "I'm proud to have watched Drumgrange become the company it is today," says Howe, "and I look forward to future exciting opportunities."

Safe as houses

Police Crime Prevention Initiatives are working behind the scenes to keep businesses and homes secure

www.policecpi.com

Few crime-busting initiatives can boast an 87 per cent reduction in targeted offences, and those that do certainly grab the headlines — which makes the understated success of Secured by Design (SBD) all the more remarkable. The SBD project works to achieve sustainable reductions in crime, both through design and by benchmarking the quality of doors, windows and locks.

First launched by a group of police forces in 1989, SBD was taken up by the Association of Chief Police Officers (ACPO) for the UK in 1999, becoming Police Crime Prevention Initiatives (PCPI) in 2016. Over the past 20 years more than one million new homes have been built to certified SBD standards; although PCPI Chief Executive Officer Guy Ferguson believes the true impact of the initiative has been even greater. "I think we've had a positive influence across the construction sector — and particularly in social housing — regardless of certification," he says. "Developers are using better products because the market has shifted that way, to keep up with the standards we have set."

Working as an operational arm of policing, SBD collaborates with the private security industry, planners, architects, developers, local authorities and housing associations. These last include Haig Housing, a housing trust which offers assistance to ex-service people and/or their dependants. "I'm very proud of our work with Haig Housing and some of the recent developments are fantastic," says Ferguson. "These are homes built for people we owe a massive debt to." SBD also promotes the Sanctuary Scheme, which allows thousands of victims of domestic violence to stay in their own homes. This is made possible by the installation of protective safe rooms.

The initiative also works with counterparts across Europe and the USA, and will soon be taking part in a Developing Cities event in Kenya. But while it accounts for around 75 per cent PCPI's work, there are numerous other initiatives. These include the Police Crime Prevention Academy (PCPA), which was set up in 2017 to take over the College of Policing crime-prevention courses. These revamped, independently accredited courses are delivered at cost to policing. There's also the Police Digital Security Centre (PDSC), which works with small and medium enterprises on cyber security.

"I think we've achieved a huge amount for a not-for-profit organisation," says Ferguson, "but there's still plenty more to do."

Gold standard

From protected spaces to facilities for the London Olympics, Bastion Security Products offer unprecedented levels of protection

www.bastionprotects.com

From secure military facilities to safe spaces capable of protecting people, objects and information from terrorist and state-sponsored attack, Bastion Security is one of the world's leading specialists in physical security structures and systems. Launched in London in 1982, with its primary base relocating to Newcastle shortly afterwards, the company built a solid reputation for anti-robbery facilities to protect staff and cash in banks and businesses, and heavy-armour glazing for docks in courtrooms across the UK. But its highly versatile modular room systems have proved most successful among military and commercial clients, as Managing Director Tom Deevy explains.

"The development of our ultra-secure 'flat-pack' room building systems led to us achieving the 'Approved for Government Use' tag for our most secure system, which was first used to protect data centres containing critical security intelligence at the 2012 London Olympics," says Deevy. "We develop products that have different uses in different sectors, and which can be tailored to meet the needs of the individual client. Our systems can also be easily dismantled and moved: we can get something through a standard-sized doorway, assemble the parts easily once inside, and create the right level of protection with minimal fuss. A garage-sized room can be built in 72 hours and dismantled in 24 hours, with only a 50mm wall thickness."

Bastion's trademarked and patented Protean concept provides systems that can be easily upgraded. The concept means that additional performance against changed threats can be met by simply swapping out a component, allowing a rapid upgrade to mitigate improvised explosive devices, ballistic, blast fragmentation or cyber threats, meeting a very high MoD security standard. Such innovations have led to considerable business growth, with Bastion's turnover doubling from March 2019 to 2020.

"All of our personnel are security vetted, with a high proportion being ex-services," says Deevy, "and we plough a lot of our profits back into research and development — it's an important pathway, because the threats and levels of protection required are always evolving. We are very proud of our role in protecting our defence, police, critical national infrastructure and justice system infrastructure, and look forward to the development of new products to meet new and emerging global threats."

Dogged determination

Kopek Security is the brainchild of two women dog handlers who knew they could go one better

www.kopeksecurity.com

When expert dog handlers Gennine Cope and Sue Yildiz decided to launch their own security firm, they were confident that their experience and professional approach would yield positive results. Yet the success of Kopek Security, which has grown to a team of more than 120 contractors since launching in March 2018, has astonished even them. The firm earns more each month that it was forecast to turn over in the first year.

"The speed we've grown at has really surprised us," says Cope. "We're ambitious, and we want to be a household name — for all the right reasons — but we thought the expansion would happen further down the line."

Cope and Yildiz are certainly equipped to succeed. Both are trained Level 3 dog handlers, with backgrounds in recruitment and enforcement respectively, and had worked together on several major security contracts. "We'd said on a few jobs that things could be done better," says Yildiz, "and when someone replied, 'Well, why don't you two set up a company?', we looked at each other and thought, 'Why not?'

"Starting a business as two women in the male-dominated security sector was a massive challenge. But we're tough, we stuck together and kept to our principles, and now we have a really strong team in place."

While security dogs and manned guarding are the firm's core services, other activities like close protection and vehicle escorts have become increasingly important. The firm is attracting plenty of female contractors, as well as clients looking for women in specific security roles.

Cope and Yildiz are understandably proud of the brand. "Köpek is Turkish for dog," says Yildiz. "My husband is Turkish, Gennine's surname is Cope, and as former dog handlers it seemed the perfect name. Replacing the umlaut with dog ears — on the 'O' of the company logo — was the final touch!"

The business, which took a silver award after signing the Armed Forces Covenant, is not resting on its laurels. It recently launched a new subsidiary with ex-services personnel (over half Kopek's staff are ex-military) to deliver accredited training.

"It's been an incredible journey," says Cope. "Now we're just starting to enjoy it, and there's lots more to come."

APPENDICES

About SSAFA

www.ssafa.org.uk

SSAFA, the Armed Forces charity, has been providing lifelong support to our Armed Forces and their families since 1885. In 2019 alone, the charity's teams of volunteers and employees helped more than 85,000 people in need, from Second World War veterans to the young men and women who have served in more recent conflicts, and their families. SSAFA understands that behind every uniform is a person. "And we are here for that person — any time they need us, in any way they need us, for as long as they need us."

When the Soldiers' and Sailors' Families Association (or SSFA, as it was then called) was established in 1885 by Major James Gildea, it was intended to support the military families left behind during the Second Expeditionary Force in Egypt. The Princess of Wales, later to become Queen Alexandra, became the charity's first president, establishing a tradition of royal patronage that the charity remains privileged to receive to this day, with The Queen residing as the charity's patron and Prince Michael of Kent its current president. By the end of its first year in operation in 1885, the association had awarded grants to 231 women and 466 children.

Following the establishment of the RAF in 1918, Queen Alexandra suggested the inclusion of airmen into the association's title, and so in 1919 the charity was renamed the Soldiers, Sailors, Airmen and Families Association. It would not be until the Second World War that the use of the acronym SSAFA (rhymes with "Jaffa") would become the preferred way to refer to the charity.

Throughout its history, the charity has worked hand-in-hand with the military, but it was the Second World War that would see it operate wherever the British military was deployed. It's a duty that it performs to this very day, providing health, welfare and support services to the British military serving personnel, veterans and their families, both in the UK and overseas.

In 2020, the charity's volunteer network spans every county of the UK, with 90 branches across the UK and operations in 11 other countries around the world. The present-day needs of the military community — both serving and veteran — have become increasing complicated and diverse, requiring more specialised support than ever before. SSAFA is continually adapting to these changing needs to ensure that whatever challenges they face, members of the Armed Forces community can rely on it for unfailing support.

SSAFA is a registered charity in England and Wales (210760), Scotland (SCO38056) and the Republic of Ireland (20202001). Established 1885.

About the publisher

www.sjhgroup.com

Headquartered in London, UK, the SJH Group is a world-leading creative media group that delivers bespoke publishing solutions to a global client base. Comprising five unique publishing companies — namely, St James's House, Artifice Press, Black Dog Press, SJH Publishing and Cargo Media — the Group embodies a wide range of specialisms that include history, autobiography, art, architecture, luxury lifestyle, global business and charitable causes. Collectively, since it was founded in 2002, the Group has also raised more than £2 million for charities in the UK and abroad.

"As publishers, our mission is to create beautiful books that engage, educate and entertain, and we're constantly evolving," says Richard Freed, Founder and CEO of the SJH Group. "The publishing industry of today was utterly unimaginable two decades ago. We've seen the rise of eBook, app and online formats, as well as social media as an important channel for reaching consumers. However, other changes are less obvious to industry outsiders. For instance, as publishers, increasingly we serve as consultants and strategic partners to event and communication professionals who are looking for creative ways to communicate their messages."

To this end, the SJH Group's wider network is key. Each year, in addition to retail sales, the Group distributes tens of thousands of books on a controlled-circulation basis to influential audiences that include members of Parliament and the House of Lords, C-suite executives in the private and third sectors, members of leading industry bodies, media executives, journalists and academics, among other readerships.

Globally, the SJH Group has also distinguished itself as a champion of print media, commanding the attention and respect of readers. "Somewhat counterintuitively, the status of high-quality print publications is actually on the rise," says Richard. "In a world in which digital media has come to feel like wallpaper to most people, enduring print formats such as the coffee-table book have become more prestigious and sought after than ever before — akin to monuments in a landscape of otherwise fleeting formats."

In addition to its digital output, the Group now prints more than 300,000 books annually, placing it among the UK's top companies for print media distribution, and making it one of the most influential producers of high-quality published content in its field.

Acknowledgements

This book is dedicated to all the men, women and children of the wartime generation who endured so much, whether in foreign fields or on the home front.

Thank you to all those who shared their memories for inclusion in this book, including Ann Pont, Bert Turner, Daniel Harrison, Janet Humphries, Joan Blair, Kathleen Tozer, Leslie Edward Kershaw, Leslie Norman Collins and Norman Lewis. Thanks also to those SSAFA staff and branch representatives who helped facilitate the interviews – Harry Ellis, Kathy Munslow, Anna MacKinnon, Trevor Bailey, Geoff Harriman, Emlyn Phennah, Roger Wilson and Peter Blair – as well as to Joel Chamberlin, and Dr Ellen Murgitroyd for their contributions.

Special thanks to those SSAFA team members who made this book possible: Selina Cuff, for her rigourous research and substantial written contributions; Bryony Waite, who conducted the interviews with the VE Day veterans; Juliet Chaplin, SSAFA Archivist, who delved into the charity's annuals, letters, photographic collections and records; the PR team, namely Emily Housden, Natasha Bennett and Victoria Demetriou, who consulted on early drafts and provided invaluable support; and SSAFA's Head of PR and Public Affairs, Alice Farrow, for all her assistance on the project. Selina Cuff would also like to thank Niall, Ellen and Ruardih Copeland, who provided not only a writing bothy but also moral support, and Mac for being a sounding board and her champion.

Additional thanks to: British Newspaper Archives, The National Library of Scotland, BBC News, BBC History, British Zone Review, Declassified Podcast, Mrs Jill Giles and Mr Giles, Mike and Angela Carr, Movietone archive footage, Pathé News, SSAFA Marketing & Communications and Fundraising Departments, SSAFA News and its team over the decades, The Imperial War Museum, The Ministry of Defense; and those partner organisations that made this book possible (see p. 256).

The last note of thanks goes to Margaret Thomas (or Petty Officer Margaret Stringfellow of the Women's Royal Naval Service, as she was then) who, on 8 May 1945, found herself on top of one of the lion statues in Trafalgar Square with her dear friend and fellow Wren Joan and other revellers. The moment was captured by a press photographer and has since become an iconic image of VE Day – one that features on the cover of this very book.

Contributors

Robert Jobson is a best-selling and award-winning author and royal correspondent who has chronicled the story of the House of Windsor for the past 30 years, and is internationally recognised for his in-depth and historical knowledge of the Royal Family. In addition to making regular appearances as an on-screen expert for Sky News, the BBC, ITV and Channel 5, Robert is Royal Editor of the *London Evening Standard* in the UK; Royal Contributor for NBC's *Today Show* and *Forbes* magazine in the US; and is a regular on national television in Australia and New Zealand.

Selina Cuff began her career in journalism in East Africa reporting for *The Independent*, *Global Post* and *New African* periodicals. Upon returning to the UK she wrote for *The Sunday Times* before becoming one of the country's youngest female news editors. Selina's increasing involvement with the Armed Forces community brought her to SSAFA, the Armed Forces charity, as Research and Content Development Officer. Selina is inspired by her grandparents Horace and Joan Cuff who lived through the war and who, along with her father, Tim Cuff, nurtured and encouraged her love of history and people's stories.

Credits

SSAFA, the Armed Forces charity

SSAFA, the Armed Forces charity
Elizabeth House
4 Saint Dunstans's Hill
London
EC3R 8AD

Registered charity in England and Wales (210760),
Scotland (SCO38056) and the Republic of Ireland
(20202001). Established 1885.

HM Queen Elizabeth II, Patron

HRH Prince Michael of Kent, President

Lieutenant General (retd) Sir Gary Coward
KBE CB, National Chairman

Lieutenant General (retd) Sir Andrew Gregory
KBE CB, Chief Executive

Jonathan Sandall, Director of Fundraising

Lisa Shattock, Director of Marketing and
Communications

Rebecca Keaveney, Head of Commercial
Operations

Alice Farrow, Head of PR and Public Relations

Publisher

SJH Group
298 Regent's Park Road
London
N3 2SZ

T: +44 (0)20 8371 4000
E: publishing@stjamess.org
W: www.sjhgroup.com

Richard Freed, Chief Executive
richard.freed@stjamess.org

Stephen van der Merwe, Managing Director
stephen.vdm@stjamess.org

Richard Golbourne, Sales Director
r.golbourne@stjamess.org

Stephen Mitchell, Head of Editorial
stephen.mitchell@stjamess.org

Aniela Gil, Head of Design
aniela.gil@stjamess.org

John Lewis, Deputy Editor
john.lewis@stjamess.org

Jochen Viegener, Designer
jochen.viegener@stjamess.org

Photography

Alamy
Getty Images
PA Images
SSAFA
Lizzie Henshaw Photography (pp. 194—97)
David Harper, Tim Winter (p. 218)
The R&A, St Andrews University,
 Special Collections (p. 219)
Lieutenant Simon Crossley; Peter Russell
 (pp. 240—41)

Other images are the copyright of individual
organisations.

Patrons index

A special thank you to the following organisations, without whose support this publication would not have been possible